AFRICAN AMERICAN BIOGRAPHY

AFRICAN AMERICAN REFERENCE LIBRARY

African American Biography

VOLUME 6

Phillis Engelbert

South Huntington Pub. Lib.
145 Pidgeon Hill Rd.
Huntington Sta., N.Y. 11746

AN IMPRINT OF THE GALE GROUP

African American Biography, volume 6

Phillis Engelbert

Staff

Jane Hoehner and Betz Des Chenes, *U•X•L Senior Editors*
Carol DeKane Nagel, *U•X•L Managing Editor*
Thomas L. Romig, *U•X•L Publisher*

Keryl Stanley, *Permissions Associate (Pictures)*

Rita Wimberley, *Senior Buyer*
Evi Seoud, *Assistant Production Manager*
Dorothy Maki, *Manufacturing Manager*
Mary Beth Trimper, *Production Director*

Cynthia Baldwin, *Product Design Manager*

Gary Leach, *Graphic Artist*
Barbara J. Yarrow, *Graphic Services Manager*

Marco Di Vita, Graphix Group, *Typesetting*

This publication is a creative work protected by all applicable copyright laws, as well as by misappropriation, trade secret, unfair competition, and other applicable laws. The editors of this work have added value to the underlying factual material herein through one or more of the following: unique and original selection, coordination, expression, arrangement, and classification of the information. All rights to this publication will be vigorously defended.

Copyright © 2000
U•X•L, an imprint of the Gale Group

All rights reserved, including the right of reproduction in whole or in part in any form.

ISBN 0–7876–3563–4
ISSN 1522–2934

The front cover photographs were reproduced by permission of the following sources (clockwise from top right): Elijah Muhammad (Archive Photos, Inc.); Josephine Baker (AP/Wide World Photos); Althea Gibson (Schomburg Center for Research in Black Culture)

Printed in the United States of America

10 9 8 7 6 5 4 3 2

*To Joyce Dixson, my friend and inspiration,
who provides hope to people during troubled times*

Contents

Entries by Field of Endeavor ix

Reader's Guide. xxv

Volume 6
Robert S. Abbott 1
Augusta Baker (update) 9
Ella Jo Baker 13
Romare Bearden 21
Julian Bond (update) 31
Clive O. Callender 37
Stokely Carmichael (update) 45
Shirley Chisholm (update) 51
Eldridge Cleaver (update). 57
Ruby Dee 63
Joyce Dixson 73

Lewis Howard Latimer

Portrait: Reproduced by permission of the Schomburg Center for Research in Black Culture.

vii

Joycelyn Elders	81
Father Divine	91
T. Thomas Fortune	101
Josh Gibson	111
Frances Ellen Watkins Harper	119
Charles Hamilton Houston	127
Jesse Jackson (update)	137
Vernon E. Jordan Jr. (update)	143
Lewis Howard Latimer	149
Spike Lee (update)	157
Elijah McCoy	163
Audley Moore (update)	171
Bernice Johnson Reagon	177
Philippa Duke Schuyler	185
Assata Shakur	193
Nina Simone	203
Maxine Waters	211
William Julius Wilson	221
Coleman Young (update)	233

Index . . . . **xxix**

Entries by Field of Endeavor

Joyce Dixson

Includes African American Biography, volumes 1–6. **Boldface** *type indicates volume number; regular type indicates page numbers; (u) indicates update to original entry.*

Art

Romare Bearden **6:** 21

Clementine Hunter **2:** 366

Jacob Lawrence **3:** 464

Gordon Parks **3:** 575

Henry Ossawa Tanner **4:** 696

Business

Dave Bing **1:** 65

Elleanor Eldridge **2:** 225

Arthur Gaston . . . . **2:** 258, **5:** 89 (u)

Portrait: Reproduced by permission of Joyce Dixson

Berry Gordy Jr.	**2:** 286
Alexis Herman	**5:** 115
John H. Johnson	**2:** 405
Jesse Owens	**3:** 570
Barbara Gardner Proctor	**3:** 594
Dudley Randall	**3:** 607
Naomi Sims	**4:** 672
Madame C. J. Walker	**4:** 750
Maggie L. Walker	**4:** 752
Oprah Winfrey	**4:** 792
Andrew Young	**5:** 249

Dance

Alvin Ailey	**1:** 8
Katherine Dunham	**1:** 215
Gregory Hines	**2:** 349
Bill T. Jones	**2:** 411

Education

Molefi Kete Asante	**1:** 23
Augusta Baker	**1:** 31, **6:** 9 (u)
Amiri Baraka	**1:** 37
Marguerite Ross Barnett	**1:** 43
Mary McLeod Bethune	**1:** 63
Shirley Chisholm	**1:** 138, **6:** 51 (u)
Joe Clark	**1:** 140
Jewel Plummer Cobb	**1:** 148
Johnnetta Betsch Cole	**1:** 151
Marva Collins	**1:** 160
Anna J. Cooper	**1:** 165
Ellen Craft	**1:** 175
Angela Davis	: 180
Juliette Derricotte	**1:** 193
Irene Diggs	**1:** 196
William Edward Burghardt (W. E. B.) Du Bois	**1:** 209

Mary Hatwood Futrell	**2:** 250
Henry Louis Gates Jr.	**2:** 261
Anita Hill	**2:** 344
Elma Lewis	**3:** 473
Naomi Long Madgett	**3:** 484
George Marion McClellan	**3:** 512
Elsanda Goode Robeson	**3:** 618
Charlemae Hill Rollins	**3:** 627
Gloria Scott	**4:** 654
Betty Shabazz	**5:** 189
Shelby Steele	**4:** 686
Niara Sudarkasa	**4:** 693
Mary Church Terrell	**4:** 707
Booker T. Washington	**4:** 758
William Julius Wilson	**6:** 221
Carter G. Woodson	**4:** 798

Exploration and adventure

Bessie Coleman	**1:** 158
Matthew Henson	**2:** 338
Mae C. Jemison	**2:** 394
Ronald McNair	**5:** 159

Fashion

Naomi Campbell	**1:** 116
Whitney Houston	**2:** 359
Beverly Johnson	**2:** 397
Elizabeth Keckley	**3:** 441
Patrick Kelly	**3:** 443
Annie Turnbo Malone	**3:** 490
Naomi Sims	**4:** 672

Film

Harry Belafonte	**1:** 55
Halle Berry	**1:** 61, **5:** 13 (u)

Naomi Campbell	**1:** 116
Dorothy Dandridge	**5:** 47
Ossie Davis	**1:** 188
Sammy Davis Jr.	**1:** 191
Ruby Dee	**6:** 63
Robin Givens	**2:** 273
Danny Glover	**2:** 276
Whoopi Goldberg	**2:** 278
Dick Gregory	**2:** 289
Arsenio Hall	**2:** 304
Gregory Hines	**2:** 349
Lena Horne	**2:** 357
Whitney Houston	**2:** 359
Ice-T	**2:** 371
Janet Jackson	**2:** 376
Beverly Johnson	**2:** 397
James Earl Jones	**2:** 413
Spike Lee	**3:** 467, **6:** 157 (u)
Hattie McDaniel	**3:** 515
Thelma "Butterfly" McQueen	**3:** 525, **5:** 165 (u)
Eddie Murphy	**3:** 552
Gordon Parks	**3:** 575
Sidney Poitier	**3:** 580
Richard Pryor	**3:** 597
Paul Robeson	**3:** 621
Diana Ross	**3:** 629
Tupac Shakur	**5:** 197
O. J. Simpson	**5:** 207
John Singleton	**4:** 674
Wesley Snipes	**4:** 680
Robert Townsend	**4:** 721
Tina Turner	**5:** 217
Mario Van Peebles	**4:** 737
Denzel Washington	**4:** 761

Entries by Field of Endeavor

Keenen Ivory Wayans. **4:** 769
Oprah Winfrey **4:** 792

Government and politics

Marion Barry . . . . **1:** 45, **5:** 9 (u)
Mary McLeod Bethune **1:** 63
Julian Bond . . . . **1:** 67, **6:** 31 (u)
Moseley Carol Braun **1:** 80
Edward W. Brooke, III **1:** 83
Ron Brown . . . . **1:** 95, **5:** 17 (u)
Ralph Bunche. **1:** 104
Yvonne Burke Brathwaite **1:** 106
Shirley Chisholm. . . . . **1:** 138, **6:** 51 (u)
David Dinkins **1:** 198
Marcus Garvey **2:** 255
Zelma Watson George . . . . **2:** 263, **5:** 93 (u)
W. Wilson Goode. **2:** 281
Patricia Harris. **2:** 328
Alexis Herman **5:** 115
Jesse Jackson . . . . **2:** 378, **6:** 137 (u)
Jesse Jackson Jr. **5:** 121
Barbara Jordan . . . . **2:** 424, **5:** 133 (u)
Sharon Pratt Kelly **3:** 445
Alan Keyes **5:** 147
Jewel Stradford Lafontant **3:** 462
Constance Baker Motley **3:** 544
Hazel O'Leary **3:** 565
Adam Clayton Powell Jr **3:** 583
Maxine Waters **6:** 211
L. Douglas Wilder **4:** 773
Andrew Young **5:** 249
Coleman Young. . . . . **4:** 803, **6:** 233 (u)

Law

Carol Mosely Braun **1:** 80

Entries by Field of Endeavor | xiii

Yvonne Braithwaite Burke **1:** 106
Marian Wright Edelman **2:** 223
Patricia Harris. **2:** 328
Anita Hill **2:** 344
Benjamin L. Hooks **2:** 354
Charles Hamilton Houston **6:** 127
Barbara Jordan . . . . **2:** 424, **5:** 133 (u)
Vernon E. Jordan Jr. . . . . **2:** 430, **6:** 143 (u)
Flo Kennedy **2:** 448
Jewel Stradford Lafontant **3:** 462
Thurgood Marshall **3:** 504
Constance Baker Motley **3:** 544
Pauli Murray **3:** 555
Edith Sampson **4:** 647
Althea T. L. Simmons **4:** 667
Juanita Kidd Stout **4:** 691
Clarence Thomas **4:** 710

Literature and journalism

Robert S. Abbott. **6:** 1
Maya Angelou **1:** 17
Molefi Kete Asante. **1:** 23
James Baldwin **1:** 34
Amiri Baraka. **1:** 37
Ida B. Wells Barnett **1:** 40
Daisy Bates. **1:** 50
Arna Bontemps. **1:** 73
Ed Bradley **1:** 78
Gwendolyn Brooks. **1:** 86
Claude Brown **1:** 88
H. Rap Brown **1:** 91
Ed Bullins **1:** 99
Octavia E. Butler **1:** 109
Stokely Carmichael . . . . **1:** 118, **6:** 34 (u)

Charles Waddell Chesnutt	**1:** 132
Alice Childress	**1:** 135, **5:** 27 (u)
Eldridge Cleaver	**1:** 143, **6:** 57 (u)
Anna J. Cooper	**1:** 165
Countee Cullen	**1:** 178
Ruby Dee	**6:** 63
Delany Sisters	**5:** 59
William Edward Burghardt (W. E. B.) Du Bois	**1:** 209
Paul Laurence Dunbar	**1:** 212
Ralph Ellison	**2:** 232, **5:** 67 (u)
John Hope Franklin	**2:** 247
Ernest J. Gaines	**2:** 253
Henry Louis Gates Jr.	**2:** 261
Nikki Giovanni	**2:** 271
Charles Gordone	**2:** 284, **5:** 97 (u)
Angelina Weld Grimké	**2:** 291
Alex Haley	**2:** 301
Virginia Hamilton	**2:** 309
Lorraine Hansberry	**2:** 317
Frances Ellen Watkins Harper	**6:** 119
Robert Hayden	**2:** 330
Chester Himes	**2:** 346
Langston Hughes	**2:** 362
Zora Neale Hurston	**2:** 368
James Weldon Johnson	**2:** 402
Alan Keyes	**5:** 147
Naomi Long Madgett	**3:** 464
Paule Marshall	**3:** 501
George Marion McClellan	**3:** 512
Claude McKay	**3:** 517
Terry McMillan	**3:** 522, **5:** 155 (u)
Ron Milner	**3:** 530
Toni Morrison	**3:** 541
Willard Motley	**3:** 546

Gloria Naylor	3: 557
Huey Newton	3: 560
Gordon Parks	3: 575
Dudley Randall	3: 607
William Raspberry	3: 613
Ishmael Reed	3: 616
Charlemae Hill Rollins	3: 627
Carl T. Rowan	3: 632
Sonia Sanchez	4: 649
Philippa Duke Schuyler	6: 185
Bobby Seale	4: 657
Ntozake Shange	4: 662
Carole Simpson	4: 670
Shelby Steele	4: 686
Mildred Taylor	4: 699
Susan Taylor	4: 702
Jean Toomer	4: 713
William Monroe Trotter	4: 724
Mario Van Peebles	4: 737
Alice Walker	4: 747
Phillis Wheatley	4: 771
John A. Williams	4: 782
Sherley Anne Williams	4: 787
August Wilson	4: 790
Carter G. Woodson	4: 798
Richard Wright	4: 800
Whitney M. Young	4: 806

Medicine

Clive O. Callender	6: 37
Benjamin Carson	1: 121
Charles Richard Drew	1: 207
Joycelyn Elders	6: 81
Effie O'Neal Ellis	2: 230

Lucille C. Gunning	**2:** 297
Mae C. Jemison	**2:** 394
Daniel Hale Williams	**4:** 779

Military

Benjamin O. Davis, Sr.	**1:** 183
Marcelite J. Harris	**2:** 325
Daniel James Jr.	**2:** 392
Colin Powell	**3:** 586, **5:** 171 (u)
Tuskegee Airmen	**5:** 225

Music

Marian Anderson	**1:** 14
Louis Armstrong	**1:** 20
Pearl Bailey	**1:** 28
Josephine Baker	**1:** 32
Count Basie	**1:** 48
Kathleen Battle	**1:** 53
Romare Bearden	**6:** 21
Harry Belafonte	**1:** 55
Chuck Berry	**1:** 58
James Brown	**1:** 93
Grace Bumbry	**1:** 101
Cab Calloway	**1:** 111, **5:** 23 (u)
Naomi Campbell	**1:** 116
Ray Charles	**1:** 130
Natalie Cole	**1:** 155
Nat "King" Cole	**1:** 153
John Coltrane	**1:** 163
Elizabeth Cotten	**1:** 173
Miles Davis	**1:** 186
Sammy Davis Jr.	**1:** 191
Thomas A. Dorsey	**1:** 201
Duke Ellington	**2:** 227
Ella Fitzgerald	**2:** 242, **5:** 77 (u)

Aretha Franklin	**2:** 245
Zelma Watson George	**2:** 263, **5:** 93 (u)
Dizzy Gillespie	**2:** 268
Berry Gordy Jr	**2:** 286
Hammer	**2:** 312
Lionel Hampton	**2:** 314
Jimi Hendrix	**2:** 336
Billie Holiday	**2:** 351
Lena Horne	**2:** 357
Whitney Houston	**2:** 359
Ice-T	**2:** 371
Janet Jackson	**2:** 376
Mahalia Jackson	**2:** 382
Michael Jackson	**2:** 384
Beverly Johnson	**2:** 397
Robert Johnson	**2:** 409
Quincy Jones	**2:** 416
Sissieretta Jones	**2:** 419
Scott Joplin	**2:** 421
B. B. King	**3:** 451
Coretta Scott King	**3:** 453
Little Richard	**3:** 476
Branford Marsalis	**3:** 495
Wynton Marsalis	**3:** 498
Hattie McDaniel	**3:** 515
Thelonious Monk	**3:** 533
Jessye Norman	**3:** 562
Leontyne Price	**3:** 589
Charley Pride	**3:** 592
Public Enemy	**3:** 599
Queen Latifah	**3:** 605
Bernice Johnson Reagon	**6:** 177
Paul Robeson	**3:** 621
Diana Ross	**3:** 629

Philippa Duke Schuyler	**6:** 185
Tupac Shakur	**5:** 197
Nina Simone	**6:** 203
Bessie Smith	**4:** 677
William Grant Still	**4:** 689
Tina Turner	**5:** 217
Sarah Vaughan	**4:** 739
Sippie Wallace	**4:** 755
André Watts	**4:** 766
Stevie Wonder	**4:** 795

Religion

Ralph David Abernathy	**1:** 5
George Clements	**1:** 146
Louis Farrakhan	**2:** 239, **5:** 71 (u)
Father Divine	**6:** 91
Barbara Harris	**2:** 323
Benjamin L. Hooks	**2:** 354
Jesse Jackson	**2:** 378, **6:** 137 (u)
Martin Luther King Jr.	**3:** 456
Malcolm X	**3:** 487
Eugene A. Marino	**3:** 493
Elijah Muhammad	**3:** 549
Adam Clayton Powell Jr.	**3:** 583
Al Sharpton	**4:** 664
George Stallings	**4:** 683

Science and technology

Benjamin Banneker	**5:** 1
George Washington Carver	**1:** 124
Jewel Plummer Cobb	**1:** 148
Shirley Ann Jackson	**2:** 387
Mae C. Jemison	**2:** 394
Lewis Howard Latimer	**6:** 149
Elijah McCoy	**6:** 163

Ronald McNair	**5:** 159
Garrett Morgan	**3:** 538
Lloyd Albert Quarterman	**3:** 602
Eslanda Goode Robeson	**3:** 618
Daniel Hale Williams	**4:** 779

Social issues

Robert S. Abbott	**6:** 1
Ralph Abernathy	**1:** 5
Arthur Ashe	**1:** 25
Ella Jo Baker	**6:** 13
Amiri Baraka	**1:** 37
Ida B. Wells Barnett	**1:** 40
Daisy Bates	**1:** 50
Harry Belafonte	**1:** 55
Mary McLeod Bethune	**1:** 63
Julian Bond	**1:** 67, **6:** 31 (u)
H. Rap Brown	**1:** 91
Stokely Carmichael	**1:** 118, **6:** 45 (u)
Cinque	**5:** 31
Eldridge Cleaver	**1:** 143, **6:** 57
George Clements	**1:** 146
Johnnetta Betsch Cole	**1:** 151
Bill Cosby	**1:** 170, **5:** 41 (u)
Ellen Craft	**1:** 175
Angela Davis	**1:** 180
Ruby Dee	**6:** 63
Irene Diggs	**1:** 196
Joyce Dixson	**6:** 73
Frederick Douglass	**1:** 204
William Edward Burghardt (W. E. B.) Du Bois	**1:** 209
Katherine Dunham	**1:** 215
Marian Wright Edelman	**2:** 223
Joycelyn Elders	**6:** 81

Medgar Evers	**2:** 234
James Farmer	**2:** 237
Father Divine	**6:** 91
T. Thomas Fortune	**6:** 101
Marcus Garvey	**2:** 255
Zelma Watson George	**2:** 263, **5:** 93 (u)
Dick Gregory	**2:** 289
Clara Hale	**2:** 299
Fannie Lou Hamer	**2:** 307
Frances Ellen Watkins Harper	**6:** 119
Dorothy Height	**2:** 333
Aileen Hernandez	**2:** 341
Anita Hill	**2:** 344
Benjamin L. Hooks	**2:** 354
Roy Innis	**2:** 374
Jesse Jackson	**2:** 378, **6:** 137 (u)
John Jacob	**2:** 389
James Weldon Johnson	**2:** 402
Vernon E. Jordan Jr.	**2:** 430, **6:** 143 (u)
Flo Kennedy	**3:** 448
Alan Keyes	**5:** 147
Coretta Scott King	**3:** 453
Martin Luther King Jr.	**3:** 456
Yolanda King	**3:** 459
Joseph E. Lowery	**3:** 482
Malcolm X	**3:** 487
Biddy Mason	**3:** 507
Floyd B. McKissick	**3:** 520
James Meredith	**3:** 527
Audley Moore	**3:** 536, **6:** 171 (u)
Elijah Muhammad	**3:** 549
Pauli Murray	**3:** 555
Huey Newton	**3:** 560
Rosa Parks	**3:** 578

A. Philip Randolph **3:** 610
Bernice Johnson Reagon **6:** 177
Eslanda Goode Robeson **3:** 618
Paul Robeson **3:** 621
Bayard Rustin **3:** 639
Dred Scott **4:** 652
Bobby Seale **4:** 657
Attalah Shabazz **4:** 659
Betty Shabazz **5:** 189
Assata Shakur **6:** 193
Al Sharpton **4:** 664
Althea T. L. Simmons **4:** 667
Nina Simone **6:** 203
Shelby Steele **4:** 686
Susie Baker King Taylor **4:** 704
Mary Church Terrell **4:** 707
Toussaint-Louverture **4:** 718
William Monroe Trotter **4:** 724
Sojourner Truth **4:** 727
Harriet Tubman **4:** 730
Nat Turner **4:** 733
Denmark Vesey **4:** 742
Charleszetta Waddles **4:** 744
Madame C. J. Walker **4:** 750
Maxine Waters **6:** 211
Faye Wattleton **4:** 763
Roy Wilkins **4:** 776
William Julius Wilson **6:** 221
Andrew Young **5:** 249
Whitney M. Young **4:** 806

Sports

Hank Aaron **1:** 1
Kareem Abdul-Jabbar **1:** 3

Muhammad Ali	**1:** 11
Arthur Ashe	**1:** 25
Dave Bing	**1:** 65
Bobby Bonilla	**1:** 71
Riddick Bowe	**1:** 75
Roy Campanella	**1:** 114
Wilt Chamberlain	**1:** 127
Dominique Dawes	**5:** 53
George Foreman	**5:** 81
Althea Gibson	**2:** 266
Josh Gibson	**6:** 111
The Harlem Globetrotters	**2:** 320
Florence Griffith Joyner	**5:** 101
Earvin "Magic" Johnson	**2:** 400, **5:** 127 (u)
Michael Jordan	**2:** 427, **5:** 139 (u)
Jackie Joyner-Kersee	**2:** 432
Carl Lewis	**3:** 471
Joe Louis	**3:** 479
Willie Mays	**3:** 509
Shaquille O'Neal	**3:** 567
Jesse Owens	**3:** 570
Satchel Paige	**3:** 573
Jackie Robinson	**3:** 624
Wilma Rudolph	**3:** 634, **5:** 185 (u)
Bill Russell	**3:** 637
O. J. Simpson	**5:** 207
Venus Williams	**5:** 233
Eldrick "Tiger" Woods	**5:** 239

Television

Ed Bradley	**1:** 78
Don Cornelius	**1:** 168
Bill Cosby	**1:** 170, **5:** 41 (u)
Ruby Dee	**6:** 63

Whoopi Goldberg	**2:** 278
Dick Gregory	**2:** 289
Bryant Gumbel	**2:** 294
Greg Gumbel	**5:** 109
Arsenio Hall	**2:** 304
Carl T. Rowan	**3:** 632
Carole Simpson	**4:** 670
Susan Taylor	**4:** 702
Robert Townsend	**4:** 721
Keenen Ivory Wayans	**4:** 769
Montel Williams	**4:** 784
Oprah Winfrey	**4:** 792

Theater

Ruby Dee	**6:** 63
Charles Gordone	**2:** 284, **5:** 97 (u)
Yolanda King	**3:** 459
Paul Robeson	**3:** 621
Attalah Shabazz	**4:** 659
Jackie Torrence	**4:** 716

Reader's Guide

Josh Gibson

African American Biography, Volume 6, presents the life stories 20 notable African Americans, as well as updates to 10 people who appeared in volumes 1 to 4 of *African American Biography.* Encompassing both historical and contemporary figures, the biographies present prominent African Americans from many fields of endeavor, including athletics, politics, literature, entertainment, science, religion, and the military.

In Volume 6, students will read about transplant surgeon Clive O. Callender, U.S. representative Maxine Waters, Negro League home run king Josh Gibson, and musician and historian Bernice Johnson Reagon, among others. Updated entries include those of librarian and storyteller Augusta Baker, former Detroit mayor Coleman Young, and filmmaker Spike Lee.

Other features in *African American Biography, Volume 6,* include:

- Over 45 black-and-white photos

Portrait: Reproduced by permission of Corbis-Bettmann.

- A list of African Americans from all six volumes by their field of specialization
- Sidebar boxes that highlight people and information of special interest to students
- Sources for further reading so students know where to delve even deeper
- A subject index that allows students to easily find the people, organizations, and concepts discussed in all six volumes

African American Reference Library

The *African American Biography* set is only one component of the five-part African American Reference Library. Other titles in this multicultural series are:

- *African American Almanac:* This three-volume set provides a comprehensive range of historical and current information on African American life and culture. Organized by subject, the volumes contain 270 black-and-white illustrations, a selected bibliography, and a cumulative subject index.

- *African American Breakthroughs:* This volume provides fascinating details on hundreds of "firsts" involving African Americans. Arranged in subject categories, the entries summarize events and include brief biographies of many pioneers in African American history. This volume features illustrations, a timeline of firsts, and a thorough subject index.

- *African American Chronology:* This two-volume set explores significant social, political, economic, cultural, and educational milestones in black history. Arranged by year and then by month and day, the volumes span from 1492 until June 30, 1993, and contain 106 illustrations, extensive cross references, and a cumulative subject index.

- *African American Voices:* This title presents 35 full or excerpted speeches and other notable spoken works of African Americans. Each entry is accompanied by an introduction and boxes explaining terms and events to which the speech refers. The two-volume set contains pertinent black-and-white illustrations, a timeline, and a subject index.

Acknowledgments

Special thanks to Premilla Nadasen, assistant professor of African-American history at Queens College, for helping develop the list of entries; to the youth librarians and reference librarians at the Ann Arbor Public Library for providing assistance with research; and to William F. Shea and Ryan Patrick Shea for their love and patience.

Advisors

Many thanks to the following advisors who provided valuable comments and suggestions for *African American Biography, Volume 6:*

- Du'Charm Lanese Archer
  Instructor in English as a second language
  Teach for America
  New York, New York

- Jamie Hart
  Center for Research on Learning and Teaching
  University of Michigan
  Ann Arbor, Michigan

- Frances Hasso
  Assistant professor of sociology
  Antioch College
  Yellow Springs, Ohio

- Elizabeth James
  Librarian
  Center for Afroamerican and African Studies
  University of Michigan
  Ann Arbor, Michigan

- Kidada Williams
  Doctoral candidate in history
  University of Michigan
  Ann Arbor, Michigan

Comments and suggestions

We welcome your comments on *African American Biography* as well as your suggestions for biographies to be featured in future volumes. Please write: Editors, *African American Biography,* U•X•L, 27500 Drake Rd., Farmington Hills, Michigan, 48331–3535; call toll-free: 1–800–877–4253; fax to 248–414–8066; or send e-mail via http://www.galegroup.com.

Robert S. Abbott

Born November 24, 1870
St. Simon's Island, Georgia
Died February 29, 1940
Chicago, Illinois
Newspaper publisher,
civil rights activist

With the printing press as his weapon, Robert Abbott fought to improve the lives of African Americans. At a time when white-owned newspapers ignored African Americans (except when one was involved in a crime), Abbott used the *Chicago Defender* to celebrate African American achievements, to publicize lynchings and other injustices done to blacks, and to urge blacks to stand up for their rights. Abbott influenced thousands of blacks to migrate northward, to take advantage of economic opportunities generated by World War I (1914–18). Abbott created a lasting legacy; the *Chicago Defender* is still being published today.

Abbott was born on St. Simon's Island, off the coast of Georgia. Although Abbott's generally accepted birthdate is November 24, 1870, his baptism records, published in the Parish Register of St. Stephens Episcopal Church (now St. Matthews) in Savannah, indicate that he was born on November 28, 1868.

"I wanted to create [a publication] that would mirror the needs, opinions and the aspirations of my race."

Abbott's parents were former slaves and grocers named Thomas and Flora Abbott. Thomas Abbott died when Robert Abbott was four months old. In 1874 his mother remarried John Sengstacke, a minister and storekeeper. Sengstacke was the son of a German man and a slave; he had been raised in Germany. For most of his childhood, Abbott lived above Sengstacke's store in Savannah, Georgia.

Sengstacke was the greatest influence in young Abbott's life. Sengstacke instilled in Abbott a sense of fairness and a willingness to fight for equal rights for African Americans. Abbott later took his stepfather's surname as his own middle name.

Earns degrees in printing and law

After high school, Abbott began his college career at Claflin College in Orangeburg, South Carolina. He then went to the all-black Hampton Institute in Virginia to learn the printing trade.

In 1893 Abbott traveled with the Hampton Institute Quartet to perform songs at the Columbian Exposition in Chicago. At the Exposition, Abbott heard Frederick Douglass (1817–1985; see entry in volume 1), the famous abolitionist, speak. Over the shouts of a group of white hecklers (people who harass a public speaker), Douglass strongly denounced racial injustice. That event inspired Abbott to make a personal commitment to advancing the rights of African Americans.

Upon graduating from Hampton, Abbott moved to Chicago. There he had a hard time finding employers willing to hire a black printer. Discouraged with the printing industry, Abbott decided to change fields. He enrolled at the Chicago Kent College of Law and graduated in 1899, the only African American in his class, only to find that blacks were no more welcomed in the legal profession than they were in the printing profession. After attempting to establish law practices in Gary, Indiana, and Topeka, Kansas, Abbott returned to Chicago in 1905, nearly penniless.

The *Chicago Defender's* humble beginnings

Abbott, more determined than ever to fight against racial oppression, sat down with his typewriter in his landlady's dining room on March 4, 1905, and cranked out the first edition of the *Chicago Defender*. Beneath the "Chicago Defender" banner he typed: "The World's Greatest Weekly Newspaper." Abbott's first paper was four pages long. He printed 300 copies and sold them door-to-door through black neighborhoods, and in churches, barbershops, and poolrooms.

From the start, the primary mission of the *Chicago Defender* was to provide a voice for African Americans and to denounce racial injustice. "I wanted to create an organ that would mirror the needs, opinions and the aspirations of my race," Abbott once stated.

The *Defender* grows

Abbott continued to publish the paper weekly, calling upon his friends to write articles and to make financial contributions. Before long, the *Defender* made its way to the South—home to more than 90 percent of the nation's African American population. By 1915, one decade after its founding, the *Defender's* circulation had grown to 230,000. Two-thirds of those copies were sold outside of Chicago. Each copy of the *Defender*, which contained reminders to "pass it on," was read by an estimated five people. Of the 280 or so black newspapers in the nation, the *Defender* had become the leading seller.

Abbott was bold and uninhibited in his editorials against racial oppression. He wrote opinions that no southern black paper would have been able to, without fear of its editors being killed or its office being burned to the ground. Abbott mocked the white papers for their practice of printing (Negro) after a black person's name; in the *Defender*, whenever a white person was mentioned the name was followed by (White).

It is difficult to overstate the importance of the *Defender* to African Americans during that time. The paper's influence in black communities was rivaled only by the church. For

Abbott Takes on Lynching

Robert S. Abbott frequently denounced lynching in the pages of the *Chicago Defender*. (Lynching is the extra-legal execution of a person [usually an African American] accused of a crime or a violation of social mores, often by hanging, by a group of three or more people.) In the late 1800s and early 1900s. white Americans, even supposedly "respectable" people such as pastors, condoned (approved of) lynching as a way to keep blacks submissive (humbly obedient). A black person could be lynched for attempting to vote, testifying in court, showing disrespect to a white man, or (for a black man) merely speaking to a white woman. Sometimes whites lynched blacks for no reason at all; even black women and children fell victim to lynching.

While lynchings had occurred since the time of slavery, the number of lynchings greatly increased in the late 1800s. Between 1889 and 1899, lynchings averaged 104 per year in the South and 23 per year in the North. Between 1900 and 1909, an average of 84 southern blacks, and 8 northern blacks per year lost their lives to lynching. A total of 3,000 black Americans were lynched between 1882 and 1919.

Lynchings went largely unreported in the white press. Abbott, however, reported lynchings on the front page using big, bold headlines. He described the horrors of lynchings, such as victims being burned alive or castrated. Abbott advised black people to defend themselves against lynching. He wrote: "When the mob comes, take at least one with you"; and "When the white fiends come to the door, shoot them down."

southern blacks, whose lives were completely dominated by white employers and landlords, the *Defender* provided a source of invaluable (beyond calculable value) information and advice—it gave voice to their fears and aspirations. For former slaves, the *Defender* offered proof that they were really free. The *Defender* even reached the ears of those who could not read: it was read aloud in churches, on street corners, and in barbershops.

Encourages northward migration

Prior to the outbreak of World War I (1914–18), Abbott had advised blacks to stay in the South and work for social reform. He changed his position in 1916, however, due to the boost in wartime production. Northern factories had to meet growing demands for armaments (weapons) and other goods; at the same time, white workers were going off to war. Suddenly the steel mills and packing houses of Chicago had a shortage of workers. Abbott felt that southern blacks should take advantage of the employment opportunities in Chicago and other northern cities, as well as the greater personal freedoms the North provided.

Abbott made it a personal crusade to bring as many blacks to the North as possible. He used articles, editorials, advertisements, and cartoons to get his message across. Abbott printed train schedules from southern points of origin to Chicago, gave practical information about where to find housing and employment, and wrote about movie theaters and night clubs in the black parts of town. He personally responded to the inquiries mailed to him by African Americans who were considering coming to Chicago.

In large part due to Abbott's efforts, ten thousand blacks per month left the South in 1916. Between 1916 and 1919, five hundred thousand southern blacks left their homes for the North or West. During the 1920s, one million more blacks left the South.

White southerners try to stop the *Defender*

By 1917, the exodus of African Americans from the South was making a great impact on the region's economy. White employers, who initially believed the blacks would return after experiencing the cold northern climate, realized the blacks were gone for good. It was statements like the following made by Abbott in the February 27, 1917, issue of the *Defender* that kept blacks from returning to the South: "If you can freeze to death in the North and be free, why freeze to death in the South and be a slave, where your mother, sister and daughter are raped ... where your father, brother and son are ... hung to a pole [and] riddled with bullets."

In their desperation, white employers sought to ban the *Defender*. Municipalities (cities, towns, or other districts with governing bodies) passed laws against the publication or sale of black papers (in defiance of the Constitution), police confiscated bundles of the *Defender* at railway platforms, and people were arrested for peddling the paper.

Abbott turned to black railroad porters for assistance. The porters gladly took on the task of distributing the *Defender* throughout the South. They hid bundles of the paper on trains and tossed the bundles out in the countryside. Rural people would retrieve the papers and pass them around their communities. Southern whites learned that the *Defender* could not be stopped.

Reports on the 1919 riots

During the summer of 1919, often called "Red Summer," there were race riots in at least twenty-five cities throughout the nation. Race riots—in which mobs of white people terrorized black residents and destroyed their property—had been occurring, mostly in the South, since the late 1800s. In the summer of 1919 racial tensions exploded; hundreds of people were killed, most of them black. The 1919 riots marked a turning point in race relations in that, for the first time, blacks vigorously fought back. Some of the deadliest rioting that summer took place in Chicago.

In July 1919, the Chicago riots claimed the lives of more than thirty people and caused hundreds of injuries. The rioting was sparked when a white man stoned and drowned a young African American swimmer who had allegedly crossed into the "white" swimming area in Lake Michigan. Police refused to arrest the white assailant and instead arrested a black man they accused of harassing a white man.

For two years prior to the riots, Abbott had warned that the growing anger in the black community over employment and housing conditions would one day erupt in violence. Once the rioting began, Abbott reported extensively on the events and kept a tally of fatalities. He emphatically (forcefully) advised his readership to stay home and out of harm's way.

After the riots, Abbott was named to the Chicago Commission on Race Relations. In 1922 that group published a report entitled "The Negro in Chicago." This famous report looked at the causes of the 1919 riots and assessed race relations in the aftermath of the great northward migration of African Americans.

Abbott becomes a millionaire

As the circulation of the *Defender* continued to grow, so did Abbott's personal wealth. He had acquired $500,000 by 1920 and by the early 1930s he had become a millionaire—the first black publisher to do so.

Previously humble and modest, Abbott the millionaire acquired expensive tastes. He began wearing tailor-made suits, riding in a chauffeur-driven Rolls Royce limousine, smoking Havana cigars, and carrying a gold-handled walking stick. He purchased the best seats for cultural events and traveled frequently through Europe. He insisted that everyone, even his wife, address him as "Mr. Abbott."

Abbott dies; the *Defender* lives on

Abbott died on February 29, 1940, of Bright's disease (an ailment characterized by high blood pressure and the presence of proteins in the urine). Upon Abbott's death, his nephew, John H. Sengstacke, inherited the *Defender*. Abbott had been grooming Sengstacke for the position; since 1934 Sengstacke, who graduated from Hampton Institute like his uncle, had served as Abbott's assistant.

In 1956 Sengstacke changed the weekly newspaper to a daily. Sengstacke oversaw the paper's operations until his death in 1997. The *Chicago Defender* remains the nation's largest black-owned daily newspaper.

Sources for further reading

Altman, Susan. *The Encyclopedia of African-American Heritage.* New York: Facts on File, Inc., 1997, p. 1.

The Black Press: Soldiers Without Swords (videocassette). San Francisco: Half Nelson Productions, Inc., 1998.

Celebrating 91 Years of History—The Chicago Defender. [Online] Available http://aman.interman.net/bronzeville/defend.htm (accessed April 15, 1999).

Doreski, C.K. "From News to History: Robert Abbott and Carl Sandburg Read the 1919 Chicago Riot." *African American Review.* Winter 1992: pp. 637+.

"John H. Sengstacke, Trailblazing Publisher, Dies at 84 (obituary)." *Jet.* June 16, 1997: pp. 4+.

Ottley, Roi. *The Lonely Warrior: The Life and Times of Robert S. Abbott, Founder of the Chicago Defender Newspaper.* Chicago: Henry Regnery Company, 1955.

Ploski, Harry A., and James Williams, eds. *The Negro Almanac: A Reference Work on the African American.* 5th edition. Detroit: Gale Research, 1989, p. 1265.

Smallwood, David, et. al. *Profiles of Great African Americans.* Lincolnwood, IL: Publications International, Ltd., 1996, pp. 10–11.

Augusta Baker

Born April 1, 1911
Baltimore, Maryland
Died February 23, 1998
Columbia, South Carolina
Librarian, storyteller

UPDATE

Augusta Baker was a spellbinding storyteller and influential librarian. During her thirty-seven-year career at the New York Public Library she coordinated children's services and storytelling. Baker crusaded for the publication of children's literature that portrayed African Americans in a realistic manner. After moving to South Carolina, Baker began her second career as storyteller in residence at the University of South Carolina. **(See original entry on Baker in volume 1.)**

Baker was born in Baltimore in 1911, the only child of Winfort and Mabel Braxston. Both of Baker's parents were teachers; they surrounded her with books and stressed the importance of education.

At age of sixteen Baker went to live with her aunt in Pennsylvania and enrolled in the University of Pittsburgh. There she met and married Jim Baker, a graduate of Lincoln University. Baker accompanied her new husband to Albany,

"Let the story tell itself, and if it is a good story and you have prepared it well, you do not need all the extras."

Portrait: Reproduced by permission of the Granger Collection, New York.

New York, where he had been hired to set up an interracial council for the Urban League.

Baker continued her education in Albany at the New York College for Teachers (today called the State University of New York at Albany). She was almost denied the opportunity to student-teach at the prestigious Milne School, because of the color of her skin (there had never been a black teacher or student at the school). Baker was granted a position only through the intervention of Eleanor Roosevelt, wife of Franklin D. Roosevelt (at that time governor of New York; served as president of the United States from 1933–1945) and a board member of the Urban League.

In 1933 Baker graduated with a teaching certificate. The following year she completed a degree in library science. Baker and her husband then moved to New York City.

Spearheads reforms in African American children's literature

After a short stint as a teacher, Baker was hired as a children's librarian for the New York Public Library's Countee Cullen Branch (in Harlem) in 1937. She rapidly became dismayed at the depiction of African Americans in children's literature as shiftless, happy, grinning, clownish creatures speaking ridiculous dialects.

Baker spoke out against the offensive stereotyping and began compiling lists of children's books in which blacks were realistically portrayed. Baker's first list, which came out in 1941, was made available for library visitors' use. In 1946 she published a bibliography through the New York Public Library entitled *Books About Negro Life for Children*. In later editions, this publication was called *The Black Experience in Children's Books*.

At the Countee Cullen Branch, Baker began acquiring high-quality children's books about African American lives and experiences. She placed the books in the James Weldon Johnson Memorial Collection, named for the distinguished author (1871–1938; see entry in volume 2) and first black executive director of the National Association for the

Advancement of Colored People (NAACP). Part of that collection is now housed at the Schomberg Center for Research in Black Culture, in New York.

Shares storytelling talents

When Baker began her career as a librarian, common wisdom held that storytelling was an integral component of early childhood education. Choosing folk tales set in Africa and the Caribbean, Baker captivated children and adults alike.

Baker was introduced to storytelling at an early age. "My grandmother on my mother's side was a marvelous storyteller," reminisced Baker in a 1995 interview for *Horn Book* magazine. "She told me the old English tales and of course Br'er Rabbit stories.... As an only child I was entertained for hours with her wonderful stories."

For students of storytelling, Baker offered the following advice in *Horn Book*: "Let the story tell itself, and if it is a good story and you have prepared it well, you do not need all the extras—the costumes, the histrionics, the high drama. Children of all ages do want to hear stories. Select well, prepare well, and then go forth, stand tall, and just tell."

In addition to her oral presentation of stories, Baker published four collections of stories: *Talking Tree* (1955), *Golden Lynx* (1960), *Young Years: Best Loved Stories and Poems for Little Children* (1960), and *Once Upon a Time* (1964).

Promoted to coordinator of children's services

In 1953 Baker was promoted to the position of assistant coordinator and storytelling specialist at the public library's main branch. Eight years later she was named coordinator of children's services—a top-level administrative position in which she was responsible for children's programs at all eighty-two branches of the New York Public Library.

During that era Baker served as a consultant for the television program "Sesame Street" and wrote numerous reviews of children's books for the *New York Times*. She also compiled the *New York Times Book Review*'s list of best-illustrated books and served as chairperson of the selection committee for the Newbery-Caldecott Award.

Moves South, becomes "storyteller in residence"

Baker retired from the New York Public Library in 1974. For the next five years she continued producing a weekly radio show on WNYC called *The World of Children's Literature,* and presenting lectures at Columbia University's program in library sciences. In 1977 Baker cowrote, with Ellin Green, the book *Storytelling: Art and Technique.*

In 1980 Baker moved with her second husband, Gordon Alexander, to Columbia, South Carolina. There Baker began a new position as storyteller-in-residence at the University of South Carolina (USC). In 1987 USC and the Richland County Public Library honored Baker by initiating a yearly storytelling festival called "A(ugusta) Baker's Dozen." In 1993 the Association of Library Services to Children of the American Library Association bestowed upon Baker its highest honor: the Distinguished Services Award.

In a 1995 interview Baker lamented the demise of storytelling in the modern era. "As far as storytelling goes," she commented, "it seems that young people coming out of library school today are telling themselves that children do not want to listen to stories, so they do not want to take the time to learn them. It makes me sad!"

Sources for further reading

Glick, Andrea. "Storyteller Leaves Lasting Legacy" (obituary). *School Library Journal*. April 1998: p. 13.

Saxon, Wolfgang. "Augusta B. Baker, 86, Storyteller, Editor and Children's Librarian" (obituary). *New York Times*. March 6, 1998: p. B13.

Smith, Henrietta M. "An Interview with Augusta Baker." *Horn Book*. May-June 1995: pp. 292+

Ella Jo Baker

Born December 13, 1903
Norfolk, Virginia
Died December 13, 1986
New York, New York
Organizer for the NAACP and the SCLC, advisor to the SNCC

Ella Jo Baker was a brilliant behind-the-scenes organizer, considered by many to be the "godmother" of the civil rights movement. She championed the ideal of grassroots empowerment and member-controlled leadership in civil rights organizations. She was a living example of her philosophy that the best leaders were those people who empowered others to lead.

In an activist career spanning fifty years, Baker accomplished a tremendous amount. She established numerous chapters of the National Association for the Advancement of Colored People (NAACP) and sparked the formation of both the Southern Christian Leadership Conference (SCLC) and the Student Nonviolent Coordinating Committee (SNCC). And by taking an active role in political affairs at a time when women were expected to limit their activities to taking care of the home and children, Baker served as a role model for a generation of young women.

"My theory is, strong people don't need strong leaders."

Portrait: Reproduced by permission of AP/Wide World Photos, Inc.

Baker was born in 1903 in Norfolk, Virginia, the second of three children. Her father was a waiter; her mother was a schoolteacher who was active in the church and community affairs. At the age of eight, Baker and her family moved to Littleton, North Carolina. For the next seven years Baker lived on land that her grandparents had once lived and worked as slaves, but later purchased. Baker attended high school in Raleigh, North Carolina, then stayed in Raleigh to attend the predominantly black Shaw University. She graduated from Shaw in 1927, at the top of her class.

Later that year, Baker moved to Harlem, an area in New York City. She spent the next two years working in a factory and waitressing. In 1929 Baker accepted a position on the editorial staff of the *American West Indian News*.

Early activist positions

Baker began her career as a social activist in 1932, during the throes of the Great Depression. (The Great Depression—the worst economic crisis to ever hit the United States—began in 1929 and continued through 1939.) Her first activist position was as director of the Young Negroes Cooperative League, a branch of the Works Progress Administration (WPA; one of the many social programs initiated by President Franklin Delano Roosevelt [1882–1945] to provide jobs and pull the nation out of the Depression). In that capacity, Baker helped people form buying cooperatives so they could purchase food and other goods as a group (buying large quantities of goods and dividing them up was cheaper than buying goods individually).

In the mid-1930s Baker was also active in a women's rights organization called the Women's Day Workers and Industrial League. She wrote a book in 1935 entitled *Crisis* that exposed the miserable working conditions of domestic servants.

Works with the NAACP

Baker joined the NAACP in 1938 and in 1940 was named national director of branches (also known as field secretary). Her main responsibility was to recruit members throughout the South. She also promoted job training programs for black workers. Baker resigned from the national NAACP in 1946 (but remained active on the local level), due to differences with the organization's cumbersome bureaucracy and top-down leadership style. She felt that the NAACP would be stronger if the grassroots constituency were empowered to make their own decisions, rather than taking their directions from national leaders.

In the late 1940s and early 1950s Baker worked as a freelance consultant to numerous civil rights groups, two of which were the National Urban League (an African American community service organization active primarily in cities) and In Friendship (a New York City-based organization that raised funds for civil rights activists in the South). Baker quickly earned a reputation as an effective organizer.

In 1954, Baker became president of the New York City NAACP. In the mid-1950s, she organized parents to fight for racial integration of public schools. (Although the 1954 *Brown v. Board of Education of Topeka, Kansas* Supreme Court ruling outlawed segregation in public schools, it took several more years before most school districts allowed integration to proceed.)

Formation of the Southern Christian Leadership Conference

In December 1956, Baker approached Reverend Martin Luther King Jr. (1929–1968; see entry in volume 3) with the idea of forming an organization of black ministers to coordinate civil rights activities in the South. At the time, King was president of the Montgomery Improvement Association—the organization that had coordinated the successful, 382-day-long, Montgomery bus boycott. Baker, who had been one of the boycott's strongest supporters in the North, was impressed by the ability of King and other ministers to rally large numbers of participants. Baker felt that the momentum of the boycott should be preserved.

After some debate, King agreed with Baker's idea of forming a permanent organization. The Southern Christian Leadership Conference (SCLC) was founded in January 1957 by sixty-five black ministers from eleven southern states. The group set up headquarters in Atlanta, Georgia, and selected King as president. The ministers hired Baker as acting executive director and office manager.

Baker's role in the group's success has been greatly overlooked in most history books. As an experienced activist, Baker navigated the group through the murky political waters of the period. During her two and a half years with the SCLC, Baker was the group's senior strategist, producer and distributor of literature, and public relations director. She also coordinated the group's voter registration program, called Crusade for Citizenship.

"The kind of role that I tried to play [at the SCLC]," stated Baker in the 1980 book about women activists entitled *Moving the Mountain,* "was to pick up pieces or put together pieces out of which I hoped organization might come. My theory is, strong people don't need strong leaders."

The birth of the SNCC

In April 1960, Ella Baker organized a conference at Shaw University for members of the student sit-in movement. (Sit-ins were a form of civil rights protest in which black students, sometimes joined by white students, would request service at segregated lunch counters. The students then refused to leave when denied service.) Baker felt that students, with their boundless energy and optimism, had a great potential to bring about social change. She urged them to form an organization through which they could coordinate their actions.

The three largest civil rights organizations—the SCLC, the NAACP, and the Congress on Racial Equality (CORE)—sent representatives to the conference to try to convince the students to form a wing of their respective organizations. Baker, however, steered the students away from associating with any of the established civil rights organizations. She advised them to form an independent organization that would reflect, and respond to, the needs and experiences of the students. The new student organization, she argued, should be energetic and militant, and not cautious and conservative like the established groups.

"We ended up with about three hundred people [at the conference]," stated Baker in a 1980 interview with Ellen Canterow and Susan Gushee O'Malley for *Ms.* magazine. "The Southern Christian Leadership Conference was interested in having the students become an arm of the SCLC. They were most confident that this would be their baby, because I was their functionary and I had called the meeting. The SCLC leadership made decisions about who would speak to whom to influence the students to become part of the SCLC. Well, I disagreed. I wasn't one to say yes, just because it came from the Reverend King."

Baker also sought to foster the students' natural tendency toward participatory democracy or, as Baker called it, "group-centeredness." The established civil rights organizations were all led by strong directors who made the decisions and handed down instructions to the membership. In her years with the NAACP and the SCLC, Baker had become disillusioned with the top-down leadership style. The sign of a healthy organization, according to Baker, was "the development of people who are interested not in being leaders as much as in developing leadership among other people."

The result of the Shaw University conference was the birth of the Student Nonviolent Coordinating Committee, better known by its initials, SNCC (pronounced "snick"). Baker stayed with the SNCC through the early 1960s as an informal counselor. She gave strategy advice, helped resolve conflicts between members, and introduced the students to older activists in the South she had met while working for the NAACP. The SNCC quickly rose to the fore of the civil rights movement. It's activists were recognized as hard working, fearless, and committed warriors in the fight for racial equality.

Helps found the Mississippi Freedom Democratic Party

In 1964 Baker assisted Mississippi civil rights activists in founding a new political party, the Mississippi Freedom Democratic Party (MFDP). The MFDP was organized as an alternative to the regular Democratic Party, which excluded blacks. Baker gave the keynote address at the MFDP convention in Jackson, Mississippi, and set up the MFDP's Washington, D.C., office.

On August 6, 1964, delegates from the MFDP (including legendary Mississippi civil rights organizer Fannie Lou Hamer [1917–1977]; see entry in volume 2) headed for Atlantic City, New Jersey, where they challenged the regular Democratic Party for representation of the people of Mississippi at the national Democratic presidential convention. Baker was instrumental in drumming up support in the capital for the MFDP's challenge. Although the MFDP was unable to unseat the regular Democratic Party, it forced a change in rules to favor integrated state party delegations at future conventions and dramatized the plight of black Mississippians before a national television audience.

Active in her later years

Baker remained active in the fight for civil rights and human rights even as a senior citizen. Baker worked for liberation in Africa and fought racism in America. She was also active in women's rights groups and labor organizations, and served as an advisor to students in the anti-Vietnam War movement. She served an advisor to numerous social justice organizations and was a national board member of the Puerto Rican Solidarity Committee. Baker was in constant demand as a speaker at conferences and demonstrations throughout the nation.

"Maybe there will be a new revolution," Baker remarked in *Ms*. "I don't think there's going to be one anytime soon, to be honest—I mean among blacks or whites in this country. The best country in the world, you hear them say. I guess it may be, I haven't lived anywhere else. But it's not good enough as far as I'm concerned."

Baker died of natural causes in 1986, on her eighty-third birthday, in Harlem. A few years before Baker's death, a documentary about her life entitled *Fundi: The Story of Ella Baker* aired on public television. ("Fundi" is a Swahili [a language spoken in some parts of Africa] word for "one who hands down a craft from one generation to the next.")

Sources for further reading

Cantarow, Ellen. *Moving the Mountain: Women Working for Social Change.* Old Westbury, NY: The Feminist Press, 1980.

Cantarow, Ellen, and Susan Gushee O'Malley. "NAACP, SCLC, SNCC: Ella Baker Got Them Moving." *Ms.* June 1980: pp. 56+.

Carson, Clayborne. *In Struggle: SNCC and the Black Awakening of the 1960s.* Cambridge: Harvard University Press, 1981.

Clinton, Catherine. "Ella Baker." *The Reader's Companion to American History.* Boston: Houghton Mifflin Co., 1991: pp. 71–72.

Crawford, Vicki L., Jacqueline Anne Rouse, and Barbara Woods, eds. *Women in the Civil Rights Movement: Trailblazers and Torchbearers, 1941–1965.* Brooklyn, NY: Carlson Publishing Inc., 1990.

Dallard, Shyrlee. *Ella Baker: A Leader Behind the Scenes.* Englewood Cliffs, NJ: Silver Burdett Press, Inc., 1990.

Fundi: The Story of Ella Baker. Written, produced, and directed by Joanne Grant. New York: Icarus Films, 1986.

Giddings, Paula. *When and Where I Enter: The Impact of Black Women on Race and Sex in America.* New York: Bantam Books, 1984.

Grant, Joanne. *Ella Baker: Freedom Bound.* New York: John Wiley, 1998.

Levy, Peter B. *The Civil Rights Movement.* Westwood, CT: Greenwood Press, 1998.

"Rites Held in New York for Rights Activist Ella Baker" (obituary). *Jet.* January 19, 1987: p. 18.

Robinson, Jo Ann Gibson. *The Montgomery Bus Boycott and the Women Who Started It.* Knoxville: University of Tennessee Press, 1987.

Robnett, Belinda. *How Long? How Long? African-American Women in the Struggle for Civil Rights.* New York: Oxford University Press, 1997.

Salmond, John A. *My Mind Set on Freedom: A History of the Civil Rights Movement, 1954–1968.* Chicago: Ivan R. Dee, 1997.

Wiley, Jean. "On the Front Lines; Four Women Activists Whose Work Touched Millions of Lives: Fannie Lou Hamer, Ella Baker, Amy Jacques Garvey, and Septima Clark." *Essence.* February 1990: pp. 45+.

Romare Bearden

Born September 2, 1912
Charlotte, North Carolina

Died March 12, 1988
New York, New York

Artist, composer

Romare Bearden was an extraordinary American artist, most famous for his collages that expressed the hopes and hardships of African Americans. (Collages are works of art created by pasting onto a single surface fragments of photographs, magazine and newspaper clippings, pieces of painted paper, and other materials.) Bearden's collages and paintings reflected not only the experiences of African Americans generally, including the civil rights demonstrations and urban riots of the 1960s, but also his own experiences—his youthful summers in North Carolina, his high school years in the steel mill city of Pittsburgh, his childhood and adult years living in the vibrant jazz and art mecca of Harlem, and his later years on the Caribbean island of St. Martin.

Bearden produced some five hundred collages, paintings, and murals during his lifetime. His artwork can be found in every major museum in New York City and in many museums elsewhere in the United States. In an obituary for Bearden in

"Romare Bearden was the pictorial historian of the black world, especially in the South."

—*Gallery owner Arne Eckstrom in the* New York Times

Portrait: Photograph by Carl Van Vechten.

the *New York Times,* Arne Eckstrom, owner of a gallery in which Bearden exhibited his work in 1960, called Bearden "the pictorial historian of the black world, especially in the South."

From North Carolina to Harlem

Bearden was born on September 2, 1912, in his great-grandfather's house in Charlotte, North Carolina. Both his grandfather and great-grandfather painted and drew, and his father played the piano. As a toddler, Bearden would sit on that porch and scribble with paints while watching for trains to pull into the nearby station. At the age of three Bearden moved with his parents, Richard Howard and Bessye Bearden, to Saskatchewan, Canada, fleeing the racism of the southern United States. A few years later the family moved to Harlem, an area of New York City.

It was in Harlem that Bearden spent most of his youth and adulthood. Bearden's mother worked as the New York bureau chief of the African American weekly the *Chicago Defender* (for more information about the *Defender,* see Robert Abbott entry) and served as the first president of the Negro Women's Democratic Association. His father was employed as a health inspector for the city of New York.

The Bearden family (Romare was an only child) lived in an apartment on West 131st Street, amid the vibrant music and art scene of an era known as the Harlem Renaissance (the African American cultural blossoming from 1916 to 1940). Among the family friends who frequented the apartment were poet Langston Hughes (1902–1967; see entry in volume 2), singer and actor Paul Robeson (1898–1976; see entry in volume 3), scholar and civil rights activist W.E.B. DuBois (1868–1963; see entry in volume 1), band leader Duke Ellington (1899–1974; see entry in volume 2), and jazz musician Fats Waller (1904–1943).

As a youngster, Bearden spent summers with his paternal grandparents in Charlotte, North Carolina. During his high school years Bearden lived with his maternal grandmother in Pittsburgh, Pennsylvania, in a boarding house she ran for black steel workers. Most of the steelworkers Bearden encountered had recently arrived from the South. Later in life Bearden would draw heavily on his visual memories from his youth in Harlem, Charlotte, and Pittsburgh for his paintings and collages.

Art education

While a high school student, Bearden met Elmer Simms Campbell, a prominent black cartoonist. With Campbell's encouragement, Bearden created political cartoons and sold them to the *Baltimore Afro-American, Colliers,* and the *Saturday Evening Post,* along with other publications. Drawing cartoons was Bearden's sole involvement with the arts during high school.

After high school, Bearden attended Boston University and was the star pitcher on the school's baseball team. He also played semi-professional baseball in the summers, but quit after being told that the only way he would make it to the major leagues was if he was willing to "pass" for white (like his mother, Bearden was very light-skinned).

Bearden transferred to New York University (NYU), completing a bachelor's degree in mathematics in 1935. During Bearden's senior year at NYU he drew cartoons and served as art editor for a humorous campus publication called *NYU Medley.*

While Bearden traveled in artistic circles during his college career, his formal training in art did not begin until after he graduated. In 1936 Bearden enrolled at the Art Students League and studied painting with German-born American artist and satirist George Grosz (1893–1959). (A satirist is a person who uses humor and irony to denounce a political system or other entity.) Grosz introduced Bearden to a host of European artists whose works were steeped in social commentary, including Francisco Goya (1746–1828), Jean-Auguste-Dominique Ingres (1780–1867), Albrecht Dürer (1471–1528), Käthe Kollwitz (1867–1945), and Hans Holbein (1497–1543).

In 1938 Bearden rented an art studio on West 125th Street and began producing works of art. He only painted during his spare time since, to make ends meet, he had taken a job as a caseworker for New York City's Department of Social Services. Bearden's early paintings were done on coarse brown wrapping paper—the cheapest material available. With bright, bold colors and earth tones he depicted scenes of the South.

Bearden also solidified his bonds with others in the Harlem arts community during that time. He helped organize the Harlem Artists Guild and wrote articles about African American art and other subjects of social relevance for *Opportunity* (the magazine of the National Urban League). Bearden could frequently be found hobnobbing with artists, musicians, poets, and writers at gallery exhibitions in Harlem.

Early stages of art career

Bearden's first solo art show was held in a Harlem studio in 1940. His twenty-four paintings at that show, like most of his work from 1940 to 1942, were steeped in the social-realist tradition. (Social realism is a style of painting in which people are portrayed in everyday experiences.) Bearden's early paintings depicted southern blacks picking cotton and going to church, and northern blacks working in steel mills and standing on street corners. His subjects were women, mothers and children, industrial workers, and musicians.

Bearden was drafted into the army in 1942 and served until May 1945. When Bearden returned to Harlem, his painting took on an abstract quality. He mainly created formulaic designs that resembled stained glass windows. Toward the end of the 1940s, tiring of abstract expressionism, Bearden turned to American artist Stuart Davis (1894–1964) for advice. Davis encouraged Bearden to incorporate musical themes—especially from jazz—into his paintings.

In 1950 Bearden suffered a mid-life crisis of sorts. Feeling uninspired in Harlem, Bearden sought out new ideas in Paris, France. He took advantage of the free tuition provided by the G.I. Bill (legislation that provides funds for college tuition for military veterans) and enrolled at the Sorbonne to study philosophy and art history. During the two years Bearden was in Paris, he did not paint. He did, however, make the acquaintance of such famous painters as Pablo Picasso (1881–1973), George Braque (1882–1963), and Fernand Leger (1881–1955).

Takes up jazz writing

Upon his return to Harlem, Bearden went back to work for the Department of Social Services. In 1952 and 1953 Bearden spent his evenings frequenting jazz clubs and writing musical compositions. Bearden's best-known composition was "Sea Breeze," which became a hit after being recorded by jazz greats Dizzy Gillespie (1917–1993), Billy Eckstein (1914–1993), and Oscar Pettiford.

In 1954 Bearden married artist and dancer Nanette Rohan, who encouraged Bearden to resume painting. In his paintings over the next few years, Bearden interpreted works from a wide variety of cultural sources. Among his influences were Italian Renaissance art; traditional Chinese and Japanese brush painting; twentieth-century modernist European art; African art; the Bible; blues and jazz music; and the ancient Greek poet Homer's epics, the *Iliad* and the *Odyssey*. (The Renaissance period, from the fourteenth to the seventeenth century, marked the transition from the medieval to the modern era in Europe. A modernist is a person who favors contemporary over classical styles of art.)

In the late 1950s and early 1960s, Bearden's greatest influences were Zen Buddhism and Asian brush painting. Accordingly, he produced large paintings that emphasized composition, spatial orientation, and use of colors, over realistic portrayals of people or objects.

Collages inspired by civil rights movement

In the early 1960s Bearden joined a small clique of African American artists called the Spiral Group ("spiral" symbolized

Romare Bearden produced this work, called The Family, *in 1988. (Reproduced by permission of the literary estate of Romare Bearden.)*

the path to success for black artists). The purpose of the group was to forge an African American identity through art, in light of the growing civil rights movement. At one meeting, Bearden suggested that the group compose a large, communal collage that would portray the aspirations of blacks for full acceptance into American society. Faced with disinterest from other members of the group, Bearden went ahead with the collage himself.

The civil rights movement and urban riots continued to inspire Bearden's collages throughout the 1960s. The collages were mainly composed of pictures of African Americans, clipped from the pages of *Ebony, Look,* and *Life* magazines. In some cases Bearden enlarged portions of a collage through a photographic process, producing a specific type of collage called a photomontage. Bearden's collages reflected a number of different styles: the geometric forms and shapes of cubism; the dreamlike imagery of surrealism; and the focus on societal issues typical of Dadaism (the Dadaists were a group of German writers and artists in the 1920s who shunned conventional values).

Bearden portrayed African Americans in various cultural, historical, and ceremonial events in his collages. Some of his subjects included: trains, guitar players, neighborhoods, plantations, night clubs, funerals, parades, jazz musicians, female bathers, roosters, doves, cats, and the sun and moon. In 1964 Bearden began a series of collages called "The Prevalence of Ritual," that focused on black urban life.

Bearden's collages were immediately well received. He held exhibitions at several galleries and museums, including a one-person show at the Corcoran Gallery in Washington, D.C., in 1965. His collages graced the covers of several magazines, including *Time, Fortune,* the *New York Times Magazine,* and *TV Guide.*

By 1966 Bearden had become successful enough to quit his day job. He then focused all his energies on painting, writing, and studying the history of African American art. Bearden wrote several articles for leading newspapers and magazines during this period, as well as the following books: *The Painter's Mind, A Study of the Relations of Structure and Space in Painting* (1969) with fellow artist and friend Carl Holty, and *Six Black Masters of American Art* (1972) with writer Harry Henderson.

Later years in the Caribbean

In the 1970s and 1980s Bearden focused his artwork on three primary subjects: jazz, the female nude, and St. Martin.

The latter is an island in the Caribbean—the native country of Bearden's wife—where Bearden spent much of his time during the last twenty years of his life. Bearden's paintings from that era include the bright, bold colors of the plants and animals on St. Martin, as well as the water surrounding the island. He painted the landscape of the island, as well as ceremonies and rituals performed by the islanders. He also wrote a book, published in 1983, entitled *The Caribbean Poetry of Derek Walcott and the Art of Romare Bearden.*

Bearden painted right up to the final years of his life. In 1986 he was commissioned by the Detroit Institute of Arts to create a mosaic mural. The mural, called "Quilting Time," was made of glass tiles and covered an area ten feet by thirteen feet. It depicts a groups of women making a quilt—a common activity of African Americans in the South and an important aspect of African American culture.

Bearden was the recipient of many honors and awards throughout his career, including five honorary doctorates, the State Medal of North Carolina in Art, and the National Medal of Arts. Bearden was awarded the Frederick Douglass Medal by the New York Urban League and the James Weldon Johnson Award by the National Association for the Advancement of Colored People (NAACP). (Frederick Douglass [1817–1895; see entry in volume 1] was an escaped slave who became one of the nation's most outspoken opponents of slavery. James Weldon Johnson [1871–1938; see entry in volume 2] was the NAACP's first black executive director.)

Bearden died in 1988 after an eighteen-month-long struggle with bone cancer. His remains were cremated and his ashes were ceremonially spread over St. Martin. In 1993 a book that Bearden had spent fifteen years researching and writing was published posthumously (after his death). *A History of African-American Artists: From 1792 to the Present,* coauthored by writer Harry Henderson, describes the lives and works of thirty-six notable African American artists born before 1925. Bearden and Henderson wrote the book to provide information about black artists—a group of people largely ignored by most historians.

Sources for further reading

Bearden, Romare, and Harry Henderson. *A History of African-American Artists: From 1792 to the Present.* New York: Pantheon Books, 1993.

Bearden, Romare, and Harry Henderson. *Six Black Masters of American Art.* New York: Zenith Books, 1972.

"The Block" (book review). *Publishers Weekly.* November 13, 1995: p. 60.

Brenson, Michael. "The Long Life Journey of Romare Bearden." *New York Times.* June 9, 1989: p. B1.

Brown, Kevin. *Romare Bearden.* New York: Chelsea House, 1995.

Campbell, Mary Schmidt, and Sharon F. Patton. *Memory and Metaphor: The Art of Romare Bearden, 1940–1987.* New York: Oxford University Press, 1991.

DISCovering Multicultural America. "Romare Bearden." [Online] Available http://galenet.gale.com (accessed May 6, 1999).

"Fragments of the Past." *Scholastic Art.* February 1996: pp. 4+.

Fraser, C. Gerald. "Romare Bearden, Collagist and Painter, Dies at 75" (obituary). *New York Times.* March 13, 1988: p. 19.

Schwartzman, Myron. *Romare Bearden: His Life and Art.* New York: Harry N. Abrams, Inc., 1990.

Seaman, Donna. "A History of African-American Artists: From 1792 to the Present" (book review). *Booklist.* October 15, 1993: p. 405.

Willi, Denise. "A Living Art." *Scholastic Art.* February 1996: pp. 4+.

Williams, Betty Lou. "Romare Bearden" in *Notable Black American Men,* edited by Jessie Carney Smith. Farmington Hills, MI: The Gale Group, 1999, pp. 64–68.

Yarrow, Andrew L. "The Life and Works of Romare Bearden Recalled in a Tribute" (obituary). *New York Times.* April 7, 1988: p. D21.

Julian Bond

*Born January 14, 1940
Nashville, Tennessee
Civil rights activist, politician*

UPDATE

Julian Bond was elected chairman of the board of the National Association for the Advancement of Colored People (NAACP) in February 1998. This position is the latest milestone in Bond's long and distinguished career as a civil rights activist and politician. **(See original entry on Bond in volume 1.)**

Bond made his entry into the civil rights movement in 1960 as a college student in Atlanta, Georgia. He served as the press secretary of the Student Nonviolent Coordinating Committee (SNCC) from 1963 to 1965, stepping down when he won a seat in the Georgia state legislature. In 1986 Bond lost a bitter race for U.S. representative to his old friend and comrade, John Lewis. Bond then retreated from politics and began teaching college courses, writing news columns, and hosting television shows. Bond's election to the head of the nation's largest and longest-lived civil rights organization marks his reentry into the world of civil rights activism.

Julian Bond has had a long and distinguished career as a civil rights activist and a politician.

Portrait: Reproduced by permission of Corbis-Bettmann.

Bond was born in Nashville, Tennessee, to Julia and Horace Mann Bond. Bond's father served as president of the predominantly black Lincoln College in Pennsylvania. With other professors, Horace Mann Bond successfully sued for the racial integration of the local school system. The senior Bond also participated in campaigns to desegregate theaters and restaurants in nearby Oxford, Pennsylvania.

Julian Bond attended an integrated junior high school. He was then sent to a boarding school run by Quakers, called George School. Despite being the only black student in his high school, Bond rarely experienced racial discrimination.

Coordinates civil rights campaign in Atlanta

In the late 1950s Bond moved to Atlanta, Georgia, to attend college at the historically black Morehouse College. In early 1960 Bond watched with great interest as a wave of student sit-ins, beginning in Greensboro, North Carolina, swept the nation. (Sit-ins were a form of nonviolent protest in which black students, sometimes joined by white students, would request service at whites-only lunch counters. When the students were denied service, they would refuse to leave.)

Bond joined Morehouse football star Lonnie King in organizing college students to campaign for civil rights in Atlanta. The student activists demanded the desegregation of restaurants, concert halls, movie theaters, hospitals, parks, and other public facilities, as well as housing. Beginning in March 1960, the students held sit-ins at various eateries throughout the city. On March 15, 1960, Bond was arrested (his first and only time) during a sit-in at the Atlanta City Hall Cafeteria. After more than a year of demonstrations, the students forced an end to segregation in Atlanta.

Handles media relations for SNCC

In 1961 Bond dropped out of college to devote all his time to the civil rights struggle. He joined the Student Nonviolent Coordinating Committee (SNCC), an organization of student civil rights activists that strove to achieve racial equality and integration at all levels of society, using nonviolent methods.

With his flair for writing and his charismatic manner of speaking, Bond was chosen as the SNCC's director of communications. Bond traveled throughout the South wherever SNCC was active, speaking to reporters, writing press releases, and presenting taped announcements to radio stations.

Elected to Georgia legislature

In 1965, at the age of twenty-five, Bond became the youngest member elected to the Georgia State House of Representatives. Just before Bond was to be sworn in to his new position, he endorsed an SNCC statement opposing the war in Vietnam (1954–75). His fellow lawmakers, outraged, refused to seat him. It wasn't until December 1966, when the Supreme Court ruled in Bond's favor, that Bond was allowed to take his place on the House floor. Even then, Bond was treated as an outcast—for his first five years as a representative he was not given a chance to address the assembly.

In 1968 Bond made headlines when he led a group, called the Georgia Democratic Party Forum, to challenge the 95 percent white, regular Georgia Democratic Party delegation at the Democratic National Convention. Not only were Forum members granted the majority of seats at the convention (the national party had ruled four years earlier that delegations had to reflect the racial makeup of their state), but Bond was nominated as a candidate for vice president. The nomination was merely symbolic—made in protest of the party's involvement in the Vietnam War and as an affirmation of racial equality—since at age twenty-eight Bond was too young to serve as vice president. In a poll taken two years after the convention, a majority of African Americans indicated that Bond would be their first choice for president.

Loses congressional race

Bond continued to serve in the Georgia legislature until 1986, when he stepped down to run for a seat in Congress.

Bond, considered a shoo-in for the job, was upset by his former friend and fellow civil-rights activist John Lewis (1940–). Bond's campaign was plagued by accusations of cocaine use and marital infidelity.

After losing his bid for U.S. Representative, Bond, deeply in debt and emotionally wounded, stepped back from politics. He moved to Washington, D.C., and began teaching courses at American University and the University of Virginia. He also narrated *Eyes on the Prize,* the civil rights documentary produced for public television, and hosted the television program *America's Black Forum.*

Takes over the reins of the NAACP

In February 1998 Bond was named chairman of the board of the nation's oldest and most prestigious civil rights organization, the National Association for the Advancement of Colored People (NAACP). In that position, Bond is responsible for setting policy for the 400,000-member organization. The NAACP's board of directors—weary after the financial scandals and calls for black separatism by its chief officers that plagued the group in the early 1990s—is counting on Bond to reinvigorate the organization and return it to its original mission of racial integration.

At a news conference following his election to the helm of the NAACP board, Bond voiced his support for affirmative action (a set of federal government policies that provide increased educational and employment opportunities to racial minorities and women, to overcome past patterns of discrimination) and stressed that the NAACP is not for blacks only. "I just want to send a signal that there are no racial restrictions to participation with the NAACP," he remarked in the *New York Times.*

Bond's initial period with the NAACP has been marked by a vigorous defense of affirmative action, at a time when the program is facing mounting criticism. At the NAACP's annual convention in July 1998 Bond credited affirmative action with helping establish a sizable black middle class. He dismissed claims that affirmative action does not help people at the bottom of the economic ladder, stating that "[affirmative action] ought not to be blamed for failing to solve problems it wasn't designed to solve.... Affirmative action isn't a poverty program. It is designed to counter racial discrimination."

Sources for further reading

Chappell, Kevin. "Where are the Civil Rights Icons of the 60s?" *Ebony*. August 1996: pp. 108+.

Dreifus, Claudia. "Julian Bond" (interview). *The Progressive*. August 1998: pp. 32+.

Holmes, Steven A. "N.A.A.C.P. Post Gives Julian Bond New Start." *New York Times*. February 28, 1998: p. A6.

"Moving Forward at the N.A.A.C.P." (editorial). *New York Times*. February 24, 1998: p. A20.

"N.A.A.C.P.'s Julian Bond Sees a New Civil Rights Era Ahead." *New York Times*. July 13, 1998: p. A12.

White, Jack E. "'It's Still White Supremacy': Julian Bond Restores the Focus of the N.A.A.C.P." *Time*. July 27, 1998: p. 27.

Clive O. Callender

Born November 16, 1936
New York, New York
Organ transplant surgeon

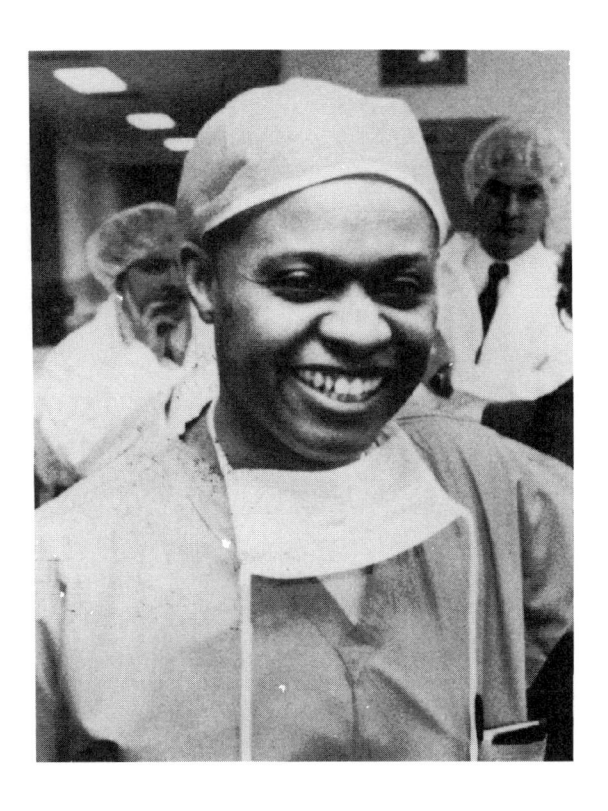

Clive Callender is a distinguished organ transplant surgeon and founder of the transplant center at Howard University Hospital in Washington, D.C. (An organ transplant is the surgical implantation of a healthy internal organ into a patient; the organ comes from a donor, who is a live or recently deceased person.) He is chairman of the Howard University Medical School's Department of Surgery and chairs the Minority Affairs Committee of the United Network for Organ Sharing.

Callender is active in promoting organ donor programs in the United States and abroad. He works to dispel myths about organ donation in minority communities and serves as a spokesman for health issues of concern to African Americans.

Education and early career

Callender was born in New York City in 1936 to Joseph Callender and Ida Burke. When Callender was eight years old,

"Institutional racism is alive and well and thriving in America.... [T]his practice of organized racism exacts a severe price."

Portrait: Reproduced by permission of AP/Wide World Photos, Inc.

he listened to a sermon about medical missionaries (people sent by a church to perform medical services in foreign countries) at New York City's Ebenezer Gospel Tabernacle. In a 1988 interview for *Black Enterprise,* Callender recalled that event as follows: "I was listening to the minister who spoke about the two greatest occupations in the world: ministering to the souls of mankind and to the bodies of mankind." During that sermon, Callender found his calling—to serve humanity through a career in medicine.

Callender attended Hunter College in New York City, graduating in 1959 with degrees in chemistry and physiology (the science of the structure of living organisms). In 1963 Callender graduated first in his class from Meharry Medical College in Nashville, Tennessee. His next step was an internship at the University of Cincinnati, where he began his training in surgery. Callender continued his surgical training while serving as chief resident at Howard University Hospital and Freedmen's Hospital.

In 1968 Callender married Fern Irene Marshall. The couple eventually had three children: Joseph, Ealena, and Arianne. Callender worked as an instructor at Howard University in 1969 and was a medical officer at D.C. General Hospital the following year. In 1971 Callender fulfilled his youthful ambition of being a missionary doctor by taking a surgical position at the Port Harcourt General Hospital in Nigeria. "It was like a dream come true," stated Callender in *Black Enterprise.* "It was [during] the Biafran Civil War. I had a chance to do the medical missionary work I wanted to do and to go to Ethiopia."

Becomes a transplant surgeon

On his return to the United States, Callender began his training in transplant surgery. He completed a fellowship in transplants and transplant immunology (study of the immune system, the body's natural defense against disease) at the University of Minnesota. He then undertook a post doctoral research fellowship at the National Institutes of Health (NIH). In 1973, Callender returned to Howard University and established a transplant center.

Callender's Testimony Before the House Commerce Committee

On June 18, 1998, Callender testified before the House Commerce Committee Subcommittee on Health and the Environment and the Senate Labor and Human Resources Committee on the matter of organ transplants. Callender stressed the need to address racism within the medical system, to shorten waiting times for patients awaiting transplants, to find the fairest allocation (assignment of organ recipients) system possible, to promote health and disease prevention in the general population, and to boost organ donations—particularly in minority communities. What follows is an excerpt from Callender's testimony:

"Institutional racism is alive and well and thriving in America. While race is irrelevant as we are all Homo Sapiens and members of the same race, this practice of organized racism exacts a severe price. The price minorities pay for this abominable practice ... may well be the major reason people of color die ten-to-fifteen years before their time.

"Yet, while the gap between people of color (minorities) and the majority widens, we continue to not allow minorities to sit at the discussion table. Yet, just last week, data released revealed that African Americans continue to wait twice as long as other Americans for kidney transplants while constituting more than 50 percent of those waiting for kidney transplants.

"This debate on allocation of organs and the secretary's proposed regulations rages and once again the minority population is excluded from the table of discussion.... For emphasis, I must restate the need for the support of the perpetuation of the national minority strategic plan which requests that institutionalized racism be treated by involving minorities at all levels of research, resource allocation and problem resolution from start to finish."

Since then Callender has traveled widely throughout the United States, the Caribbean, and Europe, lecturing on organ transplantation and promoting organ donations. He has also worked as a visiting fellow specializing in clinical liver transplantation at the University of Pittsburgh. Callender cofounded a transplant center in St. Thomas, Virgin Islands, in 1983.

In 1980 Callender was hired as a professor of surgery and elected vice chairman of the department of surgery at the Howard University College of Medicine. In 1996, he was promoted to surgery department chair. Throughout his career Callender has performed more than 300 kidney transplants.

Questions low rate of organ donations among minorities

Upon entering the field of organ transplantation, Callender noticed that the organ donation rates among racial minorities lagged far behind that of the general population. Callender explored the reasons for minorities' low donation rates and found that the following myths exist in many minority communities: a person of color would be less likely to be selected for an organ transplant than a white person; organ removal from the body precludes life after death; organ removal results in the mutilation of the body and prevents open casket viewing; and white doctors prematurely pronounce the deaths of minority organ donors in order to transplant their organs into white persons. Most of the persons of color interviewed voiced a mistrust of the largely white medical community.

"When I first got started in this," commented Callender in a 1991 interview with the *New York Times,* "I didn't realize what an emotional issue [organ donation] was for blacks. We're dealing with myths, but to the people who believe them, the myths are real."

Callender has worked diligently to dispel misconceptions about organ donations. To that end he conducts workshops for prospective donors, at which he answers questions and circulates organ donor cards for signing. Callender has also convinced Congress to allocate increased funds for community education on organ donation.

Callender argues that it is important for minorities, especially African Americans, to become organ donors because African Americans have relatively high rates of kidney failure and are frequently in need of kidney transplants. "Blacks are twenty times as likely as whites to suffer kidney disease and

30 percent of dialysis patients are black," Callender noted in the *New York Times*. (Dialysis is a procedure in which a machine performs the function of the kidneys—namely, it filters waste products out of the blood.)

Founds national minority organ transplant program

In the early 1980s, Callender founded the D.C. Organ Donor Program—a joint endeavor with African American college and hospital officials in the Washington, D.C., area to increase the numbers of minority organ donors. Callender expanded his program nationally in 1991, with the founding of the Minority Organ and Tissue Transplant Education Program (MOTTEP). The purpose of MOTTEP is to boost donation rates within various minority groups throughout the nation, using strategies that have succeeded in the Washington area.

MOTTEP received funding from the NIH's office of Research on Minority Health in 1993, to implement programs in three cities. In 1995 the NIH increased its funding to allow MOTTEP to operate in fifteen cities. Callender remains MOTTEP's principal investigator.

Due in part to Callender's efforts, organ donations by people of color have been on the rise. A Gallup poll in 1985 found that just 7 percent of African Americans had signed cards indicated they were willing to donate organs; in a similar poll in 1990, that percentage had jumped to 24.

Honors and awards

Callender has received wide recognition for his work as a surgeon and organ-donations advocate. In 1979 he became president of the National Capitol Area branch of the National Kidney Foundation. He was elected to the Hunter College Alumni Hall of Fame in 1989 and in 1994 became the first African American member of the Task Force on Organ Procurement and Transplantation. Callender was elected chairman of the Minority Affairs Committee of the United Network for Organ Sharing (UNOS) in July 1998.

In 1996 Callender was named the first LaSalle D. Leffall professor and chairman of the Howard University Medical School's Department of Surgery. Leffall, who chaired the department prior to Callender, was granted an endowed Chair in Surgery in his name. (The position was endowed, or funded, by $1.5 million in contributions.) Leffall is a surgical oncologist (surgeon specializing in the treatment of cancer) and an educator. He was the first black president of the American College of Surgeons and is past-president of the American Cancer Society.

Callender was again awarded the LaSalle D. Leffall award in 1998. Upon presenting the award at the 1998 All Surgeons Day, the Metropolitan Washington Chapter of the American College of Surgeons issued the following statement:

> The award recognizes Dr. Callender's contributions to patients in the metropolitan Washington, D.C., area, especially those with chronic renal (kidney) failure and end stage renal disease. The award further salutes Dr. Callender's outstanding leadership in the surgical community and his devotion to surgical education.

The organization further lauded Callender for his "dedication to patient care, teaching, and research; concern for the community; and leadership in the profession.... [This] award serves as special recognition of a truly outstanding individual," the statement concluded.

Sources for further reading

Callender, Clive O. *Testimony Before the House Commerce Committee Subcommittee on Health and the Environment.* [Online] Available http://207.87.26.13/Newsroom/archive_regs_testimony_callender.htm (accessed April 21, 1999).

"Clive O. Callender" in *Notable Twentieth-Century Scientists,* edited by Emily J. McMurray. Vol. 1. Detroit: Gale Research, 1995, pp. 297–98.

Delaney, Paul. "Myth Fighters Seek Organ Donors." *The New York Times.* November 6, 1991: p. B9.

"Dr. LaSalle Leffall Jr. Chair Established at Howard University Medical School; Dr. Clive Callender Named to the Chair." *Jet.* April 1, 1996: p. 16.

Howard University Medical School. "Transplant Center Staff." [Online] Available http://www.med.howard.edu/transplant/staff.htm (accessed April 21, 1999).

"Medical Expert Gives Five Reasons Blacks Aren't Organ Donors." *Jet.* February 5, 1990: pp. 38–39.

National Minority Organ and Tissue Transplant Education Program. [Online] Available http://www.imappl.org/~changa/EION/background.html (accessed April 21, 1999).

Petrucci, Peter E. "Leffall Award Presented to Clive O. Callender, MD, FACS." *Metropolitan Washington D.C. Chapter of the American College of Surgeons.* [Online] Available http://www.facs.org/chapters/mwdcacs/publications/spring98/leffall.html (accessed April 21, 1999).

"Saving Lives With New Organs: Dr. Clive O. Callender." *Black Enterprise.* October 1988: p. 90.

Stokely Carmichael

*Born June 29, 1941
Port-of-Spain, Trinidad and Tobago
Died November 15, 1998
Conakry, Guinea
Activist, author*

UPDATE

Stokely Carmichael, later known as Kwame Toure, died of prostate cancer in November 1998 in Conakry, Guinea. He was fifty-seven years old.

Carmichael was best known as a young, militant leader of the Student Nonviolent Coordinating Committee (SNCC; pronounced "snick") in the mid-1960s. Carmichael, who popularized the phrase "black power," led the SNCC away from its integrationist, nonviolent stance and toward a position of black separatism and armed self-defense. After leaving the SNCC, Carmichael served as prime minister of the Black Panther Party. He spent his final three decades in the West African nation of Guinea. **(See original entry on Carmichael in volume 1.)**

Carmichael was born on the Caribbean island of Trinidad and Tobago. When he was a toddler his parents left him in the care of his grandparents and moved to the United States. At the age of eleven Carmichael's parents brought him to live with them in Harlem. Shortly thereafter the family moved to

"The only way we're gonna stop them white men from whippin' us is to take over."

Portrait: Reproduced by permission of Archive Photos, Inc.

Morris Park, a mostly Jewish and Italian neighborhood in the East Bronx. Carmichael did well in school and gained admission to the prestigious Bronx High School of Science.

In 1961 Carmichael answered the call of the Congress on Racial Equality (CORE; an early civil rights organization) to participate in the Freedom Rides. The Freedom Rides were journeys throughout the South made by integrated groups of people to test the enforcement of a pair of Supreme Court rulings striking down the constitutionality of segregated seating on interstate (crossing state lines) buses and trains. Carmichael was among the riders sentenced to forty-nine days at the dismal Parchman Penitentiary in Jackson, Mississippi.

Carmichael enrolled in the predominantly-black Howard University in Washington, D.C., in 1960, graduating in 1964 with a bachelor's degree in philosophy. After graduation Carmichael joined the Student Nonviolent Coordinating Committee (SNCC), an organization of student civil rights activists that strove to achieve racial equality and integration (the coming together of people of all races in a shared environment) using nonviolent methods.

Advocates "black power"

As a member of the SNCC, Carmichael participated in campaigns for desegregation and voter registration throughout the South. He and his fellow activists were constantly subjected to threats, beatings, arrests, and shootings (a handful of civil rights workers were killed) at the hands of racist white individuals and law enforcement officials. The activists' progress—in terms of numbers of new black voters and the dismantling of segregation—was painfully slow.

By 1965 Carmichael, like many other embattled SNCC field workers, had given up on the notion that racial equality could be brought about by nonviolent means. In a radical departure from the SNCC's stated philosophy, Carmichael promoted separatism (the rejection of white culture and institutions, in favor of separate African American culture and institutions) over integration. He also convinced SNCC members to arm themselves in self-defense.

In 1966 Carmichael was elected leader of the SNCC. That summer he popularized the phrase "black power" during a march from Memphis, Tennessee, to Jackson, Mississippi. After being arrested and briefly detained in Greenwood, Mississippi, Carmichael addressed the marchers and assembled spectators. "The only way we're gonna stop them white men from whippin' us is to take over," he exclaimed. "We been saying freedom for six years—and we ain't got nothin'. What we gonna start now is 'Black Power!'" The term "black power" was denounced as divisive and inflammatory by Martin Luther King Jr. (1929–1968; see entry in volume 3) and the leaders of other civil rights organizations.

Joins Black Panther Party

In 1967 Carmichael explained why he felt violence was necessary to free blacks from their white oppressors in a book, coauthored with professor of political science Charles Hamilton, called *Black Power: The Politics of Liberation in America*. The authors defined "black power" as follows: "It is a call for black people in this country to unite, to recognize their heritage, to build a sense of community. It is a call for black people to define their own goals, to lead their own organizations."

Also in 1967 Carmichael joined the Black Panther Party (BPP), an organization founded in Oakland, California, in 1966, that worked to stem police brutality and offered free breakfast programs and free health clinics to African Americans in inner cities. BPP members were recognizable by their berets, black leather jackets, raised fists, and the guns slung over their shoulders. By late 1968 the BPP had established chapters in twenty-five cities and had a membership of several hundred people.

Carmichael quickly rose through the ranks of the BPP, becoming the group's honorary prime minister. Carmichael's tenure with the BPP, however, was short-lived. He left the BPP after clashing with the group's minister of information,

Eldridge Cleaver (1935– ; see entry in volume 1 and update on page 57), over Cleaver's endorsement of joining forces with white radicals (activists who believe in a radical restructuring of the social order).

Moves to Africa

In 1969 Carmichael moved to Guinea, a country located on the western coast of Africa, with his wife Mariam Makeba (a South African singer). He told reporters upon his departure: "America does not belong to the blacks." Carmichael changed his name to "Kwame Toure" in honor of two African leaders: Ahmed Sekou Toure, president of Guinea, and Kwame Nkrumah, the first leader of Ghana following that nation's independence.

In 1971 Carmichael published his second book, *Stokely Speaks: Black Power Back to Pan-Africanism.* In the book he linked the struggle of blacks in America with those of Africans.

Except for lecture tours of the United States in 1972 and in the early 1990s, Carmichael spent the remainder of his years in Africa. He continued to write and speak out about Pan-Africanism (the advocacy of a political alliance between all people of African descent) and served as chairman of the Philadelphia-based All-African People's Revolutionary Party.

Denounced for controversial remarks

Carmichael came under intense criticism in the 1990s for making antisemitic statements—a charge he denied. (Antisemitism is discrimination against Jewish people.) In a letter to the *New York Times* dated March 11, 1996, Abraham H. Foxman, national director of the B'Nai Brith Anti-Defamation League, called Carmichael an "unabashed racial separatist and anti-Semite who often uses the slogan 'the only good Zionist is a dead Zionist.'" (A Zionist is a person who advocates the establishment of a national homeland for Jews in Palestine.)

For his part, Carmichael admitted to being an anti-Zionist but claimed that that did not make him antisemitic. He explained that Zionism is a political philosophy, not a religion.

"A Jew would say the only good Nazi is a dead Nazi," Carmichael told a *New York Times* reporter in 1996. "When you condemn Nazis you don't condemn Germans, you condemn a political philosophy."

Undergoes cancer treatment

Carmichael was diagnosed with prostate cancer in 1996 and received treatment in New York City and Cuba. Carmichael's former civil rights comrades held fundraisers to cover his medical expenses. The disease claimed his life in November 1998.

"[Carmichael] was one of our generation who was determined to give his life to transforming America and Africa," stated Rev. Jesse Jackson (1941– ; see entry in volume 2 and update on page 137) upon hearing of Carmichael's death. "He was committed to ending racial apartheid in our country. He helped to bring those walls down."

Sources for further reading

Chappell, Kevin. "Where are the Civil Rights Icons of the 60s?" *Ebony.* August 1996: pp. 108+.

De Witt, Karen. "A Fighter For Rights is Treated for Cancer." *New York Times.* March 1, 1996: p. B4.

De Witt, Karen. "Formerly Stokely Carmichael and Still Ready for the Revolution." *New York Times.* April 14, 1996: p. E9.

Engelbert, Phillis. *American Civil Rights: Almanac.* Vol. 1. Farmington Hills, MI: U•X•L, 1999.

Foxman, Abraham. "Black Activist Disparages Jews" (letter to the editor). *New York Times.* March 11, 1996: p. A16.

Kaufman, Michael T. "Stokely Carmichael, Rights Leader Who Coined 'Black Power,' Dies at 57." *New York Times.* November 16, 1998: p. B10.

Shelton, Debra Hale. "'Black Power' Activist Dies." *Ann Arbor News.* November 16, 1998: p. A3.

Shirley Chisholm

Born November 30, 1924
Brooklyn, New York
Politician

UPDATE

Shirley Chisholm was appointed ambassador to Jamaica by President Bill Clinton in July 1993. The diplomatic post marks Chisholm's reentry into the world of politics.

In 1968 Chisholm became the first African American woman to be elected to the U.S. House of Representatives. She was reelected to represent her New York City district six times before retiring in 1983. Chisholm mounted an unsuccessful bid for the Democratic presidential nomination in 1972. Throughout her years in Congress, as well as in her preceding years as a state representative in the New York assembly, Chisholm championed the rights of poor people, people of color, and women. **(See original entry on Chisholm in volume 1.)**

Chisholm was born Shirley Anita St. Hill in Brooklyn, New York, in 1924. Her parents were immigrants: Charles St. Hill, from British Guiana, a factory worker; and Ruby (Seale) St. Hill, from Barbados, a seamstress and domestic worker.

"Shirley Chisholm is a true pioneer of American politics, whose passion for social justice is unparalleled."

—President Bill Clinton

Portrait: Source unknown.

When Chisholm was three years old she was sent, along with her two younger sisters, to live with her grandmother in Barbados. The girls were brought back to New York City seven years later to live with their parents.

Chisholm's parents, like her grandmother, were strict guardians who stressed education and religion. Chisholm excelled in high school and was offered two college scholarships. She chose to attend Brooklyn College, which was close to her home.

Joins Harriet Tubman Society in college

In college Chisholm prepared for one of the few careers open to women in the 1940s: teaching. She graduated with a bachelor's degree in psychology from Brooklyn College in 1946, and earned a master's degree in elementary education from Columbia University in 1951. While working toward her master's degree she also taught nursery school.

During her years at Brooklyn College, Chisholm supplemented her formal education with her participation in a political discussion group called the Harriet Tubman Society. (Harriet Tubman [1820?–1913] was an escaped slave who helped another 300 slaves reach freedom through the Underground Railroad; see entry in volume 4.) The students in the group read about and discussed African history, African American history, and current events. A frequent topic of conversation was the injustice toward African American soldiers in World War II (1939–45), who were placed in segregated (separated by race) units and subjected to discrimination when they returned home.

Introduction to electoral politics

After graduating from Columbia University, Chisholm was hired as the director of a large childcare center. From 1959 to 1964 Chisholm worked as a consultant to the New York City bureau of child welfare.

In the 1950s Chisholm became involved in local politics. She joined the local Democratic Party and worked for the election of minority candidates. In 1953 she worked on the successful campaign of a black lawyer named Lewis S. Flagg for district court judge in New York.

From state assembly to U.S. Congress

In 1960 Chisholm helped form the Unity Democratic Club, a group working for the election of African Americans to the New York state assembly. After campaigning for numerous others, Chisholm made her own bid for office in 1964. She campaigned on street corners and in community centers, appealing especially to African Americans, Puerto Ricans (whom she addressed in their native tongue of Spanish), and women. Chisholm won election to the state legislature by a landslide.

After one term in the state assembly, Chisholm ran for Congress in the newly-created twelfth district in Brooklyn. Her opponent, a moderate Republican, was James Farmer (1920– ; see entry in volume 2), former director of the Congress on Racial Equality (CORE; an early civil rights organization best known for sponsoring the Freedom Rides on segregated transportation lines throughout the South). Farmer tried to discredit Chisholm because of her gender, claiming that the black community needed "a man's voice in Washington."

Farmer's strategy backfired; Chisholm won the seat with 34,885 votes to Farmer's 13,777 in a district where female voters outnumbered male voters by more than two-to-one. Chisholm handily won reelection to the seat six times over the next fourteen years.

Runs for president

In 1972 Chisholm campaigned for the Democratic nomination to the presidency. As an African American and a woman, she knew she had little chance of succeeding. Still, Chisholm wanted to demonstrate that a black woman could mount a serious campaign for the nation's highest office. "The mere fact that a black woman dared to run for President," she wrote in her 1973 book *The Good Fight,* "... not expecting to win but sincerely trying to, is what it was all about. 'It can be done.' That was what I was trying to say."

Resigns from Congress

Throughout her years in Congress Chisholm was noted for her independence, her willingness to take unpopular positions, and her unfailing commitment to the concerns of people of color, women, and the urban poor.

Representative Chisholm came under criticism many times for her political endorsements and actions. One act for which she claimed that "black people in my community crucified me," was her visit to George Wallace (former governor of Alabama and remorseful segregationist) in the hospital after he had been shot in 1972. And Chisholm was accused of "lik(ing) whitey" when she endorsed a white representative, Hale Boggs, over black representative John Conyers for House majority leader.

In 1983 Chisholm declined to seek reelection. One reason for her retirement was to have more time to care for her husband, Arthur Hardwick, who had been seriously injured in an automobile accident two years earlier. She said that she was also tired of the demands and frustrations of the job—demands she claimed had increased since the election of President Ronald Reagan, a conservative Republican, in 1980.

"All black politicians are depressed," Chisholm stated in an interview with *Essence* shortly after her resignation. "Don't be surprised if there are others who will resign.... this president is really out to hurt black people.... Do you know what it means to have 33 percent of the employable people in your constituency needing jobs, and you as their representative can't help them?"

Continues political activities

After leaving Congress, Chisholm taught for four years at Mount Holyoke College in Massachusetts. In 1984 Chisholm founded the National Political Congress of Black Women, a group committed to organizing black women as a political force. "We are interested in giving them the 'how-to'," stated Chisholm in a 1985 interview with the *New York Times,* "how to run for political office, how to raise funds, how to prepare issues."

In July 1993 President Bill Clinton selected Chisholm, then sixty-eight years old, to serve as ambassador to Jamaica. "Shirley Chisholm is a true pioneer of American politics, whose passion for social justice is unparalleled," said Clinton in a press statement. "I am honored that she will be my ambassador to Jamaica, and confident that she will do an outstanding job." Today Chisholm divides her time between Jamaica and her home in Palm Coast, Florida.

Sources for further reading

"Clinton Selects Chisholm for Ambassador to Jamaica." *Jet.* August 16, 1993: p. 16.

"Conference for Black Women in Politics is Led by Chisholm." *New York Times.* June 9, 1985: p. 15.

Payne, Les. "Mrs. Chisholm Calls It Quits." *Essence.* August 1982: pp. 72+.

Perlez, Jane. "Rep. Chisholm's Angry Farewell." *New York Times.* October 12, 1982: p. A24.

"Post of Jamaica Ambassador to Go to Shirley Chisholm." *New York Times.* July 30, 1993: p. A3.

Scheader, Catherine. *Shirley Chisholm: Teacher and Congresswoman.* Hillside, NJ: Enslow Publishers, Inc., 1990.

Washington, Elsie B., and Marilyn Milloy. "Wise Souls: Listening to Our Elders." *Essence.* July 1996: pp. 64+.

Eldridge Cleaver

Born August 31, 1935
Wabbeseka, Arkansas

Died April 30, 1998
Pomona, California

Political activist, author

UPDATE

E ldridge Cleaver died in Pomona, California, on April 30, 1998, of complications due to diabetes and prostate cancer. He was sixty-two years old.

Cleaver, one of the best known and most controversial 1960s' radicals, rose to prominence with the 1968 publication of his best-selling book *Soul on Ice*. At the time he wrote his collection of essays on race in America, Cleaver was serving a prison sentence for assault with intent to murder.

After being paroled Cleaver joined the Black Panther Party and became the group's minister of information. He fled the country in 1968 after being charged with the attempted murder of a police officer. In the years that followed Cleaver became a political and religious chameleon, changing his identity from a socialist and Black Muslim to a conservative Republican and a Christian fundamentalist. **(See original entry on Cleaver in volume 1.)**

Cleaver (who later dropped the name "Leroy") was born in 1935 in a small town outside of Little Rock, Arkansas. As a

"[Eldridge Cleaver expressed] the profound alienation from America which black nationalists feel...."

—Jervis Anderson in Commentary

Portrait: Reproduced by permission of AP/Wide World Photos, Inc.

young child he moved with his parents to the Watts section of Los Angeles. Cleaver took to the streets at an early age, stealing bicycles and other items and selling marijuana. In 1954 he received a prison sentence for selling drugs. A few years later he was released, only to be sent back to prison for rape and assault with intent to murder. (Cleaver, who admitted to raping black women and white women, claimed that his rapes of white women were acts of revenge for the mistreatment of blacks at the hands of whites.)

Writes *Soul on Ice* in prison

While spending time in three notorious penitentiaries—Folsom, San Quentin, and Soledad—Cleaver studied and read. In addition to earning his diploma from Bay View High School, Cleaver read the works of scholarly and radical thinkers including Karl Marx (1818–1883), Vladimir Lenin (1870–1924), James Baldwin (1924–1987; see entry in volume 1), Thomas Paine (1737–1809), and Malcolm X (1925–1965; see entry in volume 3). Cleaver was most interested in the teachings of Malcolm X, which led him to convert to the Black Muslim faith and to fight for the rights of black people.

In the mid-1960s Cleaver wrote a series of essays about the plight of blacks in America, as well as his own experiences growing up and in prison. The book, called *Soul on Ice,* was published in 1968 to international acclaim. Excerpts from the book, released two years before its publication, were praised by authors and critics. A coalition of writers successfully petitioned for Cleaver's release from prison; he was paroled in 1966.

Joins Black Panther Party

Upon his release from prison Cleaver joined the Black Panther Party (BPP), an organization founded in Oakland, California, in 1966 that worked to stem police brutality and offered free breakfast programs and free health clinics to African Americans. BPP members were recognizable by their berets, black leather jackets, raised fists, and the guns slung over their shoulders.

Cleaver, nicknamed "Rage" by his fellow Panthers because of his inflammatory comments and forceful manner of speaking, was appointed the BPP's minister of information. In that position, Cleaver called for the overthrow of the United States government and its replacement by a socialist government run by African Americans. (Socialism is the theory that property and the means of production should not be controlled by owners, but by the community as a whole.)

Years in exile

In April 1968, just days after the assassination of Martin Luther King Jr. (1929–1968; see entry in volume 3), Cleaver, along with fellow Black Panther Bobby Hutton (the BPP's seventeen-year-old treasurer), was involved in a shootout with Oakland police. Hutton was killed as he tried to surrender, and Cleaver and three police officers were wounded. Cleaver was charged with assault and attempted murder.

In late 1968, when Cleaver was free on bond while awaiting trial, he fled the country. With his house under police guard, Cleaver climbed through an underground tunnel he had constructed to his neighbor's yard. Disguised as an old man, Cleaver made his way to the airport and boarded a flight to Canada. From there he went to Cuba.

Cleaver spent the next seven years visiting the socialist countries of Poland, Czechoslovakia, the Soviet Union, North Vietnam, East Germany, China, North Korea, and Algeria. Through that experience, Cleaver became thoroughly disillusioned with socialism. "I had heard so much rhetoric about their glorious leaders and their incredible revolutionary spirit," wrote Cleaver in *Soul on Fire,* "that even to this very angry and disgruntled American, it was absurd and unreal."

Returns to U.S., avoids prison term

In late 1975 Cleaver returned to the United States and turned himself in to the FBI. In exchange for pleading guilty to assault, Cleaver avoided a jail term. He was sentenced to five years probation and two thousand hours of community service.

Living in Berkeley, California, Cleaver continued to undergo drastic changes in his political and religious thinking. He eschewed his former message of social change and joined the Republican Party. He ran an unsuccessful campaign for Congress in California in 1984, on a conservative platform. He rankled many of his old colleagues when he endorsed Republican presidential candidates Ronald Reagan in 1980 and Bob Dole in 1996.

Cleaver's religious path was just as erratic as his political path. In 1975, before returning to the United States, Cleaver had converted from Islam to born-again Christianity. In the late 1970s he founded Eldridge Cleaver Crusades and spoke at fundamentalist churches. Cleaver then converted to Christlam (a religion he established that is a mixture of Christianity and Islam), and next to Mormonism. He later joined the Unification Church (whose members were commonly referred to as "Moonies"). His final religious affiliation was with a tiny church called the New Vision Center, Church of Religious Science, in Fontana, California.

Activities since mid-1970s

Cleaver's final decades in Berkeley were marked by unsuccessful money-making ventures and brushes with the law. In 1978 Cleaver designed and attempted to market men's trousers that had a pouch in the genital area called a "Cleaver's sleeve." He spent the years 1980 to 1985 in prison on burglary and drug possession charges. After his release Cleaver developed an addiction to crack cocaine. He made a meager living selling popsicles on the streets of Berkeley and selling discarded items to recycling companies.

Cleaver was placed on probation in 1988 after being convicted of burglarizing a home that was under construction. In 1994 Cleaver was robbed and clubbed in the head while attempting to buy cocaine, and had to undergo emergency brain surgery. It took two months after the surgery for him to regain consciousness.

In 1995 Cleaver began giving lectures at college campuses with fellow former Black Panther Bobby Seale. Cleaver carried with him stacks of his FBI "wanted" posters from 1968, which he autographed for students. In early 1998 Cleaver was hired by LaVerne University to be a consultant to its Coalition for Diversity. At the time of his death in April 1998 Cleaver was working on his memoirs, *The Eldridge Cleaver Reader.*

"[Eldridge Cleaver] disappointed me," stated Julian Bond (1940– ; see entry in volume 1 and update on page 31), current NAACP chairman and a civil rights activist since the 1960s, in a 1998 interview. "I like ideological consistency even when it's ideology that I don't agree with. Anybody who dances around as much as he does, you have to wonder about. It raises the question about what his beliefs were back then."

Sources for further reading

Cleaver, Eldridge. *Soul on Fire.* Waco, TX: Word Books, 1978.

Cleaver, Eldridge. *Soul on Ice* (paperback edition). New York: Dell Publishing, 1998.

"Eldridge Cleaver, Ex-Black Panther, Author, Political Conservative, Dies." *Jet.* May 18, 1998: pp. 6+.

Engelbert, Phillis. *American Civil Rights: Almanac.* Vol. 1. Farmington Hills, MI: U•X•L, 1999.

"A Fiery Soul Set Free: Eldridge Cleaver's Radical Journey Ends" (obituary). *Newsweek.* May 11, 1998: p. 72.

Grant, Joanne. "Former Black Panther Eldridge Cleaver Now Focuses on Spiritual Teaching." *San Jose Mercury News.* February 26, 1997.

Hughes, John. "A Chat With Former Black Panther Eldridge Cleaver." *Orange County Register.* April 29, 1998.

Mowatt, Raoul V. "Eldridge Cleaver: A '60s Radical Lost in the '90s." Knight-Ridder/Tribune News Service. March 7, 1994.

"Panther's Passage" (obituary). *People Weekly.* May 18, 1998: p. 70.

Pugh, Tony. "The Graying of a Black Panther: Eldridge Cleaver Touts God, Not Violence." *Miami Herald.* November 26, 1995.

Ruby Dee

*Born October 27, 1924
Cleveland, Ohio
Actress, playwright, poet, social activist*

Ruby Dee began acting in 1942, while a student at Hunter College in New York. In 1965, Dee became the first African American actress assigned to major roles at the American Shakespeare Theater in Stratford, Connecticut. Dee has acted in dozens of plays and films throughout her career. Her recent film credits include Spike Lee's *Do The Right Thing* (1989) and *Jungle Fever* (1991).

In 1948 Davis married fellow actor Ossie Davis (1917– ; see entry in volume 1). Dee and Davis have created and acted in dozens of productions together, including the Public Broadcasting System television art-anthology series *With Ossie and Ruby*. The couple have worked to provide job opportunities to low-income youth through their organization's Institute of New Cinema Artists and Recording Industry Training Program.

Dee and Davis have been active supporters of the National Association for the Advancement of Colored People (NAACP), the Southern Christian Leadership Conference

"Being black, there's a cohesion there that exists. Racism in America unites us. Racism in America demands [that] we've got to love each other."

Portrait: Reproduced by permission of AP/Wide World Photos, Inc.

(SCLC), the Student Nonviolent Coordinating Committee (SNCC), and the Congress on Racial Equality (CORE). They count among their friends such legendary black leaders as Reverend Martin Luther King Jr. (1929–1968; see entry in volume 3), Malcolm X (1925–1965; see entry in volume 3), Paul Robeson (1898–1976; see entry in volume 3), Angela Davis (1944– ; see entry in volume 1), and Huey Newton (1942–1989; see entry in volume 3).

Upbringing in Harlem

Dee was born Ruby Ann Wallace in Cleveland, Ohio, in 1924. When Dee was still an infant, she moved to Harlem with her father and stepmother, who were in search of better jobs. (Dee's natural mother left the family shortly after Dee's birth, on a religious quest.) Dee's father, Marshall Wallace, found work as a railroad porter and waiter and her stepmother, Emma (Benson) Wallace, was hired as a schoolteacher.

Emma Wallace was determined that her four children become educated so that they could someday move beyond the limited means in which they were being raised. Dee and her sisters were encouraged to study literature and music. The family spent their evenings reading aloud to one another from the poetry of American Henry Wadsworth Longfellow (1807–1882), Englishman William Wordsworth (1770–1850), and African American Paul Laurence Dunbar (1872–1906; see entry in volume 1). While a teenager, Dee wrote poetry, which she submitted to the African American weekly newspaper, the *Amsterdam News*.

Dee excelled in her studies in grammar school and passed the entrance examination to the elite Hunter High School for girls. She was one of the few black students in the mostly white, upper-class student body. Her primary studies were music, literature, art, and drama. In addition, Dee was a social activist, picketing neighborhood stores that did not hire African Americans. By the time she graduated high school, Dee had discovered the two pursuits that would remain important to her throughout her life: drama and social change.

Ruby Dee (at far right, on her knees) starred in the play A Raisin in the Sun with Sidney Poitier and Diana Sands. (Reproduced by permission of Corbis-Bettmann.)

Early acting career

After high school Dee enrolled in Hunter College as a romance languages major. She also joined the American Negro Theater (ANT), a grassroots operation housed in the basement of the West 135th Street branch of the New York Public Library. The participants not only acted, they also cleaned and maintained the facility, sold tickets door-to-door through Harlem, ushered, and built sets. Among Dee's contemporaries at the ANT were such notable performers as Sidney Poitier (1924– ; see entry in volume 3), Harry Belafonte (1927– ; see entry in volume 1), Hilda Simms (1920–), and Earle Hyman (1926–).

Dee acted in several plays with the ANT, the most important being the World War II drama *South Pacific* in which Dee portrayed a native girl named Ruth. Dee also took a course in radio training while in college, after which she was awarded roles in the radio serial *Nora Drake* and other radio plays. Before her graduation from college in 1945, Dee married public relations worker Frankie Dee.

With her bachelor of arts degree in hand, Dee went to work as a French and Spanish translator at an export company, and at a factory painting designs on buttons. Dee constantly sought ways that she could earn a living through acting. By the end of 1945, Dee's marriage had come to an end.

Partnership with Ossie Davis

Dee was given her first Broadway role in 1946, in the play *Jeb,* a work about the difficulties faced by a returning black war hero. It was during this production that she met Ossie Davis—the leading man in the play who would soon become the leading man in Dee's life. Dee and Davis became close friends. After *Jeb* the pair acted together in *Anna Lucasta*. Dee portrayed the title role and Davis was her costar. Dee and Davis again performed together, in a play called *Smile of the World*. On December 9, 1948, a Thursday (the one day of the week the actors had off), Dee and Davis slipped off to a justice of the peace and were wed.

For more than half a century, Dee and Davis have been the entertainment industry's preeminent husband-and-wife team. They have acted together in more than thirty plays, movies, radio presentations, and television documentaries (mainly focusing on human rights struggles and African American culture). In 1979 the pair acted in the musical satire *Take It from the Top,* written by Dee.

Dee and Davis appeared together in 1989 in Spike Lee's movie *Do The Right Thing*. Dee played the neighborhood's wise old woman—an actress with an unfulfilled career in white America named Mother Sister—and Davis played a drunken philosopher named "Da Mayor," who was in love with Mother Sister. For their performances in the film, Dee and Davis were inducted into the NAACP Image Awards Hall of Fame. Dee and Davis were also cast in Lee's 1991 film *Jungle Fever* as the parents of the main character.

Duo collaborates on social change

In 1974 Dee and Davis produced *The Ruby Dee/Ossie Davis Story Hour,* which promoted black heritage. The series was broadcast by sixty stations of the National Black Network. Seven years later the couple created *With Ossie and Ruby,* a television series about black artists and authors for the Public Broadcasting System. Dee and Davis appeared on the National Educational Television's series *History of the Negro People* and in 1986 produced the public television special *Martin Luther King: The Dream and the Drum, A Walk Through the 20th Century with Bill Moyers.*

Dee and Davis have also performed frequently at benefits and rallies for civil rights organizations. Together they founded the Institute of New Cinema Artists and the Recording Industry Training Program. The institute trains disadvantaged youths for jobs in film and television, and the training program provides youth with employment opportunities in the music industry. Dee, herself, established the Ruby Dee Scholarship in Dramatic Art to help aspiring young black actresses.

Dee and Davis have three children—daughters Nora and Hasna, both educators, and son Guy, a blues musician—and seven grandchildren. In February 1999, in an article paying tribute to the couple following their fiftieth wedding anniversary, journalist Joy Bennett Kinnon wrote in *Ebony* magazine: "Working, marching, and acting through decades of civil and social unrest, through several world wars, political and character assassinations, the divorces of many of their close friends and colleagues and the deaths of family members, Ossie and

Commitment to Civil Rights

Ruby Dee's first publicized protest of the denial of civil rights, in 1953, did not involve African Americans, but a Jewish couple: Ethel and Julius Rosenberg. The Rosenbergs, who were active in the Communist Party, had been convicted of passing secrets about the atomic bomb to the Soviet Union during World War II (1939–45). The Rosenbergs were sentenced to die, despite the absence of hard evidence linking them with the crime. Critics of the death sentence claimed that the Rosenbergs were being punished for their political and religious affiliations, and not for having committed the crime of which they were accused. Dee denounced the planned executions in interviews and press conferences. For her actions, Dee was labeled a Communist by many people and was shunned by some entertainment industry officials.

In August 1963, Dee emceed, with Davis, the March on Washington For Jobs and Freedom (the event at which Martin Luther King Jr. delivered his famous "I Have A Dream" speech). One month later, following the bombing of a church in Birming-

Ruby have returned again and again to the well that feeds their love and have been renewed."

Dee and Davis were granted the Silver Circle Award by the Academy of Television Arts Sciences in 1994. The following year, President Bill Clinton and first lady Hillary Clinton presented them with the presidential medal for Lifetime Achievement in the Arts.

Typecast as "the Negro June Allyson"

Many of Dee's stage and screen roles in the 1950s and 1960s cast her in the role of the patient, docile, and often suffering wife or girlfriend. This type of role was so prevalent that Dee was dubbed by critics as "the Negro June Allyson." (June Allyson, nicknamed "the girl next door," was a movie actress in the 1940s and 1950s, appearing in such movies as *Girl Crazy, Little Women,* and *The Glenn Miller Story*—always in "wholesome" roles.) In one of Dee's most famous roles, she played the tormented wife and daughter-in-law in the 1958 Broadway play *Raisin in the Sun* by African American playwright Lorraine Hansberry.

ham, Alabama, in which four young black girls were killed, Dee participated in the founding of the Association of Artists for Freedom. The group launched a campaign to convince Americans to forego Christmas shopping and donate the money they would have spent on presents to civil rights organizations.

Dee also performed in numerous benefit shows throughout the 1960s to raise funds for jailed civil rights activists and to support the Black Panther Party (BPP; an organization of black activists seeking to stem police abuse and provide social services to their community) and the Young Lords Party (a Puerto Rican-rights organization).

In 1970 the New York Urban League paid tribute to the efforts of Dee and her husband, Ossie Davis, presenting the couple with the Frederick Douglass Award for "a sense of fervor and pride to countless millions." (Frederick Douglass, [1817–1895; see entry in volume 1] was an escaped slave who became one of the nation's most outspoken opponents of slavery.)

Dee finally managed to break out of her stereotypical role in 1970, when she played Lena in the play *Boesman and Lena*. Written by white South African playwright Athol Fugard, *Boesman and Lena* was about the oppression of people of color in South Africa. In her role as Lena, Dee traveled the countryside with her husband Boesman (played by James Earl Jones [1931–]; see entry in volume 2), trying to eke out a living. Dee received rave reviews for her performance. "Ruby Dee as Lena is giving the finest performance I have ever seen," wrote critic Clive Barnes in the *New York Times*. "Never for a moment do you think she is acting.... You have no sense of someone portraying a role ... her manner, her entire being have a quality of wholeness that is rarely encountered in the theater."

Television and movie roles

The first movie in which Dee acted, released in 1946, was *Love in Syncopation*. Four years later, in *The Jackie Robinson Story,* she played the role of the legendary baseball player's wife. That same year Dee was cast alongside Sidney Poitier in the movie *No Way Out,* about a black doctor accused of killing his white patient. Dee again acted with Poitier in the 1957 film *Edge of the City,* a performance for which Dee received rave reviews. In 1961 Dee appeared in the movie version of *Raisin in the Sun.*

Dee starred in the 1963 movie *Gone Are the Days,* about a black preacher's attempts to outsmart a white plantation owner, based on a play written two years earlier by Davis called *Purlie Victorious.* Other of Dee's movie appearances in the 1960s and 1970s included: *Virgin Island* (1960), *The Incident* (1967), *Uptight* (1968), *Buck and the Preacher* (1972), *Black Girl* (1972; directed by Davis), and *Countdown at Kusini* (1976).

Dee's television career began in the early 1960s, with various roles in the *Play of the Week* series. She also appeared in episodes of *The Fugitive, The Defenders, The Great Adventure,* and *The Nurses.* Dee was the first black actress to have a role in the popular nighttime soap opera, *Peyton Place,* in 1968. She played Alma Miles, the wife of a neurosurgeon. In 1991 Dee won an Emmy for her performance in the NBC drama *Decoration Day.*

Literary accomplishments

Two of Dee's published works, *Two Ways to Count to Ten* (1990) and *Tower to Heaven* (1991), are retellings of old West African folktales for American children. In 1972 she edited the book of poems called *Glowchild and Other Poems.*

Dee has written numerous plays throughout her career, one of her more recent being *Two Hah Hahs and a Homeboy* (1995). Dee and Davis costarred in the two-act drama. The play was a tribute to Harlem Renaissance writer Zora Neale Hurston and featured the music of the couple's son, Guy Davis. The play used humor to examine the ways that discrimination impedes the social mobility of middle-class blacks.

In 1998 Dee coauthored with Davis the couple's autobiography, *With Ossie and Ruby: In This Life Together.* In 1999

Dee published a collection of her poems and short stories entitled *My One Good Nerve.*

"One facet of love is struggle," stated Dee in a 1999 interview for *Essence* magazine. "Being black, there's a cohesion there that exists. Racism in America unites us. Racism in America demands [that] we've got to love each other and that's what is taking us all wrong now. We're forgetting that. We can't afford not to love each other."

Sources for further reading

Burns, Khephra. "A Love Supreme: Actors Ossie Davis and Ruby Dee." *Essence.* December 1994: p. 76+.

Carlin, Peter Ames. "Married 50 Years, Actors Ossie Davis and Ruby Dee Have Grown Together, Not Apart." *People Weekly.* November 9, 1998: p. 153.

Davis, Ossie, and Ruby Dee. *With Ossie and Ruby: In This Life Together.* New York: William Morrow, 1998.

Dee, Ruby. *My One Good Nerve.* New York: John Wiley & Sons, Inc., 1999.

DISCovering Multicultural America. "Ruby Dee." [Online] Available http://galenet.gale.com (accessed May 6, 1999).

Goldman, Connie. "Hume Cronyn & Jessica Tandy; Ossie Davis & Ruby Dee." *Modern Maturity.* July-August 1994: pp. 64+.

Kinnon, Joy Bennett. "Ossie & Ruby: Is This The Love Affair Of The Century?" *Ebony.* February 1999: p. 48.

Lee, Felicia R. "Art and Politics: Keeping It All Fresh." *The New York Times.* April 20, 1995: p. B9.

"Ruby Dee" in *Notable Black American Women,* edited by Jessie Carney Smith. Vol. I. Detroit: Gale Research, 1996, pp. 260–62.

Joyce Dixson

Born March 23, 1951
Saginaw, Michigan
Social worker, director of Sons and Daughters of the Incarcerated (SADOI).

Joyce Dixson grew up in a poor family in Saginaw, Michigan. While her future never seemed particularly promising, few would have predicted that Dixson would spend seventeen years in prison. Yet in August 1976, Dixson was locked up for killing her abusive partner. She was forced to leave behind her two young sons.

Dixson took advantage of every educational opportunity available to her in prison. In May 1991, Dixson became the first woman behind bars to earn a bachelor's degree from the University of Michigan. Two years later, Dixson's conviction was overturned and she was set free. Dixson immediately enrolled in the University of Michigan's School of Social Work, earning her master's degree in 1995. Today Dixson directs a nonprofit agency that provides support services to children of incarcerated parents.

"Kids of the incarcerated need for people to understand us, to take time with us, and to listen to what we have to say."

—A seventeen-year-old client of SADOI.

Portrait: Reproduced by permission of Joyce Dixson.

Growing up in Saginaw

Dixson was born in 1952 in Saginaw, Michigan. She grew up in a house with a grandfather who could neither read nor write, a grandmother who scrubbed white people's floors for a living, a mother, and a brother. Her mother received welfare assistance; Dixson never knew who her father was.

"As a child growing up I was very unhappy," wrote Dixson in a 1998 *Michigan Daily Weekend Magazine* article. "I was too light-skinned for the Black kids and not light enough for the white kids. I just didn't fit in. I was very conscious of being prejudiced against for being too light (and too dark)."

Dixson had her first child while a junior in high school, and her second child two years later. She managed to graduate from high school, becoming the first member of her family in four generations to do so. A college education, however, was not within Dixson's realm of possibility. Dixson recalled in the *Michigan Daily Weekend Magazine:* "The dream of going to college was reserved for the most special people: the kids whose parents had the money, the kids who understood at an early age that going to college was automatically expected of them, or the kids with athletic scholarships. In any case, I was left out."

Fateful event leads to prison term

When Dixson was twenty-four years old she became involved with a man who peddled drugs and prostitutes. The man began to physically assault Dixson and refused to let her leave him. What began for Dixson as a fascinating affair turned into a nightmare.

"It wasn't the type of relationship that I could just walk out of," wrote Dixson in a 1994 article for *AGENDA*. "I was from a small community where most blacks lived in one area. It wasn't the kind of place where I could get away and somebody would not be able to find me....

"Then a time came when my choice came down to: 'Am I going to stand here and probably get seriously hurt—or worse—or am I going to get out of this situation?' And I shot him. I didn't want to shoot him; I didn't want to kill him.

When I did it, I wasn't thinking about if he was going to die. I was thinking about if I was going to live."

Dixson was convicted of first-degree murder in a two-day trial full of irregularities. Her court-appointed lawyer never revealed that he was also representing the man Dixson killed, at the time of the man's death. The lawyer waived Dixson's right to a jury trial and, despite Dixson having a plausible claim to self-defense, called no witnesses on her behalf. The judge found Dixson guilty and sentenced her to life in prison.

Dixson's conviction was twice overturned by the Michigan Court of Appeals, only to be reinstated by the Michigan Supreme Court. Despite pleas from many influential community members (including the prosecuting attorney in the case and the victim's own sister), Dixson was not granted a new trial.

In a 1987 affidavit supporting Dixson's appeal for pardon or commutation of sentence, attorney Kenneth Mogill wrote: "It is nothing short of an outrage to our legal system that a person whose trial was so tainted should have been denied all relief and should find herself in jail as Ms. Dixson is."

Works for self-improvement behind bars

After her first few years in prison, Dixson came to the realization that she was going to be behind bars for a very long time. She put aside her self-pity and bitterness and began to seek out educational opportunities. Dixson first enrolled in classes offered at the prison through Washtenaw Community College (in southeastern Michigan). She excelled in her studies, making the dean's honor list, and graduated with an associates degree in 1980.

The following year Dixson completed the requisite training course and became a certified paralegal. She then went to work for Prison Legal Services, assisting her fellow inmates with appeals and other legal matters. In 1985 Dixson was transferred to the Florence Crane Women's Correctional Facility in Coldwater, Michigan, where she singlehandedly ran the legal services office. She also coordinated a children's visitation program called "Kids Need Moms." In 1991 Dixson was transferred to a new women's prison, the Scott Correctional Institution, in Plymouth, Michigan, to set up the facility's legal services program.

Throughout her years in prison, Dixson assumed the role of unofficial social worker for inmates. "There are many prisoners who do not understand what caused them to end up in prison," wrote Dixson in 1988. "Many women prisoners ask: 'Why did I allow this man to abuse me so?' 'Why do I keep stealing? I'm not a bad person, I'm just a thief.' There are other questions such as, 'Why am I weak? Why can't I control my rage and anger? Why does the whole world hate me?' These people need help in addressing these issues."

Earns degree from University of Michigan

In the late 1970s, Dixson joined a small group of women prisoners fighting for their educational rights. The inmates accused the Michigan Department of Corrections of gender discrimination, pointing out that male prisoners were able to pursue bachelor's degrees while female prisoners were not. The women filed a class action suit called *Glover v. Johnson* in U.S. district court (Mary Glover was a prisoner suing for educational rights; Johnson was the director of the Department of Corrections).

In 1981 the court ruled that the Michigan corrections department had to work with four-year colleges to establish bachelor's degree programs at women's prisons. It took several years for that ruling to be put into practice at the Florence Crane Facility, where Dixson was incarcerated.

In January 1987 Dixson was finally given the opportunity to participate in a correspondence program through the University of Michigan (U-M). Dixson received audio tapes of lectures and course books through the mail. Periodically, teachers or students from U-M would make the 100-mile trek from Ann Arbor to Coldwater to tutor Dixson.

For Dixson, being a U-M student while behind bars was a remarkable experience. "I started to read [the course books], and a whole new world of thought opened up to me," wrote Dixson in the *Michigan Daily*. "I started to think about the way other people were forced to live in other parts of the world. I began thinking about this nation's economy and the society as a whole. I started thinking about the trees and deforestation.... I started having mental flashes of the aged and the homeless. Illiteracy, poor health care, and the conditions of low income families suddenly became clear issues for me. Before the symptoms and effects of these things were so familiar, but I didn't understand them. Now I do and have realized that I was a product of a lot of these social and economic conditions."

Despite the difficulties presented by her incarceration (she wrote in 1988 that "sometimes, while listening to the lecture tapes, I hear the professor writing something on the board and I just sit back and wonder what it says"), Dixson did well in her classes. On May 4, 1991, Dixson became the first woman prisoner to graduate with a bachelor's degree from the University of Michigan.

Freedom

In April 1993, after years of letter writing campaigns by her supporters, Dixson won a new trial. Circuit court judge Lynda L. Heathscott struck down Dixson's first-degree murder conviction in exchange for a guilty plea to second-degree murder, thereby paving the way for Dixson's freedom. "I'm so happy," Dixson wrote in a letter to a friend dated April 23, 1993. "Even though I don't have a thing, I'll be free. I'm just waiting for the day."

The next month the judge ruled that Dixson had served far more time than necessary for her conviction, and released her. On May 11, 1993, with the judge's words "Joyce Dixson, have a good life!" ringing in her ears, Dixson left the courthouse. Dixson's supporters, who crowded the courtroom on that day, shouted and wept tears of joy.

Dixson moved to Ann Arbor and prepared to attend graduate school in the fall. She had already been accepted by the University of Michigan School of Social Work, pending her release from prison. Dixson completed her master's of social work degree in January 1995.

Founds agency to help troubled youth

While in graduate school, Dixson formulated plans to begin a social service agency committed to helping youth of incarcerated parents. Soon after graduation, Dixson founded SADOI—Sons and Daughters of the Incarcerated. What began as a part-time pilot program has evolved into a nonprofit organization of which Dixson is executive director.

Through SADOI, Dixson gives emotional support to children who are experiencing trauma brought about by the loss of a parent to incarceration—something she wishes her own two young sons had been given when she went to prison. Dixson facilitates group sessions in which kids discuss the events that took place before, during, and after their parent's incarceration. She helps participants overcome their feelings of emotional isolation and, in many cases, to recognize and redirect emerging patterns of destructive behavior.

"Kids of the incarcerated need for people to understand us, to take time with us, and to listen to what we have to say," wrote a seventeen-year-old client of SADOI. "People on the outside don't know what we go through. I saw my mom get arrested. They arrested her at our house. They just took her. No one was concerned about us. We just stayed at home. My mother was only gone two weeks, but our family has never been the same since. I stayed at home and took care of my brothers and sisters by myself. I was only eleven years old. It was so hard."

Dixson recognizes that children of the incarcerated are at a greater risk than the general youth population of becoming criminal offenders; accordingly, one of her goals is to steer her clients away from crime.

On December 17, 1996, Joyce Dixson was featured in an exclusive interview on National Public Radio's *Fresh Air* program. Dixson has received numerous honors and awards and has given keynote addresses at the following events: the NAACP Michigan Conference (June 1997); the University of Michigan School of Social Work Commencement (December 1997); and the National Association of Social Workers conference (May 1998).

Sources for further reading

Dixson, Joyce. "The Journey of Joyce Dixson." *AGENDA: Ann Arbor's Alternative Newsmonthly.* January 1994: 5–6.

Dixson, Joyce. Letter to Phillis Engelbert. April 23, 1993.

Dixson, Joyce. "Public Holds Key to Own Safety." *AGENDA: Ann Arbor's Alternative Newsmonthly.* August 1988.

Dixson, Joyce. "Women Prisoners in Michigan." *The Michigan Daily Weekend Magazine.* November 11, 1988: 8–9.

Faber, Don. "Lifeline of Love: Former Inmate Reaches Out to Children of Incarcerated." *Ann Arbor News.* August 17, 1998: C2–3.

Littlejohn, Edward J., and Kenneth M. Mogill. "Supplement to Application for Pardon or Commutation of Sentence of Joyce Ann Dixson." 1987.

Nord, Thomas. "Judge Sets Aside Saginaw Woman's Life Sentence in '75 Slaying." *Saginaw News.* April 22, 1993: A1–2.

Treml, William B. "Educational Freedom: Two Prisoners Earn Degrees Through U-M Program." *Ann Arbor News.* May 4, 1991: A4.

Joycelyn Elders

Born August 13, 1933
Schaal, Arkansas

Professor of pediatric medicine, medical researcher, public health advocate

On September 7, 1993, Dr. Joycelyn Elders was confirmed by the U.S. Senate as the nation's first African American surgeon general. That day marked the apex of a long and arduous life's journey for the sixty-year-old Elders, who began life as the child of poor sharecroppers in rural Arkansas. Elders went on to become a college graduate, an army lieutenant, a medical doctor, head of the Arkansas health department, and ultimately the nation's highest medical officer.

Elders' outspokenness on issues of sexual education and reproductive health care led her up the ladder of success; it also, however, led to her undoing. On December 8, 1994, after making the comment at a United Nations (UN) conference that masturbation (sexual self-gratification) should be taught in schools as a form of safe sex, Elders was forced to resign her post. Today she is a professor in the Department of Pediatrics at the University of Arkansas.

"If I had it to do all over again ... I would not do it differently.... I would still be the kind of Surgeon General that I was, still speaking out."

Portrait: Reproduced by permission of AP/Wide World Photos, Inc.

Childhood in rural Arkansas

Elders was born Minnie Lee Jones on August 13, 1933, in the town of Schaal, in southwestern rural Arkansas. According to Elders, in her memoir *Joycelyn Elders M.D.*, in 1995 the town had a population of ninety-eight and was "too small for most maps." Elders was the first of eight children born to sharecropper parents Haller and Curtis Jones. (A sharecropper is a landless farmer who works a plot of land and in return gives the landowner a share of the crop.) Both of Elders's parents completed school through the eighth grade—a significant achievement for southern black sharecroppers in the early twentieth century.

At an early age, Elders's mother taught her to read. In her memoir Elders noted that her mother "held tight to the conviction that if we ever wanted to 'be something,' we had better get educated." To attend school, Elders had to walk five miles to a bus, then ride another eight miles to the segregated (separated by race) facility. When she wasn't in school or doing homework, Elders divided her time between working in the cotton fields and helping her father prepare raccoon hides for sale to department stores.

The ten-person Jones family lived in a three-room shack—a symbol of the poverty experienced by sharecroppers. There were no doctors in the vicinity, nor were there hospitals that would accept blacks. If anyone suffered an injury or illness, the only treatments were natural remedies of the family's own concoction.

Wins college scholarship

Elders excelled in her studies throughout her school years. She graduated valedictorian of her high school class and was offered a full-tuition scholarship to the all-black, liberal arts Philander Smith College in Little Rock. Elders's educational plans were nearly hijacked when her father decided he needed her to stay home and harvest the cotton crop. It was only through the intervention of her paternal grandmother and namesake, Minnie Jones, that Elders was allowed to go.

The next obstacle to be overcome was raising the $3.83 Elders needed in bus fare to Little Rock. Elders's family took to the fields, harvesting cotton bolls that had ripened early, until they had sold $5 worth.

College and army years

In college, Elders celebrated her newfound independence by changing her name from Minnie Lee to Joycelyn—the name of a sweet peppermint candy. Elders majored in biology and chemistry. Her initial career goal was to become a lab technician. Elders set her aspirations higher after attending a talk by the first black woman to attend the University of Arkansas Medical School. From that point on, Elders aspired to become a medical doctor.

Elders joined the U.S. Army's Women's Medical Specialist Corps after graduating from college. Her plan was to complete her service, then use the G.I. Bill (education assistance for veterans) to fund her medical school education. In the army she was trained as a physical therapist and rose to the rank of lieutenant.

Medical training

In 1956 Elders enrolled in the University of Arkansas School of Medicine. Although school segregation had been outlawed since the 1954 *Brown v. Board of Education of Topeka, Kansas* Supreme Court case, many traces of the ugly practice remained. For instance, Elders (one of three African American students at the medical school) was denied entrance to the regular student dining room and made to eat in a separate room with African American members of the cleaning staff. Elders tolerated the indignity so that she could accomplish the greater goal of completing medical school.

As Elders neared the end of her time in medical school, she met the man who would become her husband, Oliver Elders. Joycelyn met Oliver Elders while she was performing physicals on high school basketball players—a job she did to earn extra money. Oliver Elders was the team coach. The couple were wed in 1960 and had two sons.

Becomes expert on childhood diabetes

After completing medical school, Elders performed an internship in pediatrics (medical care for children) at the University of Minnesota. In 1961 Elders returned to Little Rock for the final stage of her medical training, her residency. Elders became chief pediatric resident, in which capacity she supervised nine white male residents and interns.

Elders then established a pediatric practice. She also conducted research at the University of Arkansas in pediatric endocrinology (the study of glands), with a focus on juvenile diabetes (a disease that impairs the body's ability to process sugars). Elders published more than 100 papers in professional journals over a twenty-year span on these topics and became regarded as an expert on juvenile diabetes.

Elders's study of diabetes led her to look at sexual behavior in young women. In particular, Elders found that when diabetics became pregnant at an early age there were serious health risks to both mother and fetus. Elders felt it necessary to discuss sexuality with her young female diabetic patients, and in some cases to prescribe birth control.

Crusades for sex education

Elders gradually became convinced of the need for sex education and birth control for all young people. She pointed to the high emotional toll on teenagers faced with raising children, as well as the high financial cost of public support for teenagers and their babies. Teenage sexual activity was further complicated, Elders recognized, by the threat of transmission of AIDS. (AIDS, which stands for acquired immunodeficiency syndrome, is a disease caused by infection with human immunodeficiency virus [HIV]. HIV works by seriously weakening the victim's immune system, leaving the body unequipped to fight off a wide range of illnesses.)

Elders was alarmed by statistics such as the following: In 1986, 20 percent of births in Arkansas were to teenage mothers; in 1987, the taxpayers of Arkansas spent $82 million in welfare benefits for teenage mothers and their children. Elders adopted the stance that teenage sexuality should be dealt with as openly and aggressively as any other public health issue.

Becomes director of Arkansas Department of Health

In 1987 Elders was appointed director of the Arkansas Department of Health by then-Arkansas governor Bill Clinton. As a state official, Elders intensified her drive for sex education. Early in her directorship, she visited a health clinic in a school in Lincoln, Arkansas, where contraceptives were distributed to students on request. The annual number of pregnancies among senior girls at the school had decreased from thirteen to one since the contraceptives had become available.

Elders advocated that every public high school establish clinics similar to the Lincoln clinic. During her tenure as health director, eighteen high schools opened health clinics. Only four, however, distributed contraceptives.

In 1989 Elders convinced the Arkansas state legislature to require sex education in public schools, from kindergarten through the twelfth grade. The curriculum included such topics as birth control, hygiene, the prevention of sexually transmitted diseases, substance abuse prevention, self-esteem issues, and the responsibility of boys—as well as girls—in preventing pregnancy. She also convinced the legislature to allocate funds for expanding the state's health services to poor people.

Conservative political and religious figures denounced Elders's actions, accusing her of promoting sexual promiscuity among teens. Elders's opponents argued that it was only appropriate to teach teenagers abstinence (restraint from sexual activity). Elders responded that it was impossible to convince teenagers to stop having sex, and that the only sensible approach was to teach them how to be responsible in their sexual behaviors.

Nominated for Surgeon General

When Bill Clinton was elected president in 1992, he vowed to construct a Cabinet that would be reflective of America in terms of race and gender. One step in the fulfillment of that promise was the March 1993 nomination of Elders, his health chief from Arkansas, to the Surgeon General position. (The Surgeon General is the head of the U.S. Bureau of Public Health and the nation's chief medical officer.)

From the start, Elders's nomination was plagued by controversy. National religious and right-wing political forces rushed to attack Elders, playing up her endorsement of abortion rights, the RU 486 abortion-inducing pill, the medical use of marijuana, and the distribution of condoms to minors. They also disagreed with her suggestion that the ban on television advertising of condoms be lifted. In response to the latter, Elders stated in an interview with *Advertising Age*: "I find it rather strange that we can advertise cigarettes and beer to the young but then get nervous when there is talk of something [condoms] that can save lives."

At the same time, Elders won the endorsement of the American Medical Association and other national organizations of health care providers and educators, as well as former Surgeon General C. Everett Koop. The drive for her confirmation was led by Edward Kennedy, the influential Democratic senator from Massachusetts. On September 7, 1993, Elders's appointment was approved in the Senate by a margin of sixty-five to thirty-four.

A short but illustrious career as Surgeon General

As Surgeon General, Elders continued to stress efforts to reduce teen pregnancy. She campaigned against tobacco use and drug and alcohol abuse, and for AIDS research and prevention (including needle-exchange programs for intravenous drug users), the breast-feeding of infants, and preventative health care (such as immunizations and yearly physicals). Elders lobbied for gun control and a national health care plan.

Dr. Joycelyn Elders speaks to a group about the results of the Surgeon General's 1994 report on smoking. (Reproduced by permission of AP/Wide World Photos, Inc.)

She made headlines in late 1993 with her controversial proposal to study the effects on crime of legalizing street drugs (including heroin and cocaine).

Elders also looked at homophobia (fear and hatred of homosexuals) as a public health issue, and advocated the full acceptance of homosexuals in society. She asserted that the high incidence of depression, suicide, and substance abuse, especially in gay teens, was linked to discrimination against homosexuals.

Fired for controversial statement

Throughout the nearly two years spanning Elders's nomination for Surgeon General and her resignation from that position, her political adversaries never stopped trying to discredit her. For her part, Elders refused to tone down her no-holds-barred style of health advocacy. She claimed that religious and conservative forces distorted whatever she said anyway, to suit their own political agendas. Elders managed to keep her opponents at bay for a little over a year.

Elders's undoing came on December 1, 1994, following a statement she made at a United Nations World AIDS Day conference. Elders was asked, during her address before 200 people, if she felt that masturbation should be presented to children as an alternative to riskier forms of sexual activity. "I think that [masturbation] is something that is a part of human sexuality," responded Elders, "and it's a part of something that perhaps should be taught."

The response to that statement from Elders's critics was fast and furious. President Clinton, whose position was already weakened due to a Republican-dominated Congress, faced immense pressure to fire Elders. He succumbed to that pressure, stating: "Dr. Elders' public statements reflecting differences with administration policy and my own convictions have made it necessary for her to tender her resignation."

Reactions to Elders's dismissal

One week after the United Nations conference, Elders resigned. "We are extremely pleased," commented Tom Kilgannon of the Christian Action Network to a reporter. "This woman from day one has insulted traditional values and insulted the Christian community. She was a symbol of extremely liberal policies of the Clinton administration and more often than not she was an embarrassment."

Patricia Ireland, president of the National Organization for Women, lamented Elders's departure. "Joycelyn Elders was a lightning rod because she spoke the truth: That the religious right wants sex education without educating about sex," stated Ireland.

"If I had it to do all over again—knowing everything I know now—I would not do it differently," Elders proclaimed in an interview a few months after her resignation with *The Progressive*. "I would still be the kind of Surgeon General that I was, still speaking out. I never saw myself as Bill Clinton's Surgeon General, or as Congress's Surgeon General. I saw myself as the people's Surgeon General."

In January 1995 Elders returned to the University of Arkansas Children's Hospital as a professor in the Department of Pediatrics.

Sources for further reading

Barnes, Steve. "Joycelyn Elders" (interview). *The Progressive*. March 1995: pp. 34+.

Cannon, Angie et. al. "Surgeon General Joycelyn Elders is Fired After Remarks on Masturbation." Knight-Ridder/Tribune News Service. December 9, 1994.

Colford, Steven W. "New Surgeon General Backs Condom Ads: Elders Wants TV Networks to Abandon Prohibition." *Advertising Age*. January 11, 1993: pp. 3+.

Dash, Leon. "Joycelyn Elders: From Sharecropper's Daughter to Surgeon General of the United States of America." (book review). *Washington Monthly*. January-February, 1997: pp. 58+.

DISCovering Multicultural America. "Joycelyn Elders." [Online] Available http://galenet.gale.com (accessed May 6, 1999).

"Dr. Joycelyn Elders an Excellent Choice for Surgeon General." Knight-Ridder/Tribune News Service. July 15, 1993.

Elders, Joycelyn. *Joycelyn Elders M.D.: From Sharecropper's Daughter to Surgeon General of the United States of America*. New York: William Morrow and Company, Inc., 1996.

Elliott, Joan C. "Joycelyn Elders" in *Notable Black American Women,* edited by Jessie Smith Carney. Vol. 2. Detroit: Gale Research, 1996, pp. 100–03.

Harvey, Kay. "Elders Describes Bias Against Homosexuals as a Health Issue; Defends Outspokenness." Knight-Ridder/Tribune News Service: September 23, 1994.

McElwaine, Sandra. "Joycelyn Elders, M.D.: Surgeon General of the United States." *Cosmopolitan.* April 1994: pp. 122+.

"Surgeon General Elders Urges Doctors, Hospitals to Push Breast-Feeding." *Jet.* August 29, 1994.

Wilson, Paula. "Rise & Fall of the Surgeon General: The Nation Wasn't Ready for Joycelyn Elders' Blunt Messages about Sexuality." *USA Today Magazine.* May 1997: pp. 58+.

Father Divine

Born c. 1879
Rockville, Maryland (?)
Died September 10, 1965
Philadelphia, Pennsylvania
Religious leader, social activist

Although his importance is generally overlooked in history books, Father Divine is one of the most fascinating and mysterious religious figures of the twentieth century. Divine was a charismatic preacher, believed to be God by his followers. He led the largest religious movement in the northern ghettos during the Great Depression (the worst economic crisis to hit the United States, lasting from 1929 through 1939). Although his followers were mostly poor and working-class African Americans, there were also middle- and upper-class whites and people of other racial groups in his organization.

Divine was not only a religious leader, but also an early civil rights activist. Divine spoke out against racism and lynching (the extral-legal execution of a person [usually an African American] accused of a crime and or a violation of social mores, often by hanging, by a group of three or more people), and advocated integration. His "Kingdom" religious movement provides an early example of the involvement of

"Father Divine attracted ghetto residents in part because he seemed the ultimate role model for many poor, uneducated blacks seeking evidence that they could improve their lot."

—Robert Weisbrot in Father Divine

Portrait: Reproduced by permission of AP/Wide World Photos, Inc.

black churches in the civil rights movement. In many cities, the network of Peace Mission cooperatives sponsored by Divine provided thousands of people with food, housing, and employment during the lean years of the mid-1920s through the mid-1940s.

Early years in dispute

Divine's date and place of birth, as well as details about his parents and upbringing, remain in question. According to many sources, Divine was born in the South (some specifically list Savannah, Georgia). In at least one current study, however, Divine's birthplace is traced to Rockville, Maryland. Most scholars agree Father Divine's given name was George Baker Jr.

Historian Robert Weisbrot, author of *Father Divine and the Struggle for Racial Equality* (1983), asserts that Divine was most likely born between the years 1877 and 1883 in the rural Deep South, probably to sharecroppers (landless farmers who work a plot of land and in return give the landowner a share of the crop). Weisbrot also explores the possibility that Divine was born in North Carolina in 1886 to a woman named Elizabeth Mayfield, who in 1936 claimed she was Divine's mother.

"On the rare occasions when Divine discussed his origins with reporters or, more typically with trial judges," writes Weisbrot, "he was nebulous and at times hopelessly contradictory."

Author Jill Watts, in her 1992 book *God, Harlem U.S.A.*, presents a very different picture of Divine's early years. Watts claims that Divine was born in May 1879 in Rockville, Maryland. Both of Divine's parents—Nancy Smith and George Baker—had been slaves. After the Civil War (1861–65) and the emancipation (freeing) of the slaves, Smith and Baker met and married. Smith worked as a maid and cook in white people's homes and Baker worked as a farmhand.

Watts's book asserts that George Baker Jr. was the second-youngest of several children born to Smith both during and after her years enslaved. He lived as a child with his parents and three siblings, plus two other families—fourteen people in all—in a small cabin. George Jr. worked from an early age, contributing twenty-five cents a day to the family's meager income.

Beginnings as a preacher

While Divine's early adult years are also shrouded in mystery (a reliable record doesn't begin until 1917, when Divine moved to New York City), the following information has been uncovered through the efforts of Jill Watts and other historians.

Divine left his parents' home in 1899 and moved to Baltimore, where he worked as a gardener. Divine was fascinated by Baltimore's thriving world of storefront churches (informal churches, not affiliated with any major denomination, that operate in rented storefronts). He studied the styles and teachings of various preachers, and tried his own hand at preaching.

From 1902 through 1906 Divine traveled throughout the South, preaching to anyone who would listen. He then journeyed to the West Coast, where he was introduced to the Pentecostal movement (a fundamentalist religious movement characterized by participants' uninhibited expressions of faith).

Upon his return to Baltimore in 1907, Divine teamed up with two other preachers: Father Jehovia (Samuel Morris), who claimed he was God; and Reverend Bishop Saint John the Vine, who claimed that all people were God. Divine assumed the role of the Messenger—the religious instructor. Over the next five years the three men built up a significant storefront congregation.

Adventures in the South

In 1912 Divine (then calling himself "The Messenger" but giving his legal name as Anderson Baker) broke with the trio and took his political message on the road. For the next few years he traveled from town to town, (mostly in the South), holding free-form services at which worshippers sang, danced, and testified late into the night. Divine also provided meals so extravagant, the worshippers considered them to be miraculous.

As Divine's popularity grew, so did his notoriety. His claim to being the Messiah (God on Earth) drew the ire of

Father Divine and his second wife in 1949. (Reproduced by permission of AP/Wide World Photos, Inc.)

other black preachers. In fact, Divine spent sixty days on a chain gang in 1913 as a result of an altercation between himself and other preachers.

In 1914, after proclaiming himself to be God, Divine was jailed in Valdosta, Georgia, on charges of lunacy. In his sermons, Divine had impressed a number of the community's black women. He had told the women to assert their rights in the home and to stop having sexual relations with their husbands—statements that drew the ire of the women's spouses. When Divine was released from jail and ordered to leave town, a handful of female disciples went with him.

Soon thereafter Divine used prayer to "cure" a white woman of arthritis at a religious revival in Macon, Georgia. That woman, named Peninnah, married Divine and later took the name "Mother Divine." Peninnah joined Divine's group as they headed northward.

Moves to New York

In 1917 Divine and his small group of followers (most, but not all, of whom were women) moved to Brooklyn, New York. There the group lived communally in a large apartment. Some members worked outside the commune while others maintained the living quarters.

During this period Divine changed his name from "The Messenger" to "M. J. Divine." M. J. stood for Major Jealous—Jealous being another name for God. According to Exodus, verse 34:14, "for the lord, whose name is Jealous, is a jealous god." Divine later simplified his name to Father Divine.

In 1919 Father and Mother Divine, plus nine followers, moved into a home they purchased in Sayville, on Long Island. They became the neighborhood's first African American residents.

Divine slowly built his religious movement, attracting white as well as black followers. In April 1930, there were thirty people living in the Sayville house and many more attending weekend services. The activities at the house came to the attention of the police. Although an undercover sting operation turned up no wrongdoing, Divine was arrested in May 1931 on charges of operating an interracial church. He was convicted and sentenced to one year in prison, but the conviction was overturned on appeal.

Sect grows in Harlem

In 1932 Divine relocated his group's home base to Harlem, the largest and most vibrant African American community in the nation at the time. Membership in Divine's religious community, called "The Kingdom," began to grow at a remarkable rate. Fifteen hundred people attended Divine's Easter mass in 1932. Membership in the Kingdom peaked in the late 1930s, with some forty thousand to fifty thousand members in New York and another ten thousand members around the nation (one of the largest branches outside of New York was in Los Angeles, California).

Divine's religious message

In his Kingdom, Divine sought to create for his followers a heaven on Earth—one that would fulfill their spiritual, social, and material needs. "You know you want your emancipation," Divine preached. "You know you want your constitutional rights, you know you want social equality, you know you want religious liberty, you know you want health and happiness, and you know positively well you also want a chance to earn a living, the same as everybody else. That's what I came for."

Divine's followers attributed to him God-like qualities, a development that Divine encouraged. Eventually, Divine's followers came to believe Divine *was* God. Even the postal service recognized Divine's standing: he often received correspondence from his followers simply addressed "God, Harlem, U.S.A."

"Father Divine attracted ghetto residents in part because he seemed the ultimate role model for many poor, uneducated blacks seeking evidence that they could improve their lot," wrote Robert Weisbrot in *Father Divine*. "Divine was one of them—a dark-skinned evangelical preacher, with an earthy humor.... Yet he was also a man—or deity—of almost incomprehensible powers, planning deals involving millions of dollars, distributing charity funds from unknown sources, and challenging white authority with a boldness and success that surely was miraculous."

Many of Divine's adherents had earlier looked to Marcus Garvey (1887–1940; see entry in volume 2) for leadership.

Many of Father Divine's followers had earlier looked to Marcus Garvey, founder of the Universal Negro Improvement Association, for leadership. (Source unknown.)

Garvey, founder of the Universal Negro Improvement Association (UNIA), sought to unite all black peoples through the establishment in Africa of a country and government of their own. He preached economic independence, pride in blacks' heritage, and the need for all black Americans to return to Africa. Garvey had also predicted the return of a black messiah, which many former Garveyites believed to be Divine.

Members of the Kingdom had to adhere to a strict set of moral guidelines. They had to remain celibate (refrain from sexual relations) and childless, and were prohibited from drinking, smoking, swearing, and receiving gifts. Racial discrimination was expressly forbidden as well.

The growth of the Peace Mission

After relocating in Harlem, Divine initiated the Peace Mission—a charitable organization and network of cooperatives that aided poor people during the Depression. The Peace Mis-

Father Divine's Role in Housing Integration

Father Divine was legendary for his ability to cross the color line in housing. Mostly through the late 1960s, and even today to some extent, housing has been the arena of strictest segregation. (Housing segregation—the separation of the races in housing—was legally forbidden by the Fair Housing Act of 1968.) The primary purveyors of housing segregation have been Realtors, who have refused to sell blacks property in white areas, and banks, which have restricted the geographic areas in which they would approve mortgages for African Americans.

Divine got around these restrictive practices by sending white Peace Mission members to purchase property in segregated areas. The Peace Mission acquired homes, hotels, farmland, and beachfront property in exclusive areas. By the end of the 1930s the Peace Mission had purchased more than 2,000 acres of choice property—including a parcel abutting President Franklin Delano Roosevelt's (1882–1945) Hyde Park mansion. Under Divine's leadership, thousands of blacks were able to move out of the inner city and into desirable areas.

sion's first move was to buy several restaurants, which not only provided jobs for Divine's followers, but also offered nutritious meals for as little as ten cents. Also under the Peace Mission umbrella were clothing stores, other cooperative businesses, and farming cooperatives established by Divine on rich farmland in Ulster County, New York. The agricultural products from the farms were sold to the Peace Mission's urban restaurants. In each cooperative, participants shared the labor and the income.

Health and status decline

Divine's kingdom began to diminish in the 1940s, as did his health. Mother Divine died in 1943, sending Father Divine into a period of depression. In 1946 Divine married again—this time a young white Canadian woman named Edna Rose Ritchings (known in the Kingdom as "Sweet Angel").

In 1953 Father Divine and the new Mother Divine (who Divine's followers believed was a reincarnation of the first

Mother Divine) moved to a large estate near Philadelphia, called Woodmont. Divine was often ill thereafter, suffering from arteriosclerosis and diabetes. By the end of the 1950s, the Kingdom had fallen into serious decline.

Father Divine died on September 10, 1965. His remains were placed in a "Shrine to Life" at Woodmont, which continues to attract many adherents and tourists.

Sources for further reading

Burnham, Kenneth E. *God Comes to America: Father Divine and the Peace Mission Movement.* Boston: Lambeth Press, 1979.

Harris, Sarah. *Father Divine.* New York: Collier Books, 1971.

Johns, Robert L. "Father Divine" in *Notable Black American Men,* edited by Jessie Carney Smith. Farmington Hills, MI: The Gale Group, 1999, pp. 305–10.

Watts, Jill. *God, Harlem U.S.A.: The Father Divine Story.* Berkeley: University of California Press, 1992.

Weisbrot, Robert. *Father Divine and the Struggle for Racial Equality.* Urbana, Illinois: University of Illinois Press, 1983.

T. Thomas Fortune

*Born October 3, 1856
Marianna, Florida
Died June 2, 1928
Philadelphia, Pennsylvania
Journalist, civil rights leader*

Timothy (or T.) Thomas Fortune was born a slave and came of age after emancipation (the freeing of slaves following the Civil War [1861–65]). He was introduced to politics and journalism during the post-Civil War era known as Reconstruction. (Reconstruction, which lasted from 1865 until 1877, was the period during which the South was rebuilt and the rights of newly freed slaves were defined.) In the 1880s and 1890s in New York City, Fortune rose to prominence as the most influential and militant journalist of his times. Fortune used his newspaper, the *New York Age*, to defend the rights of African Americans in the South and in the North.

In 1898 Fortune spearheaded an early civil rights organization, the National Afro-American Council. That organization was the predecessor to the Niagara Movement, which ultimately evolved into the National Association for the Advancement of Colored People (NAACP). In his later years Fortune edited the *Negro World*, the publication of Marcus Garvey's

> *"No man is compelled to obey a law which degrades his manhood and defrauds him of what he has paid for."*
>
> —T. Thomas Fortune, in an editorial for the New York Age

Portrait: Reproduced by permission of the Fisk University Library.

United Negro Improvement Association. (Marcus Garvey [1887–1940] was a black nationalist who proposed that African Americans return to Africa; see entry in volume 2.)

Born into slavery

Fortune was born a slave in rural Marianna, Florida, in 1856. He was the third of Emanuel and Sarah Jane Fortune's five children. The family belonged to a farmer named Ely P. Moore.

In 1861 the Civil War began between the slaveholding southern states (the Confederacy) and the free northern states (the Union). Union troops entered Marianna in September 1864, and the slaves were freed the following May. After spending a few months in a school run by Union soldiers—his first time receiving formal education—Fortune moved with his family to the city of Jackson.

Introduction to politics

The period immediately following the Civil War, called Reconstruction, was a time of great optimism for African Americans. The Republican-dominated federal government passed three constitutional amendments between 1865 and 1870, collectively known as the Civil War amendments, that abolished slavery, gave black men the right to vote (women, of any color, were not entitled to vote until 1920), and established basic liberties for blacks.

In the late 1860s and early 1870s, under the protection of the Union army, large numbers of African Americans voted. They elected numerous blacks and sympathetic whites to all levels of government. One of those pioneering black politicians, elected to the Florida state legislature in 1868, was Fortune's father.

Following Emanuel Fortune's ascension to elected office, the family became the target of racist attacks. That was not surprising, given that Jackson County—the county in which the Fortunes were living—was a Ku Klux Klan stronghold. (The Ku Klux Klan [KKK] is an anti-black terrorist group that originally formed in the South after the Civil War [1861–65]. For decades, the KKK has intimidated and committed acts of violence against black Americans and members of other racial and ethnic minorities.) To escape persecution, Emanuel Fortune moved his family to Jacksonville.

T. Thomas Fortune, interested in his father's vocation, began working on the floor of the state senate as a page. That position enabled him to pay close attention to the political maneuverings and the legislative issues of the day. Fortune developed a disdain for white politicians who first sided with black lawmakers, then abandoned them when it suited their interests. By the late 1870s a series of racist laws, passed and enforced by all levels of government, had reduced African Americans to a status that was economically, politically, and socially indistinguishable from slavery.

Apprentices at newspapers

In his teenage and young-adult years, Fortune apprenticed at newspapers in Marianna, Jacksonville, and Tallahassee. His fascination with newspapers grew as he learned the jobs of printer and journalist. In 1874 Fortune moved to Washington, D.C., and enrolled in Howard University to study law. After two semesters, unable to afford the tuition at Howard, Fortune left school and went to work as a columnist and printer for a black weekly called the *People's Advocate*. While in Washington, Fortune made the acquaintances of famous abolitionist Frederick Douglass (1817–1895; see entry in volume 1) and educator and diplomat John Mercer Langston (1829–1897).

In 1877 Fortune married his Florida sweetheart Carrie Charlotte Smiley and returned to Jacksonville. Fortune first worked as a schoolteacher and then in the office of the *Jacksonville Daily-Times Union*. The couple had five children over the next several years, only two of whom survived to adulthood.

Newspaper career in New York

In 1879, at the age of twenty-three, Fortune left the South to work as a printer for a white-owned, religious, weekly newspaper in New York. Before long Fortune left that paper to write and set type for a weekly called *Rumor,* run by a black man named George Parker. *Rumor* changed its name to the *Globe* in July 1881 and Fortune was promoted to managing editor. For his hard-hitting editorials condemning racial discrimination and demanding full rights for African Americans, Fortune gained a reputation as a "Negro agitator." Among the *Globe's* national correspondents was sixteen-year-old W.E.B. Du Bois of Great Barrington, Massachusetts. (Du Bois [1868–1963] later became one of the nation's foremost civil rights activists and scholars.)

In 1884 Fortune started up his own newspaper, the *Freeman.* In addition to Fortune's own editorials, the paper featured a humor column and a women's column edited by suffragist Gertrude Bustill Mossell. (A suffragist is a person who advocates voting rights for women.) Also in 1884 Fortune authored a book entitled *Black and White: Land, Labor, and Politics in the South,* in which he railed against the growing tide of injustice toward African Americans in the South.

Founds the *New York Age*

Fortune reorganized the *Freeman* in 1887 as the *New York Age.* This latest publication became Fortune's most successful—it was the most widely read African American newspaper in the nation at the time. Fortune served as editor of the paper through 1907, while the paper remained in circulation until 1960. In the *Age's* pages Fortune coined the term "Afro-American," using it instead of "Negro" and "colored" (the period's most commonly used terms for blacks). Fortune once explained that "Afro-American" meant that blacks were "African in origin and American in birth."

Fortune frequently editorialized about the injustice of Jim Crow laws (the Jim Crow system was a network of laws and social customs that dictated the separation of the races at every level of society). "There are some laws which no self-respecting person should be expected to obey," asserted Fortune in an *Age* editorial about segregated (separated by race) train cars. "No man is compelled to obey a law which degrades his manhood and defrauds him of what he has paid for. When I willingly consent to ride in a 'Jim Crow Car' it will be when I am a dead Afro-American."

Fortune also championed the rights of women in his paper. He hired noted feminist activists to write articles endorsing suffrage and other rights due women. Fortune further demonstrated his support of women's rights by attending the Negro Women's Convention in Boston in 1895 (he was one of only three men to do so). The convention resulted in the formation of the National Federation of Afro-American Women, which later became part of the National Association of Colored Women.

Forms National Afro-American Council

In the late 1880s, alarmed by the continuing backlash against freedpersons' rights, Fortune decided that he had to do more than write about civil rights. In 1890 Fortune helped found the National Afro-American League, one of the nation's earliest civil rights organizations. The organization disbanded in 1893, however, due to its inability to attract members and funding.

In 1898 Fortune attempted to revive the campaign for civil rights, forming a new group called the National Afro-American Council (NAAC). The NAAC was primarily concerned with the problem of racial violence. During its few years of existence, the organization was best known for its Anti-Lynching Bureau headed by black journalist Ida B. Wells-Barnett (1862–1931; see box). (Lynching is the extralegal execution of a person [usually an African American] accused of a crime or a violation of social customs, often by hanging, by a group of three or more people).

From the membership of the NAAC, in 1905, came another civil rights group known as the Niagara Movement (named for the site of the group's founding, Niagara Falls). In turn, the Niagara Movement was the precursor to the longest-lasting civil rights organization in the history of the United States: the National Association for the Advancement of Colored People (NAACP).

Ida B. Wells-Barnett

Ida B. Wells-Barnett was born into slavery in Holly Springs, Mississippi. At the age of fourteen she became a teacher in a rural school and started writing articles for black-owned newspapers. In 1889, Wells-Barnett began writing for the *Memphis Free Speech* and soon thereafter took over as its editor.

Wells-Barnett became involved in anti-lynching activities in 1892 after three of her friends, who operated a successful Memphis business called the People's Grocery, were lynched. (Victims of lynching were often financially successful blacks who, according to whites, "didn't know their place.") One of the lynching victims, Thomas Moss, had his eyes gouged out and the fingers shot off his right hand. Wells-Barnett used her newspaper to condemn the lynchings and to encourage blacks to move out of the city. She also bought a pistol, which she kept in her belt, and urged other blacks to do the same.

Wells-Barnett then questioned the common assertion that most lynchings of black men were in retaliation for rapes of white women. She undertook a meticulous investigation of the circumstances surrounding 728 lynchings that had occurred in

Alliance with Booker T. Washington

In the 1890s Fortune began a decades-long professional relationship and political alliance with Booker T. Washington (1856–1915), a former slave and founder of the Tuskegee Normal and Industrial Institute. By some measures, Fortune and Washington were strange bedfellows. Whereas Fortune advocated full rights of citizenship for African Americans, Washington felt that blacks were better off by ignoring civil rights issues.

Washington believed that blacks could improve their status in society not by demanding political power, but by getting an industrial education. (An industrial education includes trades, such as carpentry, farming, plumbing, bricklaying, and nursing; a classical education, in contrast, includes subjects such as the arts, foreign languages, history, literature, and science.)

Although Washington's ideas were welcomed by most whites and many blacks, they were disdained by a vocal seg-

> the 1880s and early 1890s and found that most of the murdered blacks had not even been accused of rape. Examples of frequent charges against murdered blacks were "race prejudice" and "quarreling with whites." After the publication of some of Wells-Barnett's findings (which included the statement: "Nobody in this section believes the old threadbare lie that Negro men assault white women"), the *Memphis Free Speech* office was burned to the ground. Wells-Barnett left town immediately and was warned that if she returned she would be hanged from a lamppost.
>
> Wells-Barnett then began touring the country, as well as traveling abroad, giving lectures about lynching. She received help coordinating her speaking engagements from T. Thomas Fortune. Wells later coordinated the anti-lynching campaign of Fortune's National Afro-American Council and wrote news columns for his *New York Age*.
>
> In the early 1900s, Wells-Barnett was active in the movement for women's suffrage, urging white suffragists to make black women's voting rights part of their platform. In 1909, Wells-Barnett was one of two women (the other was social activist Mary Church Terrell [1863–1954]) to participate in the founding of the National Association for the Advancement of Colored People (NAACP).

ment of the black population. Washington's detractors—among the loudest W.E.B. Du Bois—decried his ideas as an acceptance of the injustice and inequality in U.S. society.

The first time Fortune openly embraced Washington's ideas was in 1895, when he printed Washington's famous speech the "Atlanta Compromise" in the *New York Age*. In that speech, delivered at the Cotton States International Exposition in Atlanta in 1895, Washington offered the following compromise: blacks would give up the struggle for equal rights if whites would give black workers a role in the economy.

Over the next twelve years Fortune edited several books and articles containing Washington's speeches or ideas. In addition, Fortune ghostwrote a book by Washington, published in 1900, called *A New Negro for a New Century*. (A ghostwriter is a behind-the-scenes writer of a book or article, for which someone else is credited as the author.)

Political differences and financial entanglements

The relationship between Fortune and Washington can be explained, in part, by their mutual support of industrial education for African Americans. Indeed, Fortune had advocated such training even before the emergence of Washington. Another reason for their partnership was money. Fortune, who was constantly strapped for cash, allowed Washington to secretly fund the *New York Age*. Fortune eventually found himself financially dependent on Washington and, therefore, forced to endorse Washington's positions in the paper—even those he personally opposed. In 1907 Washington took over the *Age* by hiring an agent to buy out Fortune's stock in the company.

Suffers a nervous breakdown

The stress caused by compromising his political integrity, plus constant financial worries, took its toll on Fortune's personal life. In the early 1900s Fortune and his wife separated, and Fortune lost contact with one of his two surviving children. According to biographer Emma Lou Thornbrough, Fortune became a heavy drinker and was given to erratic behavior. Fortune became increasingly depressed and in 1907 suffered a nervous breakdown.

Final Years at *Negro World*

After leaving the *New York Age* in 1907 Fortune held a number of temporary jobs. He worked for the U.S. Treasury Department and the New Jersey Negro Welfare Bureau, and wrote for various papers including the *Amsterdam News* (an African American paper in New York City), the *Washington Sun*, and the *Norfolk Journal and Guide*.

In 1923 Fortune took over as editor of the Universal Negro Improvement Association's *Negro World*. Most days Fortune worked at his home in Red Bank, New Jersey. In his final years, Fortune publicly broke ranks with Washington and apologized for having made unprincipled political stands.

Fortune collapsed in New York City in April 1928 and was taken to Philadelphia, Pennsylvania, where his son was a surgeon at Mercy Hospital. Fortune died there of heart disease on June 2, 1928, at the age of seventy-one.

In 1995 Fortune was recognized as a legendary newspaper publisher and defender of black rights by the county in which he was born: Jackson County, Florida. Two highway markers paying tribute to Fortune were placed at county boundaries.

Sources for further reading

Blight, David W. "T. Thomas Fortune" in *The Reader's Companion to American History,* edited by Eric Foner and John A. Garraty. Boston: Houghton-Mifflin 1991, pp. 413–14.

"Florida Highway Markers Pay Tribute to Newspaper Pioneer T. Thomas Fortune." *Jet.* September 4, 1995: p. 20.

Johns, Robert L. "T. Thomas Fortune" in *Notable Black American Men,* edited by Jessie Carney Smith. Farmington Hills, MI: The Gale Group, 1999, pp. 411–13.

Smith, Sande, ed. *Who's Who in African-American History.* New York: Smithmark, 1994, p. 58.

Thornbrough, Emma Lou. "T. Thomas Fortune: Militant Editor in the Age of Accommodation" in *Black Leaders of the Twentieth Century,* edited by John Hope Franklin and August Meier. Urbana: University of Illinois Press, 1982, pp. 19–37.

Thornbrough, Emma Lou. *T. Thomas Fortune: Militant Journalist.* Chicago: University of Chicago Press, 1972.

Josh Gibson

*Born December 21, 1911
Buena Vista, Georgia
Died January 18, 1947
Pittsburgh, Pennsylvania
Baseball player*

Josh Gibson was one of the greatest baseball players of all time, yet was barred from the Major Leagues because of the color of his skin. With a career total of some 800 home runs in the Negro Leagues, Gibson may well deserve the title of "home run king." (The Negro baseball leagues, comprised of all-black teams, were organized in the 1920s and operated until the integration of the Major Leagues in 1947.) Gibson, called the "Black Babe Ruth" and a "gentle giant" (because he was strong and lovable), was the only player ever to hit a baseball out of either the New York Yankees Stadium or Washington's Griffith Stadium; he was also a first-rate catcher. Gibson died at the early age of thirty-five, after a lengthy battle with brain cancer and substance abuse.

Childhood in Georgia

Gibson was born on December 21, 1911, in Buena Vista, Georgia—a small town near Atlanta. He grew up playing pick-

"Josh Gibson was the greatest hitter who ever lived."

—Pitcher Satchel Paige

Portrait: Reproduced by permission of Corbis-Bettmann.

up games of baseball with boys and men from his community, most of whom worked in the fields all day. There were no organized leagues, groomed diamonds, or even proper shoes—just a bat, a ball, a dusty field, and comraderie.

When Gibson was twelve years old and the eldest of three children, his family moved to Pittsburgh to escape the oppression of the Jim Crow South. (The Jim Crow system was a set of laws and social customs that dictated the separation of the races at every level of society.) Gibson's father, Mark Gibson, found work in the city's steel mills.

Leaves school to pursue baseball

Gibson started playing baseball, as well as participating in track and swimming teams, while in middle school. By the time he reached the ninth grade, his remarkable talent for baseball was obvious. Gibson left school in 1927 and worked, first in an auto manufacturing plant and then in a steel mill. In 1929 Gibson helped organize, and began playing for, a semiprofessional (a notch above sandlot teams and a notch below professional teams) ball team called the Crawford Colored Giants. Gibson was impressive both at the plate, where he powered many pitches out of the park, and behind the plate, as a first-rate catcher.

Loses wife during childbirth

At the age of eighteen Gibson married Helen Mason. Gibson had met Mason the year before and the two had fallen deeply in love. At the time of their wedding, Mason was pregnant with twins.

The happy marriage came to an early, tragic end. Mason developed kidney problems during her pregnancy and died in childbirth. Gibson was so overcome by grief that for several months he did not name his children. The twins, who were raised by their grandparents, were eventually given their parents' names—Josh and Helen.

Career in the Negro Leagues

In 1930, the same year that his wife died, Gibson made his entry into professional baseball. Legend has it that Gibson was in the stands, watching the Pittsburgh Homestead Grays play the Kansas City Monarchs, when the Grays' catcher was injured and had to leave the game. The Grays' alternate catcher was playing in the outfield. The Grays' manager, Cumberland Posey, looked out at the audience and spotted Gibson (Gibson had already come to the attention of the professional teams). He took Gibson to the dugout, gave him a uniform, and thrust him behind the plate. There began Gibson's seventeen-year-long career in the professional Negro Leagues.

Gibson played in 1930 and 1931 with the Grays, then in 1932 was recruited by the Pittsburgh Crawfords. Five years later he returned to the Grays. Gibson stayed with the Grays through 1947, except the year 1940 when he played ball in Mexico. He spent winters playing baseball, along with many other Negro Leaguers, in Cuba, Puerto Rico, and the Dominican Republic. Together with hitting star Buck Leonard, Gibson led the Grays to seven straight pennants—including the Negro Leagues' final championship.

Becomes home run king

Gibson had a career total of between 800 and 972 home runs. No one knows the exact number because African American ball games were not covered by white-owned newspapers and Negro League records were not well kept. In the 1996 HBO movie *Soul of the Game,* Gibson was credited with having 972 homers. Historian John Coates puts the total at 823 home runs, while the *Guinness Book of Records* estimates that Gibson had 900. One statistic most historians do agree on is that Gibson hit eighty-four home runs during his 1936 season.

At the peak of Gibson's career, his batting average twice topped .400 (the highest was .474 in 1943). His career average, depending on which source is consulted, was between .354 and .423.

"Josh Gibson was the greatest hitter who ever lived," stated the famed Kansas City Monarchs pitcher Satchel Paige (1906–1982; see entry in volume 3). "He couldn't play in those ballparks with the roof on 'em. He would have hit 'em through the roof."

Gibson was such a powerful hitter that he once, batting one-handed, slammed a home run into the upper deck of Yankee Stadium. According to teammate Garnett Blair, Gibson "was clowning around.... He just held the bat with one hand, swung hard, and knocked it up there. The crowd gasped. Josh, he just laughed his head off."

Denied by the Major Leagues

Segregation hung over the Negro Leagues like an ominous cloud. Although black players had a league of their own, their playing conditions and salaries lagged far behind those of white professional ballplayers. Black teams played in rented-out stadiums of white teams, when the white teams were on the road. The African American players were not allowed to use the locker rooms. Negro Leagues players earned, on average, just one-tenth what Major Leagues players earned.

Gibson was among the Negro Leagues players who aspired to play in the Major Leagues. The door to integration was opened a crack in 1945, when longtime baseball commissioner Kenesaw Mountain Landis, a staunch segregationist, died. At that time, black players pressed harder for entry into the Major Leagues.

The first team to send scouts to the Negro Leagues in search of players was the Brooklyn Dodgers. The Dodgers narrowed their choice to the three outstanding players: Gibson, Satchel Paige, and Jackie Robinson (1919–1974; see entry in volume 3), former star running back for University of California-Los Angeles (UCLA). Gibson was passed over because of his health problems, and Paige for his age (at the time, he was in his forties). The Dodgers settled on Robinson, not only for his athletic abilities, but also for his character (Robinson was a college graduate and a former army lieutenant). Robinson broke the color divide in 1947; Paige followed close behind, entering the Major Leagues in 1948.

The 1996 HBO teleplay Soul of the Game, *starring Mykelti Williamson (center) as Josh Gibson, examined the 1945 search for a black player to integrate Major League baseball. (Reproduced by permission of AP/Wide World Photos, Inc.)*

Battles alcohol addiction, health problems

Gibson developed a drinking problem in the late 1930s. During the final four years of his life, he slipped further and further into alcoholism. According to biographer Mark Ribowsky, Gibson also abused marijuana and heroin. His behavior became unpredictable and he often slurred his words. Gibson suffered a nervous breakdown in the mid-1940s and was said to be suicidal.

There were several games for which Gibson was too intoxicated to play. He sometimes drank so much that his teammates sent him to the hospital for treatment. Gibson's hospital stays ranged from one day to two weeks. On occasion, hospital attendants would drive Gibson to a game only to take him back to the hospital immediately afterward.

Remarkably, Gibson played well even when he was ill. As Ribowsky noted in *The Power and the Darkness: The Life of Josh Gibson in the Shadows of the Game,* "As though he could squeeze every ounce of strength from his weary body into his bat, Josh would wobble up to the plate and hit one out of sight." The Grays' manager managed to keep Gibson's substance abuse out of the public eye by telling reporters that Gibson's absences were "rest days."

Gibson learned he had a brain tumor in 1943, yet he refused to have the needed operation. He continued to drink heavily and play ball. As a result of his ailments gained so much weight he appeared bloated, yet he still boasted a .361 batting average in 1946.

Dies at age thirty-five

By the end of 1946, Gibson's health had seriously deteriorated. He suffered from kidney and liver disease and bronchitis. His flesh wasted away until he appeared emaciated (extremely thin). On January 18, 1947, just after his thirty-fifth birthday, Gibson complained of a terrible headache. He took a sedative and went to bed, only to die that night.

Inducted into Baseball Hall of Fame

Gibson was inducted into the Baseball Hall of Fame in Cooperstown, New York, in 1972, the second Negro Leagues player to be so honored (the first, in 1971, was Satchel Paige).

In 1996 Gibson was honored by the Pennsylvania Historical and Museum Commission with a historical marker in Pittsburgh. The marker was placed outside of Ammons Field, where Gibson played with the Crawfords.

"I don't think there's any question that Josh Gibson was one of the greatest hitters, white or black," commented Robert W. Peterson, author of the book *Only the Ball Was White,* in a 1998 interview with Gregory Clay. "I have talked to black and white players about him. Some of the black players, in particular, say he was, indeed, the finest hitter they ever saw."

Sadly, in these days when the names Babe Ruth, Hank Aaron, and Mark McGwire are household words, few people remember Josh Gibson.

Sources for further reading

Brashler, William. *Josh Gibson: A Life in the Negro Leagues.* New York: Harper & Row Publishers, 1978.

Butters, Patrick. "Meet the Unknown Slugger." *Insight on the News.* September 21, 1998: p. 43.

Clay, Gregory. "The Josh Gibson Saga: From Great Triumph to Haunting Sadness." Knight-Ridder/Tribune New Service. October 15, 1998.

"Josh Gibson, the 'Black Babe Ruth,' Honored in Pittsburgh with a Historical Marker." *Jet.* October 21, 1996: p. 49.

"Josh Gibson Was the Home Run Hero in His Day." *Jet.* October 26, 1998: p. 52.

"News Q&A: Is Baseball Legend of Negro Leagues the Home-Run Leader of All Time?" Knight-Ridder/Tribune News Service. June 5, 1996.

Peterson, Robert. *Only the Ball Was White.* Englewood Cliffs, NJ: Prentice-Hall, 1970.

Ribowsky, Mark. "In a League of His Own." *Interview.* April 1996: p. 64.

Ribowsky, Mark. *The Power and the Darkness: The Life of Josh Gibson in the Shadows of the Game.* New York: Simon & Schuster, 1996.

"Soul of the Game: HBO Movie Tells How Blacks Broke Baseball Color Barrier." *Jet.* April 29, 1996: pp. 32+.

Frances Ellen Watkins Harper

*Born September 24, 1825
Baltimore, Maryland*

*Died February 22, 1911
Philadelphia, Pennsylvania*

Abolitionist, women's rights advocate, poet, author, lecturer

Frances Ellen Watkins Harper was remarkable both for her literary capabilities and her dedication to social justice. Born a free black in the slave state (state in which slavery was permitted) of Maryland, Harper moved several times and finally settled in the free state (state in which slavery was prohibited) of Pennsylvania. There she became active in the Underground Railroad (the secret network of routes and safe houses through which slaves escaped to freedom) and established a career as an antislavery lecturer. She also joined in the struggle for women's rights.

Harper wrote several volumes of poetry, essays, and short stories, and penned one novel: *Iola Leroy; or, Shadows Uplifted*. Through her writings, Harper attacked slavery and promoted equal rights for women. She is considered a leading African American poet of the nineteenth century and one of the earliest black feminists.

> "[Frances Harper] was not a great singer, but she had some sense of song; she was not a great writer, but she wrote much worth reading.... She took her writing soberly and earnestly; she gave her life to it."
>
> —W.E.B. Du Bois

Portrait: Source unknown.

Upbringing and education

Harper was born Frances Ellen Watkins in Baltimore, Maryland, in 1825. Although Maryland was a slave state at that time, Harper's parents belonged to a colony of free blacks. Both of Harper's parents died when Harper was just three years old, leaving her in the care of her aunt and uncle. Harper attended a school for free blacks run by her uncle, a minister, called the William Watkins Academy for Negro Youth. The abolitionist (pertaining to the termination of slavery) teachings of the school had a profound impact on Harper.

At age thirteen, Harper took her first job—caring for the children of bookstore owners. That position presented Harper with the opportunity to read popular literature and inspired her to begin writing poetry (her first volume of poems was published in 1845).

Wishing to live in a free state, Harper moved to Ohio in 1850. She worked for two years as a sewing teacher—and was the first female instructor—at Ohio's all-black Union Seminary, near Columbus. The seminary, affiliated with the African Methodist Episcopal Church, was later made part of Wilberforce University.

Joins the Underground Railroad

In 1852 Harper moved to Little York, Pennsylvania, and took a job as an elementary school teacher. In Little York Harper was introduced to the antislavery movement, in particular, the Underground Railroad. From 1852–1853, Harper lived and worked at a "station" of the Railroad—the home of noted black abolitionist William Still (1821–1902). Still later wrote, in the introduction to Harper's 1892 book *Iola Leroy,* that Harper was "one of the ablest advocates for the Underground Railroad and the slave."

In 1853, Maryland passed a law that forbid free blacks to enter the state under penalty of imprisonment or enslavement. Harper, upon learning that she could not return home, went through a period of depression.

Harper made her first abolitionist speeches in 1854, in Boston and New Bedford, Massachusetts. She was immediately recognized as an effective and persuasive orator and was hired as a speaker by the Anti-Slavery Societies in Pennsylvania and Maine. For the next four years, Harper gave antislavery lectures, sometimes as many as three per day, throughout New England, Ohio, and New York. In her speeches, she also read from her growing repertoire of poetry.

In 1860, at the age of thirty-five, Harper married a farmer named Fenton Harper. She stopped her political activities and settled into the life of a homemaker. The Harpers had one child, a daughter named Mary. Fenton Harper died in 1864, after which Harper returned to the lecture circuit with little Mary in tow. Following the emancipation of the slaves in 1865, Harper began speaking up for the rights of newly liberated African Americans.

Literary accomplishments

Harper published fifteen volumes of poetry and prose, including one novel called *Iola Leroy; or, Shadows Uplifted* (see box), in the latter half of the nineteenth century and the early twentieth century. Her poetry, for which she is best known, is written in narrative form and organized into ballad stanzas. Much of Harper's work addresses the cruelty of slavery; in particular, the injustices suffered by female slaves.

Harper's first publication, *Forest Leaves* (1845), is a collection of poems and essays. Harper published two books in 1854: *Poems on Miscellaneous Subjects,* which sold more than 10,000 copies and came out in at least twenty editions, and *Eventide,* a collection of poems and short stories written under the pseudonym Effie Alton. *Poems on Miscellaneous Subjects* contains one of Harper's best-known abolitionist poems, "Bury Me in a Free Land." The introduction to the volume is by famous abolitionist William Lloyd Garrison (1805–1879).

Another of Harper's legendary poems, which has been reprinted in numerous anthologies, is "The Slave Mother." The poem describes the traumatic separation of a slave mother and daughter at the auction block. One stanza reads:

> Heard you that shriek? It rose
> So wildly on the air,
> It seem'd as if a burden'd heart
> Was breaking in despair.

Harper's two most critically acclaimed books are *Moses: A Story of the Nile,* published in 1869, and *Sketches of Southern Life,* published in 1891. *Moses: A Story of the Nile,* contains several poems and an essay. The title work, a long narrative poem, is based on the life of the Hebrew savior Moses; it focuses on the personal sacrifice required to obtain freedom for one's people. *Sketches of Southern Life* is a collection of poems, narrated by two ex-slaves, and written in African American vernacular (manner of speech). It touches on themes of importance to southern blacks: family, education, religion, slavery, and Reconstruction (the social reorganization during post-Civil War period). Harper published her final volume of poetry, *Atlanta Offering: Poems,* in 1895.

Lectures throughout the post-Civil War South

Harper conducted a speaking tour through the South from 1867 to 1871, drawing large crowds of blacks and whites. On her travels she witnessed the terrible conditions under which blacks were living in the post-Civil War period. (The Civil War took place from 1861–65.) Although they were no longer slaves, African Americans had little access to education or employment, were prevented from voting, and were victimized by racial violence.

Harper was especially concerned about the plight of black women. Not only did black women endure the oppression that white society imposed on all blacks, but many were ill-treated by their husbands. Harper once noted that black women typically worked harder than black men, pulling "double duty": a "man's share in the field and a woman's part at home."

Fights for women's rights

Motivated by a desire to improve conditions for black women, as well as to secure the vote for all women, Harper

Iola Leroy; or, Shadows Uplifted

The year 1892 saw the publication of Frances Ellen Watkins Harper's only novel, *Iola Leroy; or, Shadows Uplifted*. The protagonist of the novel, Iola, is a light-skinned young woman from a family of mixed race. Iola grows up believing she is white but, upon the death of her white father, learns that her mother was a light-skinned African American. Iola rejects the white world, in which she can easily "blend," in favor of living among blacks. This choice costs Iola her freedom, as she is captured and enslaved. Iola escapes and commits herself to abolitionism and racial justice. She is also an early feminist, believing that instead of marrying, "every woman ought to know how to earn her own living."

Iola Leroy was one of the first major literary works in which black people were portrayed in a positive manner. Harper concluded *Iola Leroy* on a hopeful note, with the following poem:

> There is light beyond the darkness,
> Joy beyond the present pain;
> There is hope in God's great justice
> And the negro's rising brain.
> Though the morning seems to linger
> O'er the hill-tops far away,
> Yet the shadows bear the promise
> Of a brighter coming day.

joined the growing women's movement in the 1860s. (Women gained the right to vote with the passage of the Nineteenth Amendment in 1920.)

In 1869, as black men stood on the threshold of enfranchisement (being allowed to vote), the women's movement split into two groups: people who supported black male suffrage unconditionally and people who supported the black male vote only if accompanied by the female vote. Harper, who had frequently argued that black women had more to fear from white racism than they did from black men, placed herself in the former camp. Harper cofounded the American Woman Suffrage Association (AWSA) in 1870, the women's group that supported the Fifteenth Amendment (the 1870 amendment granting black men the vote). Other AWSA founders were noted suffragists Lucy Stone (1818–1893) and Julia Ward Howe (1819–1910).

The other faction, led by activists Susan B. Anthony (1820–1906) and Elizabeth Cady Stanton (1815–1892), formed the National Woman Suffrage Association (NWSA). The NWSA, which counted among its members escaped slave and abolitionist Sojourner Truth (1797–1883; see entry in volume 4), lobbied for the passage of a constitutional amendment allowing women to vote.

Harper became a popular speaker at women's rights gatherings. In 1888, she addressed the conference of the International Council of Women in Washington, D.C. That gathering, organized by Susan B. Anthony, drew representatives from forty-nine countries and fifty-three women's rights groups in the United States. Harper also spoke before the National Council of Women in 1891. At the Columbian Exposition in Chicago in 1893, Harper delivered a speech entitled "Women's Political Future." In her speech Harper criticized the women's movement for ignoring the concerns of African American women.

Harper and other black feminists had long been discouraged by the racism they experienced in the white-dominated women's movement. In 1896 Harper cofounded the National Association of Colored Women (NACW), a group devoted to the self-protection, self-advancement, and social interaction of black women. Harper served as the group's first vice-president. Within ten years of its founding, the NACW boasted a membership of 50,000 women.

Harper's final years

Harper continued writing and lecturing into the final decade of her life. In 1909, Harper was dealt a tremendous emotional blow when her daughter, with whom she was extremely close, died. Two years later, Harper died of heart failure in Philadelphia.

Following Harper's death, W.E.B. Du Bois (1868–1963; see entry in volume 1), civil rights leader and editor of *Crisis* (the newsletter of the National Association for the Advancement of Colored People [NAACP]) wrote: "It is, however, for her attempts to forward literature among colored people that Frances Harper deserves most to be remembered. She was not a great singer, but she had some sense of song; she was not a great writer, but she wrote much worth reading. She was, above all, sincere. She took her writing soberly and earnestly; she gave her life to it."

Sources for further reading

Altman, Susan. *The Encyclopedia of African-American Heritage*. New York: Facts on File, Inc., 1997, p. 111.

DISCovering Authors Modules. "Frances Ellen Watkins Harper."[Online] Available http://galenet.gale.com (accessed April 29, 1999).

Giddings, Paula. *When and Where I Enter: The Impact of Black Women on Race and Sex in America*. New York: Bantam Books, 1984.

"Harper, Frances Ellen Watkins" in *Benet's Reader's Encyclopedia of American Literature*. New York: HarperCollins Publishers, 1991, p. 418.

Harper, Frances Ellen Watkins. *Iola Leroy; or, Shadows Uplifted*. Philadelphia: Garrigues Bros, 1892; reprinted by Oxford University Press, 1988.

Hine, Darlene Clark, Elsa Barkley Brown, and Rosalyn Terborg-Penn, eds. *Black Women in America: An Historical Encyclopedia*. New York: Carlson Publishing, Inc., 1993, pp. 532–36, 842–51, and 1124–28.

Smith, Jessie Carney, ed. *Notable Black American Women*. Vol. I. Detroit: Gale Research, 1996, pp. 457–62.

Smith, Sande, ed. *Who's Who in African-American History*. New York: Smithmark, 1994, p. 68.

Charles Hamilton Houston

Born September 3, 1895
Washington, D.C.
Died April 22, 1950
Washington, D.C.
Civil rights lawyer, educator

From the early 1930s until his death in 1950, Charles Hamilton Houston used the law as an instrument for social change. As special counsel for the National Association for the Advancement of Colored People (NAACP), Houston argued numerous court cases challenging the constitutionality of segregation (legal, forced separation of the races). In his capacity as vice dean and professor at Howard University Law School, he trained dozens of other civil rights lawyers. Four years after Houston's death, one of his star pupils, NAACP lawyer Thurgood Marshall (1908–1993; see entry in volume 3), successfully argued the case *Brown v. Board of Education of Topeka, Kansas* that outlawed segregation in public schools.

Upbringing in Washington, D.C.

Houston was born on September 3, 1895, in Washington, D.C. He was the only child of William LePre Houston, a lawyer

"[Houston] made it clear to all of us that when we were done, we were expected to go out and do something with our lives."

—Thurgood Marshall

Portrait: Reproduced by permission of Corbis Corporation (Bellevue).

who later became assistant U.S. attorney general, and Mary Ethel Hamilton Houston, a hairdresser (a former teacher, she switched careers to provide additional income for the family).

Houston attended segregated public schools in Washington, D.C. He excelled in his studies due to the encouragement he received from his parents and his aunt, Clotill Houston, a schoolteacher. Houston graduated valedictorian from the M Street college-preparatory high school, widely considered the best black high school in the nation, at the age of fifteen.

In 1911 Houston enrolled in Amherst College in Amherst, Massachusetts. He graduated from Amherst, one of six valedictorians, in 1915. For the next two years Houston taught English at the all-black Howard University in Washington, D.C.

In 1917, toward the end of World War I (1914–18), Houston joined the army. He served in France and Germany as an officer until 1919. During his service Houston became deeply disturbed by the racism directed at African Americans by their fellow American troops.

Legal education

Houston enrolled in Harvard Law School following his discharge from the army in 1919. Two years later Houston became editor of the *Harvard Law Review*—a distinguished scholastic honor. He earned his law degree in 1922 (becoming the first African American to graduate from Harvard Law School) and completed his legal doctorate on constitutional law in 1923. From his mentor Felix Frankfurter (1882–1965; an associate justice of the U.S. Supreme Court from 1939–1962), Houston learned that the law could and should be used to challenge societal injustices.

In 1923 Houston received a Sheldon Fellowship. He spent the following year studying civil law at the University of Madrid and traveling through northern Africa.

Law practice

In the summer of 1924 Houston returned to Washington, D.C., and joined his father's law practice, Houston and Houston. The firm handled mostly civil claims (such as personal injury, negligence, wills, and estates), and also took on some criminal cases. Soon after his arrival at the firm, Houston expanded the firm's areas of litigation to include civil rights.

Houston even acted as an advocate within the firm. When one of the firm's secretaries, Juanita Kidd Stout, voiced an interest in law, Houston encouraged her to follow her dream. Stout went to law school and subsequently became the first African American woman appointed to the Pennsylvania Supreme Court.

Active in civic and political groups

At the start of his legal career Houston was very active in civic affairs in Washington, D.C. He joined the National Bar Association (the American Bar Association, at that time, did not admit blacks) and the National Lawyers Guild (an association of activist lawyers). Houston was also a member of both the local and national NAACP, sat on the American Council on Race Relations, and was a member of the District of Columbia's Board of Education.

In 1927 and 1928 Houston, with funding by the Rockefeller Foundation, conducted a national survey of African American lawyers. He found that not only were their numbers woefully low, but there were very few with training in constitutional law—the type of law that would allow them to handle civil rights cases in federal courts.

Turns Howard into civil rights training ground

When Houston started working in his father's law firm, he taught night classes at Howard University Law School for extra income. At that time, the law school only offered a part-time program of evening courses. It had neither an adequate library nor well-trained teachers.

In 1929, when Houston was offered the position of vice dean of the law school, he leaped at the opportunity. He went

Houston's Landmark Desegregation Cases

In the late 1930s Houston successfully argued two major cases in the area of higher-education desegregation, paving the way for blacks to attend law schools at the University of Maryland and the University of Missouri. More importantly, Houston's successes chipped away at "separate but equal"—the doctrine established by the Supreme Court in the *Plessy v. Ferguson* case, which served as the legal basis of the Jim Crow system.

In their desegregation cases, Houston and other NAACP lawyers employed the remarkable strategy of using the *Plessy* decision to undermine the *Plessy* decision. In essence, the attorneys argued that under *Plessy* it is the responsibility of the states to provide educational facilities for blacks that are every bit as good as the educational facilities for whites. If that criterion was not met (which it almost never was, given the impracticality of creating two quality institutions to serve the same purpose), then white schools must admit blacks.

In 1935 Houston, together with assistant special counsel Thurgood Marshall, filed suit against the all-white University of Maryland Law School for denying admit-

---

to work transforming the school into a full-time academy and recruiting well-qualified law professors. (Many of those professors later became Houston's colleagues in the NAACP's legal department.) He also toughened admission standards, improved the library, and expanded the curriculum to include a focus on constitutional law.

Houston was roundly criticized for firing teachers he deemed incompetent and rejecting students he felt were unqualified. Many students even complained that the coursework was too rigorous. Houston remained undeterred in his mission.

The law school gained accreditation from the American Bar Association in 1931 and was admitted into the Association of American Law Schools the following year. Howard came to be considered as the best black law school in the nation.

Howard also evolved, according to Houston's vision, into a training ground for civil rights litigators. Houston believed tance to a qualified black student named Donald Murray (Marshall, himself, had been denied entry to the school years earlier). In the case, *Murray v. University of Maryland,* Houston and Marshall argued that the University of Maryland had to admit Murray since the state had no publicly supported law school for black students. The Maryland Supreme Court sided with the NAACP and ordered the school to admit the black student.

In 1938 Houston teamed up with St. Louis attorney Sidney Redmond to win the NAACP's first desegregation case in the U.S. Supreme Court. The Court, in the case *Missouri ex rel Gaines v. Canada,* ruled that the University of Missouri could not exclude a black student from its law school in the absence of an equivalent black university law school.

The victories by Houston and other NAACP attorneys in higher-education cases laid the groundwork for ending school segregation at all levels.

that the courts were the arena in which civil rights gains were most likely to take place. His reasoning was that the courts were avowedly unbiased and apolitical institutions, and therefore should be responsive to sound legal arguments regarding the unconstitutionality of discriminatory laws. Accordingly, Houston identified as Howard's single most important mission the training of its students in the use of the law as a tool for social change.

"He'd drive home to us that we would be competing not only with white lawyers but really well-trained white lawyers," Thurgood Marshall was quoted as saying in *Simple Justice.* "He made it clear to all of us that when we were done, we were expected to go out and do something with our lives." (Marshall served on the U.S. Supreme Court from 1967 to 1991.)

Houston's educational experiment was a great success. Howard Law School graduates were at the forefront of the desegregation courtroom battles of the 1930s, 1940s, and 1950s, leading to the prohibition of all Jim Crow practices. (The Jim Crow system was a network of laws and social customs that dictated the separation of the races on every level of society.)

Develops plan for fighting segregation

In 1934 the NAACP, with financial backing from the American Fund for Public Service, hired Houston to develop a litigation plan for reversing *Plessy v. Ferguson* (the 1896 case in which the Supreme Court upheld the constitutionality of the "separate-but-equal" underpinnings of Jim Crow; the case specifically endorsed a Louisiana law mandating separate railroad cars for black and white passengers). Houston prescribed a long-term, stepwise plan of strategically selected lawsuits, coupled with community involvement, that would challenge segregation on a number of specific fronts.

The NAACP accepted Houston's plan and invited him to lead their legal campaign against segregation in education and transportation. Houston accepted the offer and served as special counsel to the NAACP, in Washington, D.C., and New York City, from late 1934 through 1940.

Puts plan into action

As special counsel to the NAACP, it was Houston's job to execute the desegregation campaign he had outlined. His main objective was the elimination of segregation in public education. "These apparent senseless discriminations in education," stated Howard in a 1935 address before the National Bar Association, "against Negroes have a very definite objective on the part of the ruling whites to curb the young and prepare them to accept an inferior position in American life without protest or struggle."

For six years Houston argued cases in state and federal courts while providing advice to other civil rights attorneys. Houston also traveled throughout the South filming conditions in black schools and white schools. He then presented this documentary, highlighting the inequities between the two sets of schools, to NAACP chapters to use for public education.

In 1936 Thurgood Marshall, then a young attorney and former student of Houston's, was named assistant special counsel for the NAACP. Houston and Marshall formed a formidable team, accumulating an impressive list of legal victories for civil rights. Marshall became the NAACP's special counsel upon Houston's resignation in September 1940.

Litigates labor discrimination cases

Houston did not limit his efforts to school desegregation; he also fought racial discrimination in employment. In the late 1930s Houston and Marshall provided legal assistance to numerous African American teachers throughout the South who were being paid significantly less than their white counterparts. The U.S. Supreme Court sided with the black teachers when it ruled in the 1940 case *Alston v. Board of Education* that it was unconstitutional for teacher salaries to be determined by race.

When Houston resigned from the special counsel position in 1940, he maintained his relationship with the NAACP as a member of the organization's National Legal Aid Committee. He continued representing victims of racial discrimination both through the NAACP and as part of his private practice.

In the early 1940s Houston served as counsel for two organizations of African American railway workers: the Association of Colored Railway Trainmen and the International Association of Railway Employees. Both groups claimed that they were being discriminated against by unions of white railway workers. In two 1944 cases (*Steele v. Louisville and Nashville* and *Tunstall v. Brotherhood of Locomotive Firemen and Enginemen*), the Supreme Court ruled that the white labor unions, recognized as collective bargaining representatives, had to fairly represent all workers regardless of race.

Serves on Truman's fair employment committee

By the 1940s Houston was well-known and well-respected in Washington, D.C., political circles. He was frequently called to testify before congressional committees on the racial consequences of proposed legislation. In 1944 Houston was appointed to serve on the Fair Employment Practice Committee—established by President Harry S. Truman (1884–1972; served as president from 1945–1953) to investigate cases of racial discrimination in the railway industry.

Houston angrily resigned from the committee in December 1945. His resignation was sparked by Truman's refusal to prohibit racial discrimination by the Capital Transit Company (a railway company) in Washington, D.C.

Civil rights work consumes final years

Throughout Houston's final years his life continued to be dominated by civil rights work, leaving him little time for family (he and his wife, Henrietta Williams, had one son, Charles Hamilton Houston Jr., born in 1944) or friends. In the late 1940s Houston was an advisor to NAACP legal teams in three cases concerning higher-education desegregation. He also wrote a column on civil rights for the *Afro-American* newspaper and served as an officer in the National Lawyers Guild.

Through his private practice Houston represented numerous Washington, D.C., residents who suffered discrimination in housing and education. Houston attacked the legality of racially restrictive convenants (clauses in property titles that mandated the property remain in the hands of white owners; the convenants were used to preserve racial segregation in housing) and presented arguments before the Supreme Court in the 1948 case *Hurd v. Hodge. Hurd* was the Washington, D.C., companion case to the more famous *Shelley v. Kraemer* suit. The Supreme Court decided in both cases, on the same day, that restrictive convenants were unconstitutional.

The final desegregation case in which Houston participated was *Bolling v. Sharpe,* a 1950 companion case to *Brown v. Board of Education of Topeka, Kansas.* The *Bolling* case, in which Houston filed litigation on behalf of Consolidated Parents Group of the District, presented a challenge to school segregation in Washington, D.C. The Supreme Court ruled in

This bust of Charles Hamilton Houston was unveiled at Howard University in 1985. Houston served as vice dean of the Howard University Law School from 1930 to 1935. (Reproduced by permission of AP/Wide World Photos, Inc.)

both *Brown* and *Bolling* in 1954 that school segregation was unconstitutional.

Houston died of a heart attack on April 22, 1950. Among the mourners at Houston's funeral were five Supreme Court justices. Today the law school at Howard University bears Houston's name.

Sources for further reading

African Americans: Voices of Triumph: Perseverance. Alexandria, VA: Time-Life Books, 1993.

DISCovering Multicultural America. "Charles Hamilton Houston." [Online] Available http://galenet.gale.com (accessed May 18, 1999).

Karst, Kenneth L., Leonard W. Levy, and Dennis J. Mahoney, eds. *Civil Rights and Equality.* New York: Macmillan Publishing Company, 1986.

Kluger, Richard. *Simple Justice.* New York: Vintage Books, 1975.

McNeil, Genna Rae. "Charles Hamilton Houston: Social Engineer for Civil Rights" in *Black Leaders of the Twentieth Century,* edited by John Hope Franklin and August Meier. Urbana: University of Illinois Press, 1982, pp. 220–40.

McNeil, Genna Rae. "Charles Hamilton Houston" in *Notable Black American Men,* edited by Jessie Carney Smith. Farmington Hills, MI: The Gale Group, 1999. pp. 575–78.

McNeil, Genna Rae. *Groundwork: Charles Hamilton Houston and the Struggle for Civil Rights.* Philadelphia: University of Pennsylvania Press, 1983.

Smallwood, David, et al. *Profiles of Great African Americans.* Lincolnwood, IL: Publications International, Ltd., 1996, pp. 94–95.

Jesse Jackson

Born October 8, 1941
Greenville, South Carolina
Civil rights leader, politician, minister

UPDATE

In May 1999, many people hailed the Reverend Jesse Jackson as a hero for securing the release of two U.S. servicemen held hostage by Serbian forces. That intervention was the latest in a string of diplomatic successes for Jackson; in the years spanning 1984 through 1990 he negotiated the liberation of captives being held by the governments of Syria, Cuba, and Iraq.

Jackson served as an aide to Rev. Martin Luther King Jr. (1929–1968; see entry in volume 3) from 1966 to 1968 and later formed the Chicago-based organization People United to Serve Humanity (PUSH). He also vied for the Democratic presidential nomination in both 1984 and 1988. Throughout the 1990s Jackson has been on the front lines of civil rights and human rights work, fighting racial discrimination, supporting striking workers, and conducting voter registration drives. **(See original entry on Jackson in volume 2.)**

"I am somebody!"

—PUSH refrain

Portrait: Reproduced by permission of AP/Wide World Photos, Inc.

Educational achievements

Jackson was born in Greenville, South Carolina, in 1941. He attended Sterling High School in Greenville, where he was president of his class and a star on the school football team. Following his high school graduation in 1959, Jackson was awarded a football scholarship to the University of Illinois. Jackson left the University of Illinois after one year, upon being told that African Americans were not eligible to play quarterback. He transferred to the all-black North Carolina Agricultural and Technical (A&T) College in Greensboro, where he became a star quarterback.

Just months before Jackson arrived in Greensboro, the town had achieved fame as the site of the first lunch-counter sit-ins (a form of nonviolent protest in which black students, sometimes joined by white students, requested service at whites-only lunch counters; when the students were denied service, they refused to leave). The Greensboro lunch-counter sit-ins sparked a wave of protests, not only at lunch counters but many segregated (separated by race) facilities, throughout the South. Jackson soon involved himself in the civil rights activities, leading marches and sit-ins at segregated hotels and restaurants.

Jackson completed a bachelor of arts degree in sociology from North Carolina A&T in 1964. He then enrolled in the Chicago Theological Seminary, to train to become a minister. Jackson mixed months of study with months of civil rights activism over the next four years, and was ordained a Baptist minister in 1968.

Works with Martin Luther King Jr.

In 1964 Jackson went to work as the southeastern field director of the Congress on Racial Equality (CORE; an organization founded in 1942 to combat discrimination against African Americans). Two years later Jackson was hired by Martin Luther King Jr. to direct the Chicago branch of Operation Breadbasket—an economic development project of the Southern Christian Leadership Conference (SCLC; a civil rights organization founded by black ministers in 1957, of which King was president).

The goal of Operation Breadbasket was to increase the number of black workers at white-owned companies, as well as to support black-owned businesses. Using boycotts as his weapon, Jackson forced many employers (most notably the A&P chain of supermarkets) to hire large numbers of black workers. Jackson was so successful that in 1967 he was appointed national director of Operation Breadbasket.

Jackson also served as an aide to King, frequently traveling with the legendary civil rights leader to sites of civil rights campaigns. Jackson was standing next to King on the balcony of the Lorraine Hotel in Memphis, Tennessee, on April 4, 1968, when King was killed by a sniper's bullet.

After King's death Jackson had hoped to become the next SCLC president, however that honor went to another King aide, Rev. Ralph Abernathy (1926–1990; see entry in volume 1).

Forms PUSH

Jackson returned to Illinois after King's death and continued organizing civil rights demonstrations. In 1971 he resigned from the SCLC and founded his own organization, People United to Serve Humanity (better known as PUSH). The purpose of PUSH was to increase the political and economic power of African Americans and other disadvantaged groups.

In 1975 Jackson expanded PUSH's mission by launching PUSH-Excel, a program that encouraged educational achievement among black youth. Jackson secured a $1 million grant from the federal government and went on a tour of inner-city schools. He urged students to sign cards pledging to spend two hours every night on their schoolwork.

Takes fight for equality abroad

In 1979 Jackson took his fight for racial equality abroad, to South Africa. There he led protests against the system of racial segregation (or legal separation) called apartheid (first implemented in 1948, apartheid was dismantled in the early 1990s). Jackson's next international mission took him to the

Middle East, where he attempted to improve relations between Israelis and the people of occupied Palestine.

Runs for president

Jackson campaigned for the Democratic presidential nomination in both 1984 and 1988, becoming the only black man to have sought the nation's highest office. In both campaigns, Jackson attempted to bring together voters of all races in what he called a Rainbow Coalition. In 1984, numerous whites joined with Hispanic Americans, Native Americans, and the majority of black voters in securing victories for Jackson in the primaries of South Carolina, Louisiana, and Washington, D.C. At the Democratic National Convention, Jackson received the third-largest number of delegate votes.

In his 1988 campaign Jackson stressed his commitment to creating economic opportunities for all U.S. citizens. He won a surprise victory in the Michigan Democratic primary, with 54 percent of the vote. At the Democratic National Convention, Jackson came in second only to Massachusetts governor Michael Dukakis.

Activism in the 1990s

Jackson moved to Washington, D.C., following the 1988 elections. In 1990 he was elected to represent the district in the Senate—a nonvoting, observer position. Jackson used his presence to promote the issue of statehood for the District of Columbia. That same year, just prior to the start of the Gulf War, Jackson traveled to Iraq and negotiated the release of five hundred hostages that had been taken by Iraq during its invasion of neighboring Kuwait. In October 1997 President Bill Clinton appointed Jackson to be his special envoy for the promotion of democracy in Africa.

Throughout the 1990s Jackson continued his advocacy on behalf of African Americans, working people, and other aggrieved groups. In 1991 he spoke out about workplace safety following a fire in a poultry-processing plant in North Carolina that claimed the lives of twenty-five workers; he also lobbied for treatment for veterans suffering from Gulf War syndrome (a mysterious, debilitating medical condition affecting thousands of veterans of the Gulf War).

In 1996 Jackson picketed the White House over President Clinton's endorsement of welfare reform—legislation that dismantled the federal government's welfare program, Aid to Families with Dependent Children, and transferred responsibility for welfare programs to the states. (While the federal government provided an economic safety net to citizens for decades, individual states have no obligation to provide such services to their residents). The following year Jackson defended affirmative action (the set of federal government policies that provide increased educational and employment opportunities to racial minorities and women, to overcome past patterns of discrimination), mounting an unsuccessful campaign to oppose Proposition 209 (the legislation that ended affirmative action in California government agencies). Today, Jackson remains on the front lines of the battles for racial and economic justice.

Negotiates release of American hostages in Yugoslavia

In May 1999 Jackson won a diplomatic coup when he convinced Serbian president Slobodan Milosevic to release three U.S. servicemen being held hostage. The American soldiers—Andrew Ramirez, Christopher J. Stone, and Steven Gonzales—had been captured by Serb forces on March 31 while patrolling the border between Macedonia and Yugoslavia as part of a North Atlantic Treaty Organization (NATO) operation to drive the Serbian army out of the province of Kosovo.

Although Jackson's mission was not endorsed by the U.S. government, the Senate chose to honor him upon his return from Yugoslavia. By a 92–0 vote, the Senate commended him for his successful intervention on behalf of the imprisoned servicemen.

Sources for further reading
Engelbert, Phillis. *American Civil Rights: Almanac.* Vol. 1. Farmington Hills, MI: U•X•L, 1999.

Frady, Marshall. *Jesse: The Life and Pilgrimage of Jesse Jackson.* New York: Random House, 1996.

Lombardi, Frank, and William Goldschlag. "Jackson, Cuomo Vent Liberal Opposition to Clinton's Signing of Welfare Bill, but Embrace His Candidacy." *New York Daily News.* August 27, 1996.

Miller, Sabrina L. "PUSH, Rainbow Coalition Still at Heart of Jackson's Work." *The Miami Herald.* May 16, 1999.

"Rev. Jesse Jackson Announces that He Will Not Run for President in 2000." *Jet.* April 12, 1999: p. 12.

Seipel, Tracy, and Ariana E. Cha. "Protesters March Across Golden Gate Bridge to Denounce Proposition 209." *San Jose Mercury News.* August 28, 1997.

"U.S. Senate Praises Rev. Jackson for Winning Release of POWs." *Jet.* May 24, 1999: p. 6.

Williams, Nicole L. Baily. "Jesse Jackson" in *Notable Black American Men,* edited by Jessie Carney Smith. Farmington Hills, MI: The Gale Group, 1999. Pages 598–602.

Vernon E. Jordan Jr.

Born August 15, 1935
Atlanta, Georgia
Civil rights activist, lawyer

UPDATE

Vernon E. Jordan Jr. made headlines in 1998 and 1999 as a "presidential friend" and "Washington insider" during the sex scandal involving President Bill Clinton and White House intern Monica Lewinsky. Jordan, an advisor to President Clinton who chaired the president's transition team in 1992, is today a partner in one of the nation's largest and most influential law firms.

For over three decades Jordan has been a leading voice for civil rights. He began his career in the early 1960s, as an organizer for the National Association for the Advancement of Colored People (NAACP). He later conducted voter registration for the Southern Regional Council and headed the United Negro College Fund. From 1971 to 1981 he served as executive director of the National Urban League (an organization dedicated to helping the black urban poor). **(See original entry on Jordan in volume 2.)**

"Those of us in leadership in the black community have an enormous burden of clarifying and defining issues."

Portrait: Reproduced by permission of AP/Wide World Photos, Inc.

Jordan was born in Atlanta, Georgia, in 1935. His father, Vernon Jordan Sr., was a postal worker and his mother, Mary Belle Jordan, ran a catering business. The family lived in a segregated (separated by race) public housing unit. Jordan attended a segregated high school, where he excelled in academics and basketball and played in the school band.

After graduating with honors from high school Jordan headed for DePauw University in Greencastle, Indiana. As one of just five African American students at the university, Jordan majored in political science and minored in history and speech. He won several awards at oratory (public speaking) competitions, played basketball, acted in plays, and served as vice president of the university's Democratic club.

Practices civil rights law

In 1957 Jordan enrolled in Howard University Law School, a training ground for civil rights lawyers (for more information on civil rights and the law, see entry on Charles Hamilton Houston on p. 127). Jordan graduated with his juris doctorate (law degree) in 1960 and headed home to Atlanta, to practice civil rights law.

Jordan's first position was in the office of respected civil rights attorney Donald Hollowell. Jordan was assigned to represent Charlayne Hunter, a black woman who had been denied admission to the all-white University of Georgia. Jordan convinced a federal court to uphold the Supreme Court's ruling on desegregation of educational institutions. He was pictured on the front pages of many newspapers, using his six-foot-four-inch frame to shield Hunter from an angry mob as she registered for classes at the university.

Works for civil rights organizations

Jordan stepped up to the front lines of the civil rights movement in 1962, as field secretary for the Georgia NAACP. In that position he recruited members, organized new chapters, coordinated demonstrations, and made numerous speeches. He also initiated boycotts against companies that refused to hire blacks (many businesses responded to the boycotts by integrating their workforces).

In 1964, Jordan joined a law firm in Little Rock, Arkansas, and took on the directorship of the Voter Education Project (VEP). The purpose of the VEP was to register African American voters throughout the South, in defiance of racist laws and policies intended to keep blacks from voting. During this period, as Jordan succeeded in greatly increasing the numbers of registered black voters, he became a nationally recognized civil rights leader.

In 1970 Jordan was hired to be director of the United Negro College Fund, an organization that raises money for historically black colleges. During his one year with the fund, Jordan increased the fund's coffers by $10 million.

Directs the National Urban League

Jordan was recruited in 1971 to be executive director of the National Urban League (NUL). The NUL, with financial assistance from the federal government, coordinated voter registration drives and anti-poverty programs in inner cities (such as job training programs, health care, and early childhood education). Jordan established seventeen new NUL chapters during his tenure, bringing the total number of chapters to 117.

Jordan also proved to be an excellent fundraiser for the NUL. He supplemented federal dollars (which were largely eliminated in the 1980s, during the Reagan administration) with donations from wealthy individuals and corporations. Jordan solidified the relationships between the NUL and several influential corporations by securing seats for himself on their boards of directors.

Jordan's positions on corporate boards, which were salaried, not only enriched the NUL but also himself. Jordan came under fire from other civil rights leaders for flaunting his wealth through custom-made suits and expensive cigars.

Targeted for assassination

In 1980 Jordan was fired upon by a sniper in Fort Wayne, Indiana, following his speech to the local NUL affiliate. The bullet, fires from a powerful hunting rifle, left a fist-sized hole in Jordan' back and narrowly missed his spine. Jordan underwent emergency surgery, plus five operations over the next three months.

A white supremacist named Joseph Paul Franklin was charged with the assault; he was acquitted by an all-white jury in 1982. The same man, who was subsequently convicted of murdering two black joggers in Salt Lake City, Utah (and is believed by authorities to have gunned down as many as twenty people in the years 1977 through 1980), confessed in 1996 to having fired upon Jordan.

After his recovery Jordan spent one more year at the NUL. In 1981 he announced his resignation, as well as his retirement from civil rights activism. Jordan vowed to continue supporting the struggle for civil rights through his law practice.

Becomes a Washington power broker

Jordan next went to work as a partner in the Washington, D.C., office of the Dallas, Texas-based law firm of Akim, Gump, Strauss, Hauer & Feld. This powerful law firm, with 250 lawyers in its Washington office alone, represents and advises corporations, lawmakers, and lobbyists. In addition to continuing his employment as a senior partner in the law firm, Jordan sits on the boards of directors of at least nine national and three international corporations.

Jordan's influence expanded in 1991, when his long-time friend Bill Clinton, then governor of Arkansas, decided to run for president. Jordan was a close advisor to Clinton during the campaign. Following Clinton's election Jordan was named cochair of Clinton's transition team. In that capacity Jordan helped select several members of Clinton's Cabinet. He has remained a close friend to Clinton and an advisor on domestic and international affairs.

Linked to scandal

In December 1997 President Clinton asked Jordan to help him with a personal issue that threatened his presidency:

Monica Lewinsky, a White House intern with whom Clinton had been having an extramarital affair, was being subpoenaed to testify in another lawsuit against Clinton involving sexual impropriety. Jordan met with Lewinsky several times that December and the following January, helping her secure legal representation and attempting to find her employment at one of the many corporations with which he was associated.

Jordan's own role in the scandal came under scrutiny by a grand jury in January 1998. Jordan testified before the grand jury that he knew nothing about a sexual relationship between the president and Lewinsky, and that he did not urge Lewinsky to lie about her relationship with the president. Clinton backed his friend, claiming in his own grand jury testimony that he had denied to Jordan he was intimately involved with Lewinsky at the time he asked Jordan to help Lewinsky find work.

Clinton was ultimately convicted of perjury (not telling the truth) before the grand jury in the Lewinsky affair and was subsequently impeached in the House. Clinton was cleared in the Senate, however, where there were not the two-thirds votes required for impeachment.

Sources for further reading

Bai, Matt, and Howard Fineman. "The Smoothest Operator: Washington Super-Lawyer Vernon Jordan." *Newsweek*. February 2, 1998: pp. 42+.

Carter, Linda M. "Vernon Jordan" in *Notable Black American Men,* edited by Jessie Carney Smith. Farmington Hills, MI: The Gale Group, 1999, pp. 667–70.

Cottle, Michelle. "Mr. Smooth Comes to Washington; Vernon Jordan is the Ultimate Washington Insider—Rich, Powerful, and Unaccountable." *Washington Monthly*. June 1997: pp. 20+.

Greve, Frank. "Clinton Friend Vernon Jordan Vindicated in Starr Probe." Knight-Ridder/Tribune New Service. August 21, 1998.

Phillips, Andrew. "Closer to the Heart." *Maclean's*. March 16, 1998: pp. 32+.

"White Man Admits to 1980 Shooting of Vernon Jordan." *Jet*. April 22, 1996: p. 63.

Lewis Howard Latimer

*Born September 4, 1848
Chelsea, Massachusetts*

*Died December 11, 1924
Flushing, New York*

*Inventor, technical artist,
electrical engineer, author*

Lewis Howard Latimer, the son of escaped slaves, had a remarkable career in science and technology. A self-taught technical artist, Latimer made the patent drawings for Alexander Graham Bell's (1847–1922) first telephone. He was eventually promoted to the position of head draftsman for both the General Electric and Westinghouse companies.

In 1881 Latimer developed a carbon filament for the incandescent (glows with intense heat) light bulb. This filament was longer-lasting than any of those designed by electric-light inventor Thomas Alva Edison (1847–1931). Latimer's filament brought down the cost of the light bulb, making it affordable to the public. Working for the Maxim-Westin Electric Company, Latimer oversaw the installation of lighting systems in New York, Philadelphia, Montreal, and London. He was recruited to the Edison General Electric Company in 1884 and later joined the elite group of inventors known as the Edison Pioneers.

"Broadmindedness, versatility in the accomplishment of things intellectual and cultural ... a devoted husband and father, all were characteristic of him."

—The Edison Pioneers, in a tribute to Lewis Howard Latimer

Portrait: Reproduced by permission of the Schomburg Center for Research in Black Culture.

Youth and military service

Latimer was born in 1848 in Chelsea, Massachusetts, just outside of Boston. Unlike many other blacks during the pre-Civil War era, Latimer, because he was the son of escaped slaves, was born free. (The Civil War, which ended slavery, began in 1861 and ended in 1865.) Latimer attended primary school as a young child and excelled in reading, creative writing, and art.

When Latimer was ten years old his father deserted the family (by some accounts his father left for fear of being recaptured). Latimer's mother found work aboard a ship, sending Latimer and one of his brothers to live at a state-run institution and his sister to live with relatives. Latimer and his brother soon ran away from the dismal institution; they returned to the city and found their older brother, who was living alone. The brothers worked to support themselves. Latimer sold copies of William Lloyd Garrison's antislavery newspaper the *Liberator* and performed odd jobs. (William Lloyd Garrison [1805–1879] was the founder of the American Anti-Slavery Society.)

At the age of sixteen, Latimer falsely claimed he was eighteen and joined the Union navy. He fought in the final two years of the Civil War, first serving as a cabin boy on the gun boat *U.S.S. Massasoit* and later holding the rank of lieutenant in the 4th Battalion of the Massachusetts Volunteer Militia.

Learns technical illustration

After his honorable discharge from the military, Latimer returned to Boston where he found work as an office boy for a group of patent lawyers (a patent is a legal document that grants inventors the sole right to market their inventions). Latimer became interested in the technical drawings that were included in patent applications. With a second-hand set of drafting tools and library textbooks, he spent his evenings teaching himself drafting.

Latimer was hired by the company as a junior draftsman and eventually became chief draftsman. Among the firm's clients was inventor Alexander Graham Bell. Latimer's illustration graced the patent application for Bell's first telephone. The telephone was granted a patent in 1876.

After drawing numerous patent illustrations, Latimer began tinkering with inventions of his own. Between 1874 and 1896, Latimer acquired numerous patents for inventions such as: an improved train car bathroom; a locking rack for hats and coats; supports to keep books upright; and an air cooling and disinfecting machine for use in apartments and hospitals.

In 1873 Latimer married Mary Wilson of Fall River, Massachusetts. The couple had two daughters: Louise Rebecca and Emma Jeanette.

Invents carbon filament

In 1879, the year that inventor Thomas Edison patented his light bulb, Latimer went to work as assistant manager and draftsman for the United States Electric Lighting Company in Bridgeport, Connecticut (the company moved to New York City the following year). The company's owner, American-born British inventor Hiram Maxim (1840–1916), was competing with Edison for a share of the new electric-lighting market. Maxim wished to create an improved version of Edison's light bulb (Edison's bulb used a carbonized cotton filament that only burned for forty hours).

Latimer undertook an intensive study of electricity and electric lighting. He quickly mastered the science, then moved on to experimenting with materials capable of withstanding the extreme heat necessary to produce light in an incandescent bulb. After hundreds of attempts, Latimer and coworker Joseph V. Nichols developed a carbon filament that was longer-lasting than that used by Edison. Maxim's company began producing bulbs with carbon filaments called "Maxim bulbs." The Maxim bulb received a patent in 1881.

Latimer quickly rose within the ranks of the company. He was put in charge of setting up new manufacturing facilities and installing lighting in railroad stations throughout the United States and Canada. Latimer even taught himself French in order to communicate with workers in Montreal. Latimer traveled to London to establish the company's first European manufacturing plant. The plant was called the Maxim-Westin Electric Light Company (Westin was Maxim's business partner). The company begun by Maxim and Westin later became known as Westinghouse.

Recruited by Edison Company

In 1882 Latimer was recruited to work for the Olmstead Electric Light and Power Company in New York. Olmstead was one of many new electric companies competing with Edison for market share. In his two years with Olmstead, Latimer made small improvements to the filaments and mounting fixtures of incandescent bulbs.

Latimer was wooed by the Excelsior Electric Company in 1884. Excelsior, owned by Thomas Edison, was later incorporated into the Edison General Electric Company (the name was eventually simplified to General Electric). Latimer's first position with the company was as an engineer.

In 1890 Latimer was promoted to the company's legal department, where he was used as an expert witness by the Edison General Electric during bitter courtroom patent disputes. Latimer help the Edison company retain its patents, in the face of challenges by rival firms. In addition to giving courtroom testimonies, Latimer did research in preparation for patent cases, reading patent information in French and German as well as English.

During his years working for Edison, Latimer wrote the first textbook on incandescent lighting. Entitled *Incandescent Electric Lighting: A Practical Description of the Edison System,* the book was used as a guide by Edison Company engineers. From 1896 to 1911 Latimer also served as chief draftsman and expert legal witness for the Board of Patent Control—a body established by Edison and Westinghouse to resolve patent disputes.

Involvement in civil rights

Although it would be a stretch to call him an activist, Latimer did have a vested interest in civil rights. He had a long-

Thomas Edison, head of the Excelsior Electric Company (later General Electric), hired Lewis Latimer as an engineer in 1884. During his years working for Edison, Latimer wrote the first textbook on incandescent lighting. (Reproduced by permission of Corbis Corporation [New York]).

standing friendship with the famous abolitionist Frederick Douglass (1817–1895; see entry in volume 1); indeed, the two men corresponded by letter until Douglass's death. Latimer was also a critic of segregation (the forced, legal separation of the races). Although he could not attend the 1895 National Conference of Colored Men in Detroit, Latimer offered his written comments, which read: "The community which permits

Lewis Howard Latimer

a crime against its humblest member to go unpunished is nursing into life and strength a power which will ultimately threaten its own existence."

Latimer's later years

In 1912 Latimer left Edison General Electric and joined the engineering firm of Hammer and Schwartz. In addition to working part-time as an electrical and mechanical engineer, Latimer served as an advisor for companies applying for patents. Latimer remained with Hammer and Schwartz until 1924.

In 1918 Latimer joined the Edison Pioneers—a group of twenty-eight distinguished researchers who, along with Thomas Edison, founded the electrical industry. Latimer was the only African American in the group.

In his later years, Latimer taught night classes in English and mechanical drawing to recently arrived immigrants. He also devoted time to his favorite hobbies: music, painting, and poetry. In 1925, on Latimer's seventy-fifth birthday, his daughters arranged for the publication of a book of Latimer's poems called *Poems of Life and Love*.

Upon Latimer's death in 1928 at the age of eighty, the Edison Pioneers issued the following tribute to their late colleague: "Broadmindedness, versatility in the accomplishment of things intellectual and cultural, a linguist, a devoted husband and father, all were characteristic of him, and his genial presence will be missed from our gatherings."

Latimer was honored in 1968, when a public school in Brooklyn was named for him. In addition, the General Electric Foundation offers an annual scholarship called the Latimer Achievement Award to outstanding minority students.

Sources for further reading

DISCovering Multicultural America. "Lewis Howard Latimer." [Online] Available http://galenet.gale.com (accessed May 18, 1999).

Engelbert, Phillis. *Technology in Action: Science Applied to Everyday Life.* Vol. 2. Farmington Hills, MI: U•X•L, 1999, pp. 176–77.

Haber, Louis. *Black Pioneers of Science and Invention.* New York: Harcourt, Brace & World, 1970, pp. 49–60.

Hayden, Robert C. *Nine African-American Inventors.* Frederick, MD: Twenty-First Century Books, 1992, pp. 80–93.

McKissack, Patricia, and Frederick McKissack. *African-American Inventors.* Brookfield, CT: Millbrook Press, 1994, pp. 61–69.

Norman, Winifred Latimer, and Lily Patterson. *Lewis Latimer, Scientist.* New York: Chelsea House, 1994.

Smith, Jessie Carney. "Lewis Howard Latimer" in *Notable Black American Men,* edited by Jessie Carney Smith. Farmington Hills, MI: The Gale Group, 1999, pp. 698–700.

Sullivan, Otha Richard. *African American Inventors.* New York: John Wiley & Sons, Inc., 1998, pp. 31–38.

Spike Lee

*Born March 20, 1957
Atlanta, Georgia
Filmmaker, writer, actor*

UPDATE

Spike Lee directed several films in the mid-to-late 1990s, including *Crooklyn* (1994), *Clockers* (1995), *Girl 6* (1996), *Get on the Bus* (1996), *He Got Game* (1998), and *Four Little Girls* (1998). In these recent films Lee expounded on his familiar themes pertaining to the experiences of blacks in urban America. He also expanded into new territory, looking at family life, the drug trade, sports, and civil rights.

Lee, the nation's most successful and popular black film director, has been making films since the mid-1980s. His most recent work has won him recognition as a master of documentaries, as well as dramas. **(See original entry on Lee in volume 3.)**

Raised to appreciate the arts

Lee was born in 1957 in Atlanta, Georgia, the eldest of four children of parents deeply involved in music and the arts.

"An all-black film directed by a black person can still be universal."

Portrait: Reproduced by permission of AP/Wide World Photos, Inc.

Lee's father, Bill Lee, is a jazz musician, and his mother, Jacquelyn (Shelton) Lee, taught art and African American literature. Lee's parents, like his grandparents, graduated from all-black colleges in Atlanta.

Lee's family moved to the mostly black Fort Greene area of Brooklyn when Lee was a young child. With his sister and three brothers, Lee was taken to movies, museums, art galleries, jazz performances, and plays.

Studies film in college

After graduating from high school Lee enrolled in his father's (and grandfather's) alma mater, Morehouse College in Atlanta. He decided on a career in film early in his college career and majored in mass communications. Lee graduated with a bachelor of arts degree in 1979, then returned to New York to study film.

As a graduate student at New York University's Institute of Film and Television, Lee produced a controversial first film. Called *The Answer,* Lee's ten-minute film was a black screenwriter's response to *Birth of a Nation*—the 1915 racist classic that portrayed blacks as buffoons and criminals, and the Ku Klux Klan as heroes. (The Ku Klux Klan [KKK] is an antiblack terrorist group that originally formed in the South after the Civil War [1861–65]. For decades, the KKK has intimidated and committed acts of violence against black Americans and members of other racial and ethnic minorities.)

Lee won a Student Academy Award for his master's thesis film, *Joe's Bed-Stuy Barbershop: We Cut Heads.* A comedy about a Brooklyn barbershop that fronted a gambling operation, Lee's film was the first student film to be featured at the New Directors/New Films series in 1983. The film was also shown at international film festivals.

Bursts on the movie scene

After completing his master's degree, Lee set out on a course as an independent filmmaker. To support himself Lee worked in the shipping department for a film distribution company. He spent his evenings writing and producing his first commercial feature: *She's Gotta Have It*. The 1986 film, created on a budget of $175,000, is about a young, self-assured black woman in Brooklyn and her romantic encounters with three men. The cast includes Lee, his sister, and his college friends. Lee's father wrote the musical score. *She's Gotta Have It* won the prize for best film by a newcomer at the Cannes Film Festival in France and grossed more than $7 million.

Lee's next film, released in 1988, was *School Daze*. A musical comedy, *School Daze* explores racial tensions between light-skinned and dark-skinned blacks at an all-black college. While the work was in progress, it generated great controversy. Many blacks, including officials from the United Negro College Fund, did not want blacks' internal racial animosities aired in public. Faculty members at Morehouse College, where Lee began the filming, made him leave the campus. Lee completed the filming at Atlanta University. The film received mixed reviews but was a box-office smash.

Do the Right Thing

Lee continued his record of controversial and brilliant filmmaking with his 1989 masterpiece *Do the Right Thing*. This film is about the racial tensions between Italian Americans and African Americans in Brooklyn's Bedford-Stuyvesant neighborhood. In the story, those tensions boil over on the hottest day of the summer after a young black man is killed by a white police officer. A black crowd responds to this act by burning down an Italian pizzeria.

Lee claimed that his intention in making the film was to generate discussion about racial hatred. *Do the Right Thing* remains Lee's best-known and most highly acclaimed work. It won the Los Angeles Film Critics award for best picture. In 1989 *People Weekly* named Lee one of the "25 Most Intriguing People of the Year."

Lee's next two releases were *Mo' Better Blues* (1990) and *Jungle Fever* (1991). *Mo' Better Blues,* based loosely on the life of Lee's father (who provided the film's musical score), is about an African American jazz trumpeter trying to juggle two romantic relationships and his music. *Jungle Fever* explores an interracial romance.

Chronicles life of Malcolm X

In 1992 Lee completed his most ambitious project: a three-and-a-half-hour depiction of the life of black-rights champion Malcolm X (1925–1965; see entry in volume 3). Entitled *Malcolm X,* the film was based on *The Autobiography of Malcolm X* by Malcolm X and Alex Haley. While criticized as propagandistic (spreading rumors to promote a political viewpoint) by some politically conservative viewers and denounced as disingenuous by some admirers of Malcolm X, the film was warmly received by most critics; it grossed $48 million.

Lee's next three films did not match the acclaim of *Malcolm X. Crooklyn* (1994), written by Lee's sister Joie Lee, looks at a successful black family living in Brooklyn. *Clockers* (1995) is about two brothers involved in the inner-city drug trade, and about the hopelessness and violence of the ghetto. *Girl 6,* which came out in 1996 with little fanfare, tells the story of a young, aspiring actress who takes a job as a phone-sex operator.

Examines topical issues in recent films

In 1996 Lee released *Get on the Bus,* a fictional work about twelve black men from different walks of life. The event that brings the men together is a bus ride from Los Angeles to Washington D.C. to participate in the Million Man March (the October 1995 gathering of nearly one million black men in the nation's capital, with the purpose of renewing their commitment to themselves, their families, and their communities). The film's budget of $2.4 million was provided by black male investors who had taken part in the march.

Lee next wrote, produced, and directed the 1998 basketball drama *He Got Game.* A departure from his usual brand of social commentary, this film was inspired by Lee's love of basketball (he's an ardent New York Knick's fan). The film tells the story of a basketball superstar offered both a college scholarship and an NBA contract. The youth's decision is complicated when his jailed father requests that his son choose to attend the college (the warden's alma mater), so the father can score points of his own.

Recalls civil rights movement with *Four Little Girls*

Lee's next work, *Four Little Girls* (1998), was his first documentary. The film, produced for Home Box Office (HBO), consists of a series of interviews with family members of four young girls killed when a Birmingham, Alabama, church was bombed in September 1963. The girls—Denise McNair, age eleven, and Addie Mae Collins, Carole Robertson, and Cynthia Wesley, all age fourteen—had been in the church basement preparing for the monthly Youth Day service when the explosion occurred. Additional interviews with veterans of the civil rights movement and archival footage are used to place the bombing in historical context. The production has been hailed as an artful and moving tribute to the four girls and other victims of racial violence.

Summer of Sam gets mixed reviews

In 1999 Lee released *Summer of Sam*. The film, which takes place in a Bronx neighborhood during the summer of 1977, explores how various residents react to a series of violent murders. Based on the real crimes of David Berkowitz—better known by his nickname, "Son of Sam"—*Summer of Sam* received mixed reviews and low box office receipts, despite boasting an all-star cast and high production values.

Works to create positive portrayals

In all his movies, Lee has attempted to portray African Americans in a realistic and positive manner. "You can take an unknown, all-black cast," Lee once stated, "and put them in a story that comes from a black experience, and all kinds of people will come to see it if it's a good film. I wish Hollywood would get that message."

In 1993 Lee married attorney Tanya Lewis. The couple have a daughter, Satchel Lewis Lee, born in 1994, and a son, Jackson Lee, born in 1997.

Sources for further reading

Collins, James. "4 Little Girls" (movie review). *Time*. February 23, 1998.

Cuneen, Joseph. "He Got Game" (movie review). *National Catholic Reporter*. May 15, 1998: p. 15.

Dick, Jeff. "4 Little Girls" (movie review). *Booklist*. May 15, 1998: p. 1638.

Fretts, Bruce. "Get on the Bus" (video recording review). *Entertainment Weekly*. May 9, 1997: p. 90.

Rea, Steven. "With 'Clockers,' Spike Lee Tries for a Final Take on the Gangsta Genre." Knight-Ridder/Tribune News Service. September 14, 1995.

"The 25 Most Intriguing People of the Year—Spike Lee." *People Weekly*. December 25, 1989: pp. 78+.

Wise, Flossie E. "Spike Lee" in *Notable Black American Men*, edited by Jessie Carney Smith. Farmington Hills, MI: The Gale Group, 1999, pp. 705–09.

Elijah McCoy

Born March 27, 1843
Colchester, Ontario, Canada
Died October 10, 1929
Eloise, Michigan
Inventor, mechanical engineer

Through his creation of the lubricator cup, Elijah McCoy increased the productivity of industrial machines. McCoy was educated as a mechanical engineer in Scotland. Upon returning to the United States, he was unable to find suitable employment based on his training because of the color of his skin. Resigning himself to working on train locomotives, McCoy attempted to make the best of the situation. He used his mechanical expertise to design a device that automatically lubricated the locomotive's moving parts, thus improving the performance of engines and the efficiency of rail transportation.

Upbringing in Canada

McCoy was born in Colchester, Ontario, Canada, on March 27, 1843. He was the third of twelve children born to George and Mildred Goins McCoy. McCoy's parents were both former slaves from Kentucky who had escaped to Canada

Elijah McCoy invented the automatic lubricator for train engines, a device that increased the efficiency of rail transportation.

Portrait: Reproduced by permission of the Fisk University Library.

via the Underground Railroad (the secret network that assisted fugitive slaves to freedom) in 1837. George McCoy had served in the Canadian Army, after which he was granted 160 acres of farmland.

During Elijah McCoy's youth he worked on the family farm and attended the local grammar school for black children. From an early age McCoy was fascinated by the workings of mechanical devices and had an aptitude for repairing tools and machines.

Receives training in Scotland

When McCoy was sixteen his parents sent him to Edinburgh, Scotland, to study mechanical engineering. McCoy's parents made the financial sacrifice to send him overseas because the educational opportunities for blacks in Canada and the United States at the time were very limited. During McCoy's five years in Scotland he was trained to be an engineer and master mechanic.

While McCoy was away, the Civil War (1861–65) was being waged in the United States. When the war ended and emancipation had been decreed, the McCoy family moved to Ypsilanti, Michigan. McCoy joined them there in 1865.

Works on Michigan railroad

McCoy spent several frustrating months in Ypsilanti seeking employment. He found that professional positions were off-limits to black people, regardless of their credentials. McCoy finally resigned himself to taking the best job he could find, despite its being significantly below his level of training—that of a fireman on the Michigan Central Railroad. His duties as fireman included keeping the firebox of the steam-powered locomotive filled with wood and using an oil can to lubricate the engine parts.

Like other railroad firemen, it was part of McCoy's job to pour oil into the engine each time the train came to a stop. The purpose of the lubrication was to reduce friction between the moving parts of the engine (such as screws, gears, and levers);

the oil provided a slick layer on which the parts would glide past one another. Without sufficient lubrication, the friction produced by the moving parts could cause the engine to overheat or even catch fire (indeed, this often happened even when the parts had been manually lubricated). Manual lubrication was also dangerous; from time to time workers were injured or killed while working on engines.

McCoy noted the inefficiency, the danger, and the limited effectiveness of manual lubrication. He became convinced that a better method of lubrication could be created.

Invents lubricating cup

For two years McCoy spent his evenings in his makeshift workshop tinkering with experimental lubricating devices. McCoy's hard work paid off in 1870 with the invention of the "lubricating cup"—a mechanism that automatically lubricated the sliding components of engines. When fitted into the steam cylinder of a locomotive, the device continuously oiled all moving parts of the machine.

The lubricating cup consisted of a metal or glass cup with a hollow stem running from the bottom of the cup into the cylinder. Inside the stem was a piston and valve; as steam entered the stem, the piston would rise, causing a valve to open and release a trickle of lubricant.

McCoy's lubricator was capable of functioning while the train was in motion—thereby eliminating the need for lengthy delays. As a result, the efficiency of rail transport greatly increased. (In that era, when newly constructed railroad tracks connected the nation from coast to coast and rail transport was the primary means of moving goods, increased rail efficiency had a tremendous impact on the national economy.)

Sells patent to fund invention process

In 1872 McCoy received a patent for his invention (a patent is a legal document granting a product's inventor the sole right to manufacture and market that product). In order to finance improvements to his workshop and his ongoing experiments, McCoy sold the patent to a pair of businessmen in Ypsilanti. Throughout his career as an inventor McCoy repeatedly sold his patents in order to fund new inventions.

In 1873 McCoy married Mary Eleanora Delany Brownlow, a community activist and fundraiser for charitable causes. Brownlow was influential in McCoy's own community involvement in his later years.

"The Real McCoy"

Railroad officials initially objected to using a device invented by a black man. Before long, however, they recognized the value of the automatic lubricator and put aside their racial prejudice. McCoy was hired to supervise the installation of automatic lubricators on engines, as well as to instruct the mechanical staff in their use.

McCoy's invention was so successful that between 1872 and 1915, the majority of train locomotives in the United States, as well as trains in many other countries, were fitted with the lubricators. The lubricators also became standard equipment in steamships (including transatlantic liners) and stationary steam engines (such as those used in factories).

McCoy's lubricating device was dubbed "the real McCoy" by railroad officials. Prospective buyers of lubricators, wary of being sold one of the cheaper imitations that flooded the market in the wake of McCoy's invention, would insist on "the real McCoy." The term "the real McCoy" now has a general usage in our language, meaning something that is "genuine," "worthy," or "of the highest quality."

Continues career as an inventor

McCoy left his job with the Michigan Central Railroad in 1882 to devote more time to his inventions. He and his wife moved to Detroit, where McCoy worked as a mechanical consultant for the Detroit Lubricating Company and other manufacturing firms.

Between 1872 and 1926 McCoy received some fifty patents for revised versions of his lubricator, as well as for other steam-engine devices (such as a steam dome and a valve and plug-cock). McCoy also developed lubrication systems for air brakes (system of brakes that operates using compressed air) in locomotives and other vehicles. He improved the safety of air brakes through an advanced lubrication formula—a mixture of oil and graphite (a solid form of carbon; a major component of pencil lead).

McCoy's list of inventions also included items unrelated to steam engines, such as lawn sprinklers, folding ironing boards, tire treads, rubber heels for shoes, and a portable scaffold support. (A scaffold is a temporary structure used to hold workers and materials during building construction.) His creation of the ironing board resulted from his wife's need for a place to do ironing. When McCoy tired of watering his grass by walking around with a hose, he came up with the idea for a lawn sprinkler.

Invents graphite lubricator

In 1915 McCoy created what he considered his best invention: the graphite lubricator. The purpose of this device was to effectively lubricate a new type of locomotive called the superheater engine, which operated on great quantities of steam. Graphite, a slippery powder, proved a better lubricant than oil on the new engines.

The graphite lubricator was warmly received by engineers operating superheater locomotives. "We have found the Graphite Lubricator of considerable assistance in the lubrication of locomotives equipped with superheaters," wrote one railroad superintendent. "There is a decided advantage in better lubrication and reduction in wear in valves and piston rings, and as a well-lubricated engine is more economical in the use of fuel, there is unquestionably a savings in fuel."

McCoy patented the graphite lubricator (as well as other inventions) not only in the United States, but also in Great Britain, France, Germany, Austria, and Russia. McCoy founded the Elijah McCoy Manufacturing Company in 1920, to manufacture and market the graphite lubricator and numerous other devices.

Efforts hindered by racism

Despite McCoy's success as an inventor, racism continued to hinder his career. On certain occasions, for example, McCoy was invited to give a lecture or presentation only to be turned away at the door when the sponsoring organization discovered the color of his skin. In other instances, companies canceled orders for McCoy's products when they learned the products had been developed by a black man.

Community involvement in final years

In his later years McCoy volunteered a great deal of his time counseling troubled youth in Detroit, Michigan, and encouraging the young people to pursue careers in science and technology. McCoy remained active in the community until the age of eighty, when he was beset by health problems and depression over the death of his wife.

As his life drew to a close, McCoy was a poor man. While his inventions had made other people millionaires, McCoy—who gave up most of his patents—did not enjoy the financial fruits of his labors. In 1928 McCoy entered the Eloise Infirmary, a nursing home for low income elderly people. He died there on October 10, 1929, at the age of eighty-six, and was buried in Detroit.

McCoy did not receive the recognition his achievements merited until long after his death. In 1975 the city of Detroit honored McCoy by placing a historic marker where his home once stood and naming a nearby street "Elijah McCoy Drive."

Sources for further reading

Amram, Fred M.B. *African-American Inventors.* Mankato, MN: Capstone Press, 1996, pp. 28–33.

DISCovering Biography. "Elijah McCoy." [Online] Available http://galenet.gale.com (accessed May 18, 1999).

Engelbert, Phillis. *Technology in Action: Science Applied to Everyday Life.* Vol. 3. Farmington Hills, MI: U•X•L, 1999, pp. 520–21.

Haber, Louis. *Black Pioneers of Science and Invention.* New York: Harcourt, Brace & World, 1970, pp. 34–40.

Hayden, Robert C. *Nine African-American Inventors.* Frederick, MD: Twenty-First Century Books, 1992, pp. 94–105.

McKissack, Patricia, and Frederick McKissack. *African-American Inventors.* Brookfield, CT: Millbrook Press, 1994, pp. 55–60.

Smith, Frederick Douglass Jr. "Elijah McCoy" in *Notable Black American Men,* edited by Jessie Carney Smith. Farmington Hills, MI: The Gale Group, 1999, pp. 787–89.

Sullivan, Otha Richard. *African American Inventors.* New York: John Wiley & Sons, Inc., 1998, pp. 27–30.

Towle, Wendy. *The Real McCoy: The Life of an African-American Inventor.* New York: Scholastic, 1992.

Audley Moore

Born July 27, 1898
New Iberia, Louisiana

Died May 2, 1997
Brooklyn, New York

Human rights activist

UPDATE

Audley Moore died on May 2, 1997, two months shy of her ninety-ninth birthday. Moore, a longtime resident of Harlem, spent her final three years in a Brooklyn nursing home. Her health had been in decline since she broke her hip during a trip to Africa in the mid- 1990s.

Better known as "Queen Mother" (an honorary titled bestowed upon her in Ghana in 1972), Moore spent seven decades fighting for the rights of African Americans and poor people. Her first foray into activism was in the 1920s, as a member of Marcus Garvey's Universal Negro Improvement Association (UNIA). In the 1950s Moore became a leader in the movement to secure reparations for the descendants of slaves. Virtually unknown to whites, Moore was regarded as a hero by many African Americans. **(See original entry on Moore in volume 3.)**

"[Audley Moore] was "very famous, a great saint of civil rights…. A great humanitarian and a woman with no fear."

—Reverend Bobby Marshall

Portrait: Reproduced by permission of AP/Wide World Photos, Inc.

Family victimized by racial violence

Moore was born in 1898 in Iberia, Louisiana, to a family that bore the scars of racial violence. Moore's grandfather, a former slave, had been killed by a white mob; her grandmother, while enslaved, had been raped by a white man. In the community in which Moore's grandparents lived, the police routinely detained African American men so they could rape the men's wives and daughters.

Moore was five years old when her mother died, and she and her two younger sisters were placed in the care of their grandmother. A few years later the girls were sent to New Orleans, to live with their father. The girls' father died when Moore was in the fourth grade and the children were left to fend for themselves. Moore found work at a hair salon and supported her sisters. Moore's childhood afforded little time for formal education.

Inspired by Marcus Garvey

As a teenager, Moore was fascinated by the message of Marcus Garvey (1887–1940; see entry in volume 2), a Jamaican immigrant and founder of the Universal Negro Improvement Association (UNIA). Garvey sought to unite all black peoples through the establishment in Africa of a country and government of their own. He preached economic independence, pride in blacks' African heritage, and the need for black Americans to return to Africa.

Moore was brought firmly into the Garveyite fold following an incident in the summer of 1919 when New Orleans police officers refused to allow Garvey to address a crowd at the Longshoreman's Hall. Moore was among the African Americans who stood on benches and threatened police with guns, causing the police to retreat.

Three years later Moore moved to Harlem, an area of New York City, only to find that she had traded the stifling racism of the South for the overcrowding, unemployment, and poverty of a northern big city. She became a prominent organizer for the UNIA, but ended her activities with the group in 1927 when Garvey was convicted of mail fraud and deported.

Joins the Communist Party

In 1933 Moore joined the Communist Party, the largest organization at that time fighting poverty and racism in New York City. As a party member, Moore organized poor people to conduct a "rent-strike" (a withholding of rent) to force landlords to lower rents.

Moore was a regular speaker at the Communist Party rallies in Harlem, denouncing the economic exploitation of black female domestic workers and other issues. She climbed the ranks of the Party, becoming secretary of the New York state branch. After unsuccessfully running for state assembly on the Communist ticket, she helped Benjamin Davis, a black leader of the Communist Party, get elected to the New York City Council. Moore parted ways with the Communists in 1950, accusing them of racism.

Champions reparations for slavery

Moore traveled to the South in the early 1950s, to assist poor people in Louisiana who had been cut off from state welfare assistance. Moore recognized that in order to save tax dollars, lawmakers had penalized their least powerful constituents. Through the efforts of Moore and others, welfare benefits were restored to twenty-three thousand people.

In 1955 Moore, back in New York, initiated a movement for U.S. government reparations (compensation) to descendants of slaves. "They owe us more than they could ever pay," she once commented. "They stole our language, they stole our culture. They stole our mothers and fathers and took our names away from us.... The United States will never be able to pay us all they owe us."

Moore never gave up the quest for reparations for the suffering of blacks under the slavery system. In 1994 she gave a rousing speech to a gathering in Detroit of the National Coalition of Blacks for Reparations in America. Among Moore's demands was the construction of a national monument paying tribute to the millions of Africans who died on slave ships while crossing the Atlantic. In July 1999, two years after Moore's death, Middle Passage monuments were unveiled in various locations along the Atlantic coasts of Africa and the United States.

Demonstrates for improved education

Moore was active in many causes throughout the 1950s and 1960s in New York City. She organized domestic workers to demand higher wages, worked to prevent evictions of black tenants, stood up for prisoners' rights, and lobbied for an end to segregation (separation by race) of the armed forces and Major League baseball.

Moore also fought for improved education for African American children. To that end, she participated in a series of sit-ins in 1966 at the Board of Education headquarters in Brooklyn. Moore gave fiery speeches, accusing the school board of neglecting African American students in poor areas. "Run them out," Moore stated in the *New York Times,* in reference to the members of the Board of Education. "They're perpetuating idiot factories among us."

Visits Africa

In 1966 Moore made her first of several visits to Africa. In 1972 she attended the All-Africa Women's Conference and visited Ghana, where the Ashanti tribe paid tribute to her for decades of service to people of African heritage with the honorary title "Queen Mother." Moore was present in South Africa in 1990 to witness the release of Nelson Mandela, a political prisoner who spent twenty-seven years in confinement. (Mandela served as the first black president of South Africa from 1994 to 1999.)

Active through her final days

Moore, wheelchair-bound in her later years, remained a common sight at Harlem rallies. One of her final public appearances was at the Million Man March (an event at which black men pledged to better themselves and their communities) in Washington, D. C., in 1995, where she shared the stage with Reverend Jesse Jackson (1941– ; see entry in volume 2 and update on page 137).

Moore's outrage over the treatment of blacks in America never subsided. "They not only called us Negroes, they made us Negroes," she remarked in a 1997 *New York Times* article, "things that don't know where they came from and don't even care that they don't know. Negro is a state of mind, and they massacred our minds."

Moore died on May 2, 1997, and was buried at Ferncliff Hartdale Cemetery in Westchester, New York—also the final resting place of black nationalist Malcolm X (1925–1965; see entry in volume 3) and human rights activist/performer Paul Robeson (1898–1976; see entry in volume 3). In 1989 Moore was honored in a photo exhibition at the Corcoran Gallery of Art in Washington, D.C., featuring prominent African American women. At Kent State University, a permanent exhibit paying tribute to Moore's life of activism occupies an entire floor of a campus building.

Reverend Bobby Marshall of Memphis, Tennessee, in an obituary for Moore, stated that Moore was "very famous, a great saint of civil rights.... A great humanitarian and a woman with no fear."

Sources for further reading

"Audley Moore, 98, Civil Rights Leader." *Chicago Sun-Times.* May 7, 1997: p. 82.

Boyd, Herb. "In Memoriam: Longtime Activist Queen Mother Moore, 98, Dies." *The Black Scholar.* Summer 1997: pp. 2+.

Downing, Shirley. "Queen Mother Moore of N.Y. Inspired African Pride." *The* [Memphis, Tennessee] *Commercial Appeal.* May 6, 1997: p. B4.

Pace, Eric. "Queen Mother Moore, 98, Harlem Rights Leader, Dies." *New York Times.* May 7, 1997: p. B15.

"Rights Leader Dead at 98." [The Raleigh, North Carolina] *News & Observer.* May 7, 1997: p. B6.

Bernice Johnson Reagon

Born October 4, 1942
Albany, Georgia
Musician, historian, civil rights activist

Bernice Johnson Reagon uses music as a political medium, singing out against racism, sexism, and other social ills. Reagon's first exposure to music came in the form of hymns, sung in the Baptist church where her father was the minister. She was introduced to the civil rights movement while a college student in the early 1960s in Albany, Georgia. Reagon joined the protest marches and, when she and other students were jailed, filled the cells with freedom songs. Reagon and three other activists from the Student Nonviolent Coordinating Committee formed the Freedom Singers and took their message of social justice on the road.

Today Reagon is still singing for human rights as director of the a cappella group Sweet Honey In The Rock. She is also a history professor at American University in Washington, D.C., curator emeritus at the Smithsonian Institution, and a radio producer. Reagon has been instrumental in documenting

"I don't accept the world the way it works. I take on the world. I want to make the world the way it should be."

and preserving the songs and stories of the civil rights movement, as well as African American cultural traditions.

"I don't accept the world the way it works," stated Reagon in a 1994 interview with Mary H. J. Farrell of *People Weekly*. "I take on the world. I want to make the world the way it should be."

Upbringing in rural Georgia

Reagon was born in 1942 in rural Dougherty County, in southwest Georgia, seven miles outside of Albany. She was the third of eight children. Reagon's mother, Beatrice Wise Johnson, worked as a housekeeper during the week and in the cotton fields on weekends. Reagon's father, Reverend Jessie Johnson, presided over the Mt. Early Baptist Church. In addition to conducting services in his own church, he preached at three other backwoods churches every Sunday. During the week he worked as a carpenter.

Reagon began singing in her father's church at the age of five. "I grew up in a region that had developed a strong sacred music singing tradition, in a Black Baptist community," wrote Reagon in *We Who Believe in Freedom*. "For my first eleven years, our church ... had no piano.... we did all of our singing unaccompanied except for our feet and hands; to this day I am an a cappella singer."

Albany College and the Freedom Movement

In 1959 Reagon enrolled in the all-black Albany State college as a music major. At the same time she served as secretary of the youth chapter of the local National Association for the Advancement of Colored People (NAACP).

In 1961 activists from the Student Nonviolent Coordinating Committee (known by its initials, SNCC; a student civil rights organization formed in 1960 to coordinate activities throughout the South) set up an office in Albany. The SNCC organizers joined with local civil rights organizations to form a coalition called the Albany Movement, and began working to end segregation (the forced, legal separation of the races) in Albany. Protest marches and boycotts became part of daily life.

Reagon found she preferred the bold, direct action tactics of the SNCC over the courtroom strategies of the NAACP. In December 1961, Reagon was expelled from Albany State College for her part in a protest march. Later that month she was arrested during another march and spent two weeks in jail. Reagon led the jailed protesters in songs. "The civil rights movement is where I found song as a language," stated Reagon in her *People Weekly* interview.

In the 1993 memoir entitled *We Who Believe in Freedom,* Reagon described "being born again during the Civil Rights Movement." She continued, "I got a new walk! I got a new talk! I got a new song! I got a new taste in my mouth, which I still use to know if I am walking the path of freedom."

The SNCC Freedom Singers

Reagon joined with three other SNCC members of the Albany Movement to form a singing group called the Freedom Singers. The quartet, with their powerful renditions of spirituals and protest songs, became the musical inspiration of the civil rights movement. The Freedom Singers traveled around the nation in a Buick station wagon giving performances in homes, churches, schools, and theaters, including such celebrated venues as Carnegie Hall and Town Hall in New York City and the Ash Grove in Los Angeles. The group also performed at large events such as the Newport Folk Festival and the August 1963 March on Washington for Jobs and Freedom (the march at which Martin Luther King Jr. [1929–1968; see entry in volume 3] delivered his famous "I Have a Dream" speech). The Freedom Singers' purpose was to educate and energize civil rights supporters, as well as to raise funds for the movement.

The Freedom Singers carried on the deeply spiritual musical tradition born in the African American church. Among the songs in the Freedom Singers' repertoire were: "We Shall Overcome," "This Little Light of Mine, I'm Going to Let it Shine,"

"Ain't Gonna Let Nobody Turn Me —Round," "Go Tell it on the Mountain," and "Over My Head I See Freedom in the Air."

Marriage, motherhood, and the move to Washington, D.C.

In 1963 Reagon wed another member of the Freedom Singers, a SNCC field secretary named Cordell Hull Reagon. Over the next two years the couple had two children: a daughter, Toshi, and a son, Kwan Tauna. After the birth of her daughter in 1964, Reagon left the Freedom Singers.

From 1964 through 1966 she collaborated with folk singer Guy Carawan to organize conferences for civil rights song leaders. At the same time, Reagon joined a folk trio called the Harambee Singers and performed at various East Coast venues.

In 1967 Reagon and her husband were divorced. The following year, with the financial support of an anonymous benefactor, Reagon enrolled at Spelman College in Atlanta to pursue an undergraduate degree in nonwestern history.

Reagon was accepted to a doctoral program in history at Howard University in Washington, D.C., in 1971. With her two young children in tow, Reagon headed for the nation's capital. Soon after her arrival she got a job at the Smithsonian Institution's National Museum of American History; that position was complementary to her formal study of oral (spoken) history at Howard. In 1975 Reagon completed her Ph.D. Her dissertation was about songs of the civil rights movement.

Founds Sweet Honey In The Rock

In 1971 Reagon was hired as the vocal director of the D.C. Black Repertory Company. The following year a handful of musicians in the company approached Reagon with the idea of forming a singing group. After a few rehearsals, the group disbanded. Reagon and three other singers rekindled the idea in the fall of 1973; that time they stayed with it. Reagon named the group Sweet Honey In The Rock, after the first spiritual she taught the group. The spiritual was about a land so sweet that honey poured from the rocks.

Members of Sweet Honey In The Rock perform at a concert in New York City. (Reproduced by permission of Corbis Corporation [Bellevue]).

Sweet Honey In The Rock is popular in many parts of the world today, with its combination of gospel, jazz, folk (African and African-American), reggae, rhythm-and-blues, and rap music. The performers accompany their singing, chanting, and humming with African rhythm instruments such as shakeres (gourds covered in strings of beads) and rainsticks (sticks containing beads that make the sound of falling water). The group members wear traditional, colorful African clothing. Through its songs, Sweet Honey In The Rock denounces racism, sexism, and other forms of social and economic injustice.

Over the last twenty-six years the group has made fourteen recordings and has played countless concerts worldwide. In 1991 it won a Grammy Award for two songs—"Sylvie" and "Gray Goose"—on the album *Vision Shared*. More than twenty musicians have participated in the group since its founding; Reagon has been a constant presence.

Alice Walker Pays Tribute to Sweet Honey

In 1993, Bernice Johnson Reagon and other members of Sweet Honey In The Rock celebrated the group's twentieth anniversary with a retrospective book entitled *We Who Believe in Freedom: Sweet Honey In The Rock ... Still on the Journey*. Pulitzer Prize-winning novelist and poet Alice Walker was among the Sweet Honey fans who contributed to the volume. In her essay, "Sweet Honey In The Rock—The Sound of Our Own Culture," Walker recalled the first time she heard Sweet Honey perform, in Washington, D.C., in 1978:

"By the fifth song I knew why people travel hundreds of miles to attend a Sweet Honey concert. Why people get married to Sweet Honey's songs. Why people give birth with Sweet Honey's music blessing in the delivery room. It is inoculation against poison, immunization against the disease of racist and sexist selfishness, envy, and greed. By now my heart had reached my solar plexus, and when I heard the old songs from my grandmother's Hardshell Baptist Church ring out as the freedom songs they always were, I heard all the connectedness that racist oppression and colonial destruction tried to keep hidden. I heard the African beat, yes, and all the African tones. But I also heard the Native American 'off-the-note' harmony that used to raise the hair at the back of my neck when my grandmother moaned in church. I heard the White words of the old, nearly forgotten hymns, and felt how the irresistible need of Black people to give contemporary witness to struggle infuses them with life."

In 1993 Sweet Honey in the Rock celebrated its twentieth anniversary with the publication of a book of memoirs by present and past group members called *We Who Believe in Freedom: Sweet Honey In The Rock ... Still on the Journey*; a musical recording entitled *Still on the Journey*; and a world concert tour.

Solo musical recordings

In addition to her recordings with Sweet Honey In The Rock, Reagon has made numerous solo albums, including *Songs of the South* (1966); *The Sound of Thunder* (1967); and *River of Life* (1986). In 1972, Reagon, together with her daughter Toshi Reagon, produced a record entitled *On River of Life/Harmony: One*. On that recording Reagon dubbed over every part on several Sweet Honey In The Rock songs, singing up to sixteen different vocal parts. Reagon also sang back-up vocals on Toshi Reagon's 1990 debut album, *Justice*.

Preserves African American history

Reagon has specialized in the preservation of African American history at the Smithsonian Institution's National Museum of American History since she was hired in 1971. In her position as curator of the Division of Community Life (which she assumed in 1988), she specialized in African American oral, performance, and protest traditions. Reagon also founded the Smithsonian's program in African American culture. Even in retirement, Reagon remains involved with projects at the Smithsonian. According to James Weaver, a curator at the Smithsonian, the institution has three treasures: "Thomas Jefferson's desk, a Stradivarius cello, and Bernice Reagon."

Reagon has taken on several projects over the last two decades documenting African American history; and in particular, the social roots of her songs. She served as music consultant for two award-winning documentaries: *Eyes on the Prize* (1987) and *We Shall Overcome* (1989). She received a MacArthur Fellowship in the amount of $285,000 in 1989, for her work as an artist and historian of African American culture.

In the early 1990s, Reagon edited the book *We'll Understand It Better By and By: Pioneering African American Gospel Composers*. Reagon then adapted parts of the book into a twenty-six-part radio series called *Wade in the Water: African American Sacred Music Traditions* for National Public Radio. The series, which aired in 1994, covered 200 years of African American gospel music. It won the 1994 Peabody Award for Significant and Meritorious Achievement in Broadcasting. Reagon also compiled songs from the series into a four-CD set by the same name.

The title "Wade in the Water" was taken from an old spiritual. In her *People Weekly* interview Reagon explained why she chose that name. "To me [the song] 'Wade in the Water' meant, go ahead because God's going to control the water. It meant, don't avoid trouble. If you see trouble, go through trouble."

In 1994, a documentary hosted by Bill Moyers entitled *The Songs Are Free: Bernice Johnson Reagon with Bill Moyers* featured interviews with Reagon, as well as excerpts from traditional African American songs. In 1997 Reagon produced a CD entitled *Voices of the Civil Rights Movement: Black American Freedom Songs 1960–1966*. The recording contains forty-three songs produced on location at civil rights meetings throughout the nation.

In 1995 Reagon was presented with a presidential medal, the Charles Frankel Prize, for outstanding contribution to public understanding of the humanities. Reagon is also currently the Distinguished Professor of History at American University in Washington, D.C.

Sources for further reading

Comer, Brooke. "Still on the Journey" (sound recording review). *Down Beat*. January 1994: p. 14.

Farley, Christopher John. "Wade in the Water: African American Sacred Music Traditions" (radio program review). *Time*. January 17, 1994: p. 63.

Farrell, Mary H. J. "Raising Her Voice: Sweet Honey in the Rock's Bernice Johnson Reagon Sings Out for Change." *People Weekly*. December 12, 1994: pp. 149+.

Giddings, Paula. *When and Where I Enter: The Impact of Black Women on Race and Sex in America*. New York: Bantam Books: 1984.

Reagon, Bernice Johnson, and Sweet Honey in the Rock. *We Who Believe in Freedom: Sweet Honey in the Rock ... Still on the Journey*. New York: Anchor Books, 1993.

Smith, Jessie Carney, ed. *Notable Black American Women*. Vol. I. Detroit: Gale Research, 1996, pp. 926–28.

Walters, Neal, and Brian Mansfield, eds. *MusicHound Folk: The Essential Album Guide*. Detroit: Visible Ink Press, 1998, pp. 652–53, 776–77.

Washington, Elsie B. "Bernice Johnson Reagon: Cultural Warrior." *Essence*. February 1994: p. 55.

Philippa Duke Schuyler

Born August 2, 1931
New York, New York
Died May 9, 1967
Da Nang Bay, South Vietnam
Pianist, composer, author, journalist

Philippa Duke Schuyler was a remarkable child, capable of accomplishments well beyond her years. She learned to play piano at age three, won her first gold medal in a piano competition at age four, and completed eighth grade at age ten. At the age of twelve she wrote an orchestral composition that was performed by the New York Philharmonic and the Chicago Symphony Orchestra.

As a young adult, Schuyler gave performances in some eighty countries. She also wrote five books about her life and travels. Schuyler toured Vietnam in 1967, during the height of the Vietnam War (1954–75). While evacuating children from an orphanage in the war zone, the helicopter in which Schuyler was flying crashed. Schuyler, just thirty-five years old at the time, died in the accident.

"I am a woman of color, with all its accompanying sadness and suffering. I was born in New York, but I never truly felt like other Americans."

Portrait: Reproduced by permission of AP/Wide World Photos, Inc.

An unusual conception

Schuyler was conceived by well-to-do parents under rather unusual circumstances. In the most celebrated interracial marriage of the era, Schuyler's father, George Schuyler, an African American author, journalist, and editor of the *Pittsburgh Courier,* wed Schuyler's mother, Josephine Cogdell, a white artist and journalist from Texas.

Cogdell had moved to New York in 1927 to further her journalistic career and to meet George Schuyler, the black journalist whose writing she had long admired. Cogdell wished to marry and have a child with a black man because she believed that interracial children provided the nation's best hope for overcoming racial disharmony.

Cogdell was also convinced that a mixed-race child would be genetically superior to a child of same-race parents, in the same way that hybrid (the offspring of two organisms of different varieties or species) plants and livestock demonstrated "hybrid vigor," or a greater strength than their pure strain counterparts. (The scientific soundness of Cogdell's assumption is doubtful, however, since "race" is not equivalent to "variety" or "species." People of different races, on average, have no more genetic variability than people within a single race.)

A remarkable childhood

Schuyler turned out to be the superior specimen her parents had hoped for. By the age of two-and-a-half, Schuyler could read and write. She began to play the piano at age three and the next year started composing music. At age four Schuyler won a gold medal in the National Piano Teacher Guild competition for her performance of ten pieces by memory, seven of which she had composed herself. At age five she played a concert for a radio audience. Schuyler's IQ, tested at Fordham University, was 185 (a person with an IQ of 140 is considered a genius).

Although Schuyler's father often traveled on journalistic assignments, Schuyler's mother managed Schuyler's upbringing with the utmost attention to detail. Young Schuyler was only fed raw foods, such as wheat germ, unpasteurized milk, cod liver oil, vegetables, fruit, and Vitamin C tablets. Her mother believed that cooking food diminished the food's nutritional value. Schuyler's mother kept the home free of meat, sugar, artificial ingredients, alcohol, and tobacco. Schuyler shunned those items even in her adult years.

Except for a brief stint at the Convent School on the grounds of Manhattanville College, Schuyler was educated at home by private tutors. She was largely shielded from the outside world; she had no friends her own age and was completely unaware of the Great Depression and racial conflict that marked the era. (The Great Depression, which began in 1929 and continued through 1939, was the worst economic crisis in the history of the United States.) In an essay entitled "My Black and White World," published in *Sepia* magazine in 1962, Schuyler wrote: "I was born and grew up without any consciousness of America's race prejudices."

Well into Schuyler's adult years, her mother served as her business manager and personal advisor. Schuyler kept in close touch with her mother even while traveling abroad, typically writing detailed letters every day.

Musical career blossoms in adolescence

When Schuyler was nine, she gave two piano recitals at the New York World's Fair. Her performances prompted New York Mayor Fiorello LaGuardia to declare June 19, 1940, "Philippa Duke Schuyler Day." At age ten, Schuyler became the youngest member of the National Association of American Composers and Conductors.

When Schuyler was thirteen years old, with more than 100 piano compositions to her credit, she wrote the score to *Manhattan Nocturne* for 100 instruments. She then performed the piece with the New York Philharmonic at Carnegie Hall. The next year, her symphonic scherzo (light or playful composition) *Rumpelstiltskin* was performed by the New York Philharmonic, the New Haven Symphony Orchestra, the Boston Pops, and the Dean Dixon Youth Orchestra. At age fifteen, Schuyler gave a solo piano performance with the New York Philharmonic before twelve thousand people at Lewisohn Stadium.

Throughout her youth, Schuyler won numerous prizes for her compositions and performances. She was the subject of features in the *New York Herald Tribune, The New Yorker, Look Magazine,* and *Time* magazine. In addition, Schuyler's father tracked Schuyler's progress in his newspaper, *The Pittsburgh Courier.* "If Josephine Schuyler 'created' [Schuyler's] image," wrote Kathryn Talalay in *Notable Black American Women,* "George Schuyler, through the black press, was able to perpetuate it."

Takes her talents abroad

As Schuyler grew older, she ceased to attract white America's attention in the same way she had as a child. Schuyler found it increasingly difficult to find venues willing to host her concerts. For the first time, Schuyler experienced the painful reality of racism in the United States.

"I became intellectually aware of race prejudice," she wrote in "My Black and White World," "when I grew up and entered the world of economic competition.... Then I encountered vicious barriers of prejudice ... because I was the offspring of what America calls a mixed marriage. It was a ruthless shock to me that, at first, made the walls of my self-confidence crumble. It horrified, humiliated me."

Schuyler responded to the limitations imposed by American racist attitudes by seeking out sympathetic audiences in other nations. In Europe, for instance, race was not a barrier for Schuyler. There she became known there as "the exotic beauty with the jade complexion and the Dutch name."

Schuyler spent the better part of her final decade abroad, performing in more than eighty countries. In her position as goodwill ambassador for the U.S. State Department, she performed in some fifty countries, playing for such dignitaries as Emperor Haile Selassie of Ethiopia, Queen Elizabeth of Belgium, the president of Madagascar, the prince of Malaysia, at three presidential inaugurations in Haiti, and for President Nkrumah at the celebration of Ghana's independence.

From Schuyler's own account, her constant travels reflected her quest for a place to call home. "I am a woman of color," wrote Schuyler in a letter near the end of her life, "with all its accompanying sadness and suffering. I was born in New York, but I never truly felt like other Americans. An invisible wall surrounded me from others.... Wounds and hurt. I'm a beauty but I'm half colored, so I'm not to be accepted anyplace. I'm always destined to be an outsider, never, never part of anything."

Career as an author and a journalist

Schuyler, who was proficient in at least seven languages, embarked on a career as an international news journalist in 1960. She wrote for several newspapers in the United States and Europe, as well as for United Press International (UPI) and other news syndicates. In all, Schuyler wrote over 100 newspaper and magazine articles between 1960 and her death in 1967.

Schuyler also wrote five books between 1960 and 1967. *Adventures in Black and White,* published in 1960, was autobiographical, yet historians concur that the book was a sugar-coated version of Schuyler's real life story. In her book *Who Killed the Congo?,* published in 1962, Schuyler wrote about the aftermath of the Congo's independence from Belgium (the Congo was subsequently renamed Zaire, and is currently called the Democratic Republic of Congo). *Jungle Saints,* published in 1963, was about missionaries in Africa. Schuyler's final book published during her lifetime was *Kingdom of Dreams,* in which Schuyler explained her theory of dream interpretation. The year 1969 witnessed the posthumous (after-death) publication of Schuyler's *Good Men Die,* a book about Vietnam.

Final days in Vietnam

In 1967 Schuyler traveled to war-torn Vietnam as a correspondent for the New Hampshire *Manchester-Union Leader.* In addition to reporting on the war and writing her book, *Good*

Men Die, she performed concerts in theaters, hospitals, and schools, and served as a lay missionary (a person, not a member of the clergy, who performs educational, hospital, or religious work in a foreign country).

Schuyler was also working on a novel while in Vietnam. (While Schuyler produced many fictional pieces during her lifetime, none were ever published.) The novel, called *Dau Tranh,* was full of references to Schuyler's own life. The protagonist in the story was a mixed-race American musician who had been a child prodigy and was in Vietnam as a foreign correspondent.

"Her skin was light enough for her to be accepted as a second-class white in Rhodesia, Kenya, or South Africa, and its color made no difference in Europe," wrote Schuyler in the unpublished manuscript *Dau Tranh.* "But to Americans, it was the most important characteristic. It categorized one as a person to be insulted, to be treated as a pariah, to be deprived of respect in all deeper relationships."

On May 9, 1967, Schuyler set out in a U.S. Army helicopter to rescue children, nuns, and priests from a Catholic orphanage in the war zone village of Hue. Schuyler's helicopter crashed in the Bay of Da Nang, just ten minutes from her destination, bringing her remarkable life to an untimely end.

Schuyler's body was returned to New York where a funeral mass was held for her on May 18. After the mass, Schuyler's coffin was transported down Fifth Avenue by a military honor guard. All traffic came to a halt and thousands of people lined the street to pay their final tribute to the famed pianist and writer.

Sources for further reading

DISCovering Multicultural America. "Philippa Duke Schuyler." [Online] Available http://galenet.gale.com (accessed May 3, 1999).

Microsoft Encarta Africana. "Schuyler, Philippa Duke." [Online] Available http://www.africana.com/tt_056.htm (accessed May 3, 1999).

"Philippa Duke Schuyler: August 2, 1931." *Jet*. August 8, 1994: p. 20.

Schuyler, Philippa. *Good Men Die*. New York: Twin Circle Publishing Company, 1969.

Smith, Jessie Carney, ed. *Notable Black American Women*. Vol. 1. Detroit: Gale Research, 1996, pp. 983–87.

Talalay, Kathryn. *Composition in Black and White: The Life of Philippa Schuyler*. New York: Oxford University Press, 1995.

Assata Shakur

*Born 1947
Jamaica, New York
Political activist*

Assata Shakur became a participant in the struggle for black liberation in the 1960s. She joined the Black Panther Party and other black nationalist organizations and, in deference to her African heritage, changed her name from JoAnne Chesimard to Assata ("she who struggles") Olugbala ("love for the people") Shakur ("the thankful").

In the early 1970s Shakur (like many other militant persons of color) became a target of harassment by the Federal Bureau of Investigation (FBI). She was falsely accused of numerous crimes, including armed robbery, kidnaping, attempted murder, and murder. In every case, either the charge was dismissed for lack of evidence or Shakur was acquitted (found not guilty).

In 1973 the government finally leveled a charge at Shakur that stuck. Shakur was accused and convicted by an all-white jury of murdering a New Jersey highway patrolman. The evidence in the case was questionable and the atmosphere

"The basic reality in the United States is that being black is a crime, that black people are always 'suspects' and that an accusation is usually a conviction."

in which the trial took place was politically charged. Shakur was sentenced to life in prison, but escaped in 1979. She was granted political asylum in Cuba, where she presently resides.

Early years in North Carolina

Shakur was born in Jamaica, in the Queens section of New York City. The FBI's "wanted" poster for Shakur lists her birthdate as July 16, 1947 (a date not substantiated by birth records). "Anyway, I was born," quips Shakur in her autobiography *Assata*. "The name my momma gave me was JoAnne Deborah Byron."

Shakur's parents divorced shortly after she was born. She lived her first three years in New York with her mother, aunt, and maternal grandparents. Then Shakur moved with her grandparents to Wilmington, North Carolina, into the large wooden house in which her grandfather grew up.

Shakur's grandparents taught Shakur to conduct herself with dignity, even around white people. In the segregated South of the 1950s, where African Americans were expected to cast their eyes downward and address whites with "yes, sir" and "yes, ma'am," Shakur was taught to look people in the eye and drop the "sirs" and "ma'ams." "I was told to speak in a loud, clear voice and to hold my head up high, or risk having my grandparents knock it off my shoulders," recalled Shakur in her autobiography.

Shakur spent much of her childhood at the oceanfront resort for blacks operated by her grandparents. When she wasn't doing chores or playing with other children, she was reading stacks of books her grandfather checked out for her at the "colored" library. Occasionally the idyllic setting would be disrupted by white men, resentful at having in their proximity a successful black-owned business and carloads of African Americans enjoying themselves. "The parking lot was made of dirt, and cars spinning around on it at breakneck speed would ruin it in no time," recalled Shakur in her autobiography. "Two or three of them would ride around in the parking lot, spinning and skidding, while they shouted curses and racial insults. One time they fired guns in the air."

Attends school in New York City

After attending a segregated school in Wilmington through the second grade, Shakur returned to New York. Her grandparents and her mother felt that she would receive a better education in New York's integrated schools. Shakur lived with her mother and her sister (five years her junior) in an apartment in a small African American enclave in Queens, surrounded by a white, middle-class area. At the school Shakur attended, the overwhelming majority of pupils were white.

As Shakur progressed in school she became increasingly aware of the differences between herself and her white classmates. Most of the white students were wealthier than Shakur and lived in houses rather than apartments. They traveled to Europe or other exotic locations during summer vacations, while Shakur headed South to stay with her grandparents. As the white students grew older, they became more outwardly hostile toward Shakur and other African American students.

Activism in college years

At age seventeen Shakur, disillusioned with high school, dropped out. She rented a small apartment and began working clerical jobs. A couple of years later friends convinced her to go back to school. Shakur enrolled in Manhattan Community College and studied psychology, history, and sociology. She later transferred to the City College of New York.

During her college years Shakur became active in antiracism and civil rights causes, the movement to end the war in Vietnam (1954–75), and the students-rights movement. Among the groups Shakur was most involved in was the Black Panther Party for Self-Defense, better known as the Black Panther Party, or BPP.

The BPP was founded in Oakland, California, in 1966. BPP members—recognizable by their berets and black leather jackets, and the guns slung over their shoulders—were dedicat-

A Black Panther Party member at a BPP office. Like many other members of the Black Panthers, Assata Shakur was targeted by the FBI's notorious COINTELPRO domestic terrorism program. (Reproduced by Corbis Corporation [Bellevue]).

ed to countering police brutality. Panthers carrying guns and law books often followed the police through the streets at night, to make sure that the officers did not deprive black people of their rights. The Panthers published a weekly newspaper in which they reported incidents of police brutality and editorialized against racism. The BPP also served the community through a free breakfast program, a free health clinic, and other programs. By late 1968, the BPP had established chapters in twenty-five cities and had a membership of several hundred people.

Targeted by COINTELPRO

Shakur rose within the ranks of the BPP, becoming one of its most outspoken and celebrated leaders. Like other Black Panther notables, Shakur was targetted by the FBI's notorious COINTELPRO (counterintelligence program). The stated purpose of COINTELPRO was to combat domestic terrorism. In actuality, COINTELPRO was used to weaken or destroy the Black Panther

Party, the anti-Vietnam War movement, civil rights organizations, the American Indian Movement, and other militant organizations of people of color. (One of the programs earliest targets was the Reverend Martin Luther King Jr. [1929–1968]; see entry in volume 3.) Under the guise of COINTELPRO, the FBI—aided by local and state police—harassed thousands of activists. Many black nationalists ended up in prison or dead.

Shakur was near the top of the FBI's list of "domestic terrorists." The agency hampered Shakur's activism by leveling a series of false charges against her between 1971 and 1973. In April 1971 Shakur was charged with armed robbery at the Hilton Hotel in New York City. Four months later the police accused her of robbing a bank in Queens, and in September 1972, of robbing a bank in the Bronx. In December 1972 Shakur was charged with kidnaping a drug dealer. In January 1973 Shakur was accused of both killing the drug dealer and trying to kill a police officer. In none of those cases was Shakur convicted—either the charges were dropped for lack of evidence or Shakur was acquitted in jury trials.

"The FBI, and the New York Police Department in particular, charged and accused Assata Shakur of participating in attacks on law enforcement personnel and widely circulated such charges," stated a 1978 petition to the United Nations (UN) on behalf of Shakur by the National Conference of Black Lawyers, the United Church of Christ Commission for Racial Justice, and other organizations. The petition continued: "As a result of these activities by the government, Ms. Shakur became a hunted person; posters in police precincts and banks described her as being involved in serious criminal activities; she was highlighted on the FBI's "most-wanted" list; and to police at all levels, she became a 'shoot-to-kill' target."

Shot during highway incident

On May 2, 1973, Shakur was driving with two friends—Zayed Shakur (no relation) and Sundiata Acoli—when the trio was pulled over by two New Jersey highway patrolmen. At that time, Shakur was on the FBI's "most wanted" list; officers were under orders to bring her in, dead or alive. The police stopped the car under the pretense of its having a broken tail light, but one officer conceded that his suspicions were aroused by three African Americans traveling in a car with Vermont license plates. The driver, Zayed Shakur, was ordered out of the car and a shoot-out ensued. When the shooting ended, one patrolman and Zayed were dead; Assata Shakur was seriously injured.

The details of the shooting remain murky to this day. Shakur gave the following account of the incident in an open letter published in *Canadian Dimension* in 1998: "[State trooper Harper] then drew his gun, pointed it at us and told us to put our hands up in the air, in front of us, where he could see them. I complied. In a split second, a sound came from outside the car, there was a sudden movement and I was shot once with my arms held up in the air, and then again from the back."

Convicted of murder in controversial trial

As Shakur lay near death in the hospital, with one bullet lodged near her heart (it remains there today) and her arm mangled by a second bullet, she was questioned in association with the shootings. A detective tested her hand for residue to determine whether she had fired a gun, and found none. Shakur's injuries were consistent with a person who had raised their arms in surrender. Nonetheless, Shakur was charged with killing the officer and placed in prison.

After delays due to a change of venue in October 1973 (from multi-racial Middlesex County to mostly white Morris County) and a mistrial in February 1974, Shakur was convicted by an all-white jury in March 1977. She was sentenced to life in prison. And because Shakur refused to stand when the sentence was read (standing for the judge is a show of respect), the judge tacked an additional thirty-three years onto her sentence.

"The basic reality in the United States," wrote Shakur in her letter to *Canadian Dimension*, "is that being black is a crime, that black people are always 'suspects' and that an accusation is usually a conviction. Most white people still think that being a 'black militant' or a 'black revolutionary' is tantamount to being guilty of some kind of crime."

"The Tradition"

What follows is an excerpt from a poem by Assata Shakur entitled "The Tradition," published in *Assata: An Autobiography*:

There were Black People since the childhood of time
who carried it on.
In Ghana and Mali and Timbuktu
we carried it on.
Carried on the tradition.
We hid in the bush
when the slavemasters came
holding spears.
And when the moment was ripe,
leaped out and lanced the lifeblood
of would-be masters.
We carried it on....
In tales told to children.
In chants and cantatas.
In poems and blues songs
and saxophone screams,
We carried it on....
On soapboxes and picket lines.
Welfare lines, unemployment lines.
Our lives on the line,
We carried it on....
Carried a strong tradition.
Carried a proud tradition.

Escapes from prison

From 1973 to 1979 Shakur was kept imprisoned under horrible conditions. Much of the time she was kept in solitary confinement, was harassed by guards, and feared for her life.

Shakur escaped from the maximum-security wing of New Jersey's Clinton Correctional Facility for Women in 1979, seemingly without a trace. To this day she has not revealed how she accomplished her Houdini-like feat, for fear of reprisals against those who aided her. (Houdini was a magician famous for his "impossible escapes.") "I plotted day and night," commented Shakur in a June 1997 *Essence* article. "There was no way I was going to spend the rest of my life in prison for something I didn't do."

Shakur's whereabouts remained a mystery until 1987, when her asylum in Cuba—where she had been residing since 1984—was made public.

Still pursued by U.S. law enforcement

Shakur admits that her adjustment to living in Cuba, an underdeveloped country, was difficult at first and that she misses her home and African American people and culture. Nonetheless she learned to speak Spanish (the language of Cuba), figured out how to limit her water usage ("hot running water whenever you turn on the tap [is] not always available here," she told *Essence* in 1997), enrolled in political science courses, and settled into life in Cuba. In 1987, shortly before the publication of Shakur's autobiography, her fourteen-year-old daughter, Kakuya, joined her on the island.

Shakur has many good things to say about the socialist nation that has become her home. "I think racism in its institutional form has really been all but squashed in Cuba," stated Shakur in a February 1988 interview with Cheryll Y. Greene of *Essence*. "My experience here has given me a chance to see some of the possibilities of black and white people working together that were very difficult for me to see before."

From her refuge in Cuba Shakur continues to write and speak in support of political, economic, and social justice for African Americans. "Black people are still oppressed and exploited," she stated to *Essence* in 1997. "So I still struggle against the system in whatever way that I can, and that's why the government is fixated on trying to capture and kill me."

Shakur remains a wanted woman by U.S. law enforcement officials, and there is a $100,000 reward for her capture. In 1995 Colonel Carl Williams of the New Jersey State Police remarked that "we would do everything we could to get [Shakur] off the island of Cuba, and if that includes kidnaping, we would do it." In 1997 Congress passed a resolution calling on the Cuban government to return Shakur to the United States so that she could complete her sentence.

Former Black Panther member Bobby Seale continues to defend Shakur. "She's there [in Cuba] in exile," Seale stated in a 1997 newspaper article. "She's there after being falsely and wrongly accused and railroaded into prison in the first place. Political revolutionaries and others active in that era were literally being attacked and murdered by law enforcement officials. Because of that, they deserve amnesty outright regardless of who they were and what they did in the 1960s."

Sources for further reading

"Asylum for Assata Shakur." *Workers World.* October 15, 1998: p. 1.

Emling, Shelley. "American Criminals Call Cuba Home" [Albany, NY] *Times Union.* February 6, 1999: A7.

Essence. June 1997.

Greene, Cheryll Y. "Word from a Sister in Exile." *Essence.* February 1988: pp. 60+.

McCaslin, John. "Political Persecution." *The Washington Times.* October 13, 1998: A6.

Shakur, Assata. *Assata: An Autobiography.* Westport, CT: Lawrence Hill & Company, 1987.

Shakur, Assata. "Open Letter from Assata Shakur." *Canadian Dimension.* July-August 1998: pp. 17+.

Shipp, E. R. "Assata: An Autobiography." *New York Times Book Review.* March 6, 1988: p. 21.

"State Police Ask Pope to Help Find Cop Killer." *Bergen Evening Record.* December 25, 1997: A18.

White, Evelyn C. "Prisoner in Paradise." *Essence.* June 1997: pp. 72+.

Nina Simone

Born February 21, 1933
Tryon, North Carolina
Singer, composer, pianist

Nina Simone is one of the world's most celebrated musicians in the realms of soul, jazz, and pop. Simone was trained in classical piano and gospel music. To those genres she added boogie-woogie, bebop, blues, and jazz to create a unique and eclectic musical style. In the 1950s Simone became a smashing success on the East Coast nightclub circuit. In the 1960s Simone recorded scores of albums and earned the title the "high priestess of soul."

Simone was an active supporter of the civil rights movement and dedicated her performances to those people working for racial equality. Her hit song "Mississippi Goddam"—written in protest of the deaths of civil rights leader Medgar Evers (1925–1963; see entry in volume 2) and four young girls killed in a church bombing in Birmingham, Alabama—was a powerful denunciation of racial violence in the South.

In the late 1960s Simone began her voluntary exile from the United States, living for periods in the Caribbean, Africa,

"I think it's hopeless for the majority of black people.... Slavery has never been abolished from America's way of thinking."

Portrait: Reproduced by permission of Archive Photos, Inc.

and Europe. Simone, who gained international recognition during her decades abroad, currently resides in southern France. She has recorded fifty-eight albums and composed more than five hundred songs.

Shows an early aptitude for music

Simone was born Eunice Kathleen Waymon in Tryon, North Carolina in 1933. She was the sixth of eight children. Her parents were children of slaves, with a combination of African, European, and Native American ancestry. Simone was born during the Great Depression—a time when her family, like many others, had difficulty making ends meet. (The Great Depression was the worst economic crisis to ever hit the United States; it began with the stock market crash in 1929 and ended in 1939.)

Before the Depression, the Waymon family lived comfortably. Simone's father, John Divine Waymon, was a barber and part-owner of a dry cleaning store and a hauling company. Simone's mother, Mary Kate Waymon, stayed at home to take care of her growing brood. In the early 1930s, with the onset of the Depression, both parents worked at a variety of menial jobs. Shortly after Simone's birth, Mary Kate Waymon was ordained a Methodist minister.

Despite economic hardships, Simone recalls that her family never went hungry and that their house was filled with music. At the age of two and a half, Simone was playing hymns on the piano. By the time she was three years old, Simone regularly accompanied her mother to church services. There Simone, to the shock of the congregation, would play the opening hymn on the organ.

When Simone was eight years old she began taking piano lessons from an Englishwoman named Muriel Massinovitch. Simone's first year of lessons were paid for by the white woman for whom Simone's mother worked as a housekeeper. Thereafter, the entire town contributed to Simone's continuing musical education. In return, Simone periodically performed public recitals.

Educational opportunity and disappointment

Simone spent her teenage years at a boarding school in Asheville, North Carolina. After graduating as valedictorian of her class, Simone was awarded a scholarship to the prestigious Juilliard School of Music in New York City (a rare achievement for an African American woman in the 1950s). Simone planned to hone her skills at Juilliard for one year, after which she would take the scholarship examination for the Curtis Institute of Music in Philadelphia. Simone's dream was to become the nation's first black classical concert pianist. A music education at Curtis could make that dream come true.

In late 1950 Simone took the Curtis scholarship exam and soon thereafter learned she had been rejected. Simone was crushed by the news. What she did not know at the time was that Curtis had no black students. Several people later told Simone that she had been turned down not because she lacked ability, but because of who she was—black, female, and from a poor family. Simone was faced with the painful reality that she would never become a classical concert pianist.

Success on the nightclub circuit

After recovering from her disappointment at Curtis, Simone sought out places where her musical talents would be welcomed. She auditioned to be a pianist/singer in an Atlantic City, New Jersey nightclub and was hired on the spot. To styles of gospel and classical she knew so well, Simone added elements of blues, jazz, and boogie-woogie.

In East Coast night clubs and cocktail lounges, Simone became an instant success. She changed her name from Eunice Waymon to the more stage-savvy Nina Simone. "Nina" was a nickname given to her by a childhood boyfriend; she picked "Simone" because she admired the French actress Simone Signoret and liked the way the name sounded.

Career as a recording artist

In 1959 Simone made her first musical recording: "I Loves You, Porgy" (written by George Gershwin for his black opera

Porgy and Bess). Simone's soulful rendition, released on the small, independent Bethlehem record label, sold more than one million copies. "I Loves You, Porgy," which reached number twenty on the charts, was the sole Top 40 hit of Simone's career.

In 1961 Simone married Benjamin Stroud, a former police officer. Stroud became Simone's manager and booking agent. The couple had a daughter, Lisa Celeste Stroud, in 1962.

Soon after her recording debut, Simone signed a recording contract with Colpix, a label affiliated with Mercury Records. She made nine albums, several of them live, on the Colpix label in the early 1960s. Between 1963 and 1966, Simone made seven recordings on the Philips label. She made nine recordings with recording giant RCA between 1966 and 1973. Although classified as an adult/nightclub/jazz performer, Simone's repertoire of recorded music ranged from folk to gospel to jazz to movie themes.

The song that won Simone the greatest accolades in the mid-1960s was "Young, Gifted and Black," a tribute to Lorraine Hansberry, Simone's friend and the first successful black playwright on Broadway (Hansberry wrote *Raisin in the Sun* in 1958). Hansberry died of cancer at the age of thirty-four. At the time of her death, Hansberry had been writing a play entitled *To Be Young, Gifted and Black*. Simone's song "Young, Gifted and Black" was named the National Anthem of Black America by the civil rights organization Congress on Racial Equality (CORE).

Simone's best-selling albums include: *Wild in the Wind, High Priestess of Soul, Silk and Soul, Pastel Blue, I Put a Spell on You, Let it All Out,* and *Nina Simone Sings the Blues*. In 1966 Simone was named "Woman of the Year" by the New York City Jazz at Home Club. She was honored as Female Jazz Singer of the Year by the National Association of Television and Radio Announcers in 1967.

Sings for civil rights

Although Simone had long been troubled by the racism and discrimination directed at herself and other African Americans, it wasn't until 1963 that she formally embraced the civil rights

Mississippi Goddam

Nina Simone burst on the civil rights scene in 1963 with her song "Mississippi Goddam." The song was inspired by two events: the killing of Medgar Evers in Jackson, Mississippi, on June 11, 1963; and the bombing of a Birmingham, Alabama church on September 15, 1963, that killed four young black girls. (Medgar Evers was the head of the Mississippi NAACP; his assailant, Byron de la Beckwith, was initially acquitted by an all-white jury and allowed to walk free until his conviction nearly three decades later, in 1994.)

"The bombing of the little girls in Alabama and the murder of Medgar Evers were like the final pieces of a jigsaw that made no sense until you had fitted the whole thing together," wrote Simone in her autobiography *I Put a Spell on You*. "I suddenly realized what it was to be black in America in 1963 ... it came as a rush of fury, hatred and determination. In church language, the Truth entered into me and I 'came through.'"

Whenever Simone performed the song, she brought the audience to their feet. She also recorded "Mississippi Goddam" and released it as a single. The record sold well in the North, but, due to its poignant political message, it experienced distribution difficulties in the South. "The excuse [of southern distributors] was profanity—Goddam!—but the real reason was obvious enough," wrote Simone in *I Put a Spell on You*. "A dealer in South Carolina sent a whole crate of copies back to our office with each one snapped in half."

movement. Two events in that year—the killing of NAACP leader Medgar Evers and the church bombing that killed four young girls in Birmingham, Alabama (see box)—crystallized her commitment to the struggle for African American rights.

Simone began writing and performing protest songs such as "Mississippi Goddam" (see box) and "Old Jim Crow." (The Jim Crow system was the set of laws and customs that dictated the separation of the races on every level of society.) At her concerts, Simone would ask if anyone in the audience was a member of the Student Nonviolent Coordinating Committee (known by its initials, SNCC; a student-led civil rights organization in the South) or had participated in the Freedom Rides (journeys throughout the South by integrated groups of people who challenged segregation practices on interstate buses and trains). Simone would have those individuals stand up and would honor them for their commitment to civil rights.

"After the murder of Medgar Evers, the Alabama bombing and 'Mississippi Goddam' the entire direction of my life shifted," wrote Simone in her autobiography *I Put a Spell on You,* "and for the next seven years I was driven by civil rights and the hope of black revolution. I was proud of what I was doing and proud to be part of a movement that was changing history.... My music was dedicated to a purpose more important than classical music's pursuit of excellence; it was dedicated to the fight for freedom and the historical destiny of my people."

Simone's turbulent 1970s

The 1970s were a tumultuous period in Simone's life. She not only began the decade by divorcing her husband of nine years, but she experienced financial difficulties as well. During this time she also became increasingly embittered by racism in the United States. All of the aforementioned factors contributed to Simone's decision to leave the country. She settled for periods of time in Switzerland, Liberia, Barbados, England, and France. Although during the 1970s Simone had little contact with U.S. audiences and made few recordings, she performed concerts around the world and rose to fame in Asia, Africa, Europe, and the Middle East.

Makes a comeback in the 1980s

Simone made a triumphant return to the United States in 1985. As Simone walked on stage at New York's Town Hall, the audience stood and applauded for five minutes before the performance began. In 1987, Simone had a hit single in Europe called "My Baby Just Cares for Me." She published her autobiography, *I Put a Spell on You,* in 1991.

In 1993, with the recording of *A Single Woman,* Simone returned to Verve, a major U.S. record label. Simone again made headlines in 1993 when several of her songs were featured in the motion picture *Point of No Return* (a thriller star-

Nina Simone performs at the 1985 Kool Jazz Festival in New York City. (Reproduced by permission of AP/Wide World Photos, Inc.)

ring Bridget Fonda and Harvey Keitel). In 1996, selections from Simone's recordings from 1959 through 1963 were reissued on a two-CD set called *Anthology: The Colpix Years*, released on Rhino Records.

Simone currently resides in southern France. In 1997 she discussed the state of relations in America with a reporter from *Interview* magazine. "I think it's hopeless for the majority of black people," argued Simone, who added that "slavery has never been abolished from America's way of thinking."

"I think the rich are too rich and the poor are too poor," she continued. "I think the rich will eventually have to cave in because the economic situation around the world is not gonna tolerate the United States being on top forever."

Sources for further reading

Boyd, Herb. "I Put a Spell on You: The Autobiography of Nina Simone" (book review). *Black Enterprise.* September 1992: p. 14.

Holtje, Steve, and Nancy Ann Lee, eds. *MusicHound Jazz: The Essential Album Guide.* Detroit: Visible Ink Press, 1998.

"I Put a Spell on You: The Autobiography of Nina Simone" (book review). *Publishers Weekly.* December 13, 1991: pp. 42+.

"Nina Simone Ends Voluntary Exile from U.S." *Jet.* April 22, 1985: pp. 54–55.

The Nina Simone Web. [Online] Available http://www.boscarol.com/nina/html/ (accessed April 27, 1999).

Ploski, Harry A., and James Williams, eds. *The Negro Almanac: A Reference Work on the African American,* 5th edition. Detroit: Gale Research, Inc. 1989, p. 1159.

Powell, Allison. "The American Soul of Nina Simone." *Interview.* January 1997: pp. 76+.

Simone, Nina, and Stephen Cleary. *I Put a Spell on You.* New York: Pantheon Books, 1991.

Smith, Jessie Carney, ed. *Notable Black American Women,* Vol. I. Detroit: Gale Research, 1996, pp. 1021–22.

Smith, Sande, ed. *Who's Who in African-American History.* New York: Smithmark, 1994.

Unterberger, Richie. "Jazz: Simone." *All Music Guide Biography.* [Online] Available http://www.ddg.com/LIS/InfoDesignF96/Ismael/jazz/1980/Simone.html (accessed April 27, 1999).

Maxine Waters

Born August 31, 1938
St. Louis, Missouri
Politician, activist

Maxine Waters was first elected to the U.S. House of Representatives in 1990, and has subsequently been reelected four times. She is known as much for her combative style of politics as she is for her commitment to human rights and economic justice. Although many Americans object to Waters's confrontational manner, her constituents regard her with respect and adoration. Among Waters's strongest supporters are African American and Hispanic American youth, whom she has protected against police brutality and provided with education and job training opportunities; and women, whose economic and social interests she has consistently championed. Waters has positioned herself on the front lines against gang violence—not merely to restore order but to help young gang members to turn their lives around. Waters is widely regarded as one of the most powerful women on the American political scene today.

"Some people say I'm feisty," stated Waters in a 1984 *Ms.* magazine article. "Some say I'm tough. Combative.

"It is a real understanding I have about the unfairness [of the] inability of poor and powerless people to get a decent shake from the government and from life in general."

Portrait: Reproduced by permission of AP/Wide World Photos, Inc.

211

Bitchy. In the community where I come from, the community of survival, those were considered good qualities."

"I think she sees injustice and gets outraged," commented U.S. senator Barbara Boxer about Waters in *Los Angeles* magazine. "She puts that outrage into action, and she's consistently speaking for those who don't have a voice."

A difficult youth in the pre-civil rights era

Waters was born on August 31, 1938, in St. Louis, Missouri, the fifth of thirteen children. Waters's father left the family when Waters was two years old. She grew up poor and her mother was on and off welfare. Waters began working in a segregated restaurant (one that only served whites), clearing tables, at the age of thirteen. Like the other African American employees, Waters had to eat her meals in the basement. While in high school, Waters worked part-time in a factory.

In Waters's high school yearbook, her classmates predicted that she would one day serve as Speaker of the House of Representatives. Given Waters's modest beginnings, that prospect seemed highly unlikely to her.

Marries and moves to Los Angeles

Waters married at the age of eighteen, right after completing high school. At age twenty-one she gave birth to her first child, Edward. Two years later she had a daughter, Karen. The Waters' family moved to Los Angeles in 1961. There Waters raised her children, worked first in a garment factory and then as a telephone operator, and intermittently attended California State University.

The 1960s civil rights movement in the South, which Waters watched unfold on television, had a profound impact on her. "[Seeing] the marchers in the South, with the water hoses and the dogs turned on them" she stated in *Ms.,* "I really began to come to grips with it, to come into my own as a human being. I really began to feel very deeply that I should do something about that. I'd never marched. I'd never gone to jail."

Introduction to electoral politics

Through the late 1960s Waters worked as an assistant teacher in a neighborhood Head Start center. (Head Start is the government-funded preschool program for children from low income families.) After graduating from college in 1971 with a bachelor of arts degree in sociology, Waters was hired to be coordinator of volunteers for the Head Start center. Around the same time, Waters separated from her husband. The couple divorced in 1972.

The volunteer coordinator position brought Waters in contact with elected officials and introduced her to the world of politics. Waters was recruited to work on the campaigns of several local and state politicians, including state senator Mervyn Dymally and Los Angeles mayor Tom Bradley. In 1973 Waters was hired as chief deputy to city council member David Cunningham.

In 1976 Waters married Sidney Williams, a Mercedes Benz salesman and former pro football player with the Cleveland Browns. That same year, the California State Assembly representative from Waters's district decided not to run again. For the first time, Waters put her considerable campaign-organizing experience to work on behalf of herself, and won.

Tenure as a state representative

Waters's career in the California State Assembly spanned the years 1977 to 1990. Early on, Waters gained a reputation as a powerful player. Her "no-holds-barred" advocacy on behalf of poor people, women, and minorities cast her into the international spotlight—a rare achievement for any state-level politician.

While a state representative, Waters secured job training programs, affordable housing, withdrawal of state funds from firms doing business in South Africa (see box), state contracts for minority-owned and woman-owned businesses, a training program for the prevention of child abuse, and a ban on police strip searches of nonviolent offenders (motivated by outrage over the the strip searches of two women arrested on dog-license violations). Waters spoke out in opposition to the navy's

Waters's Stand against Apartheid

Throughout the 1980s Waters stood firm in her opposition to apartheid in South Africa. (Apartheid, which was dismantled in the early 1990s, was the South African policy of racial segregation [legal separation] and discrimination against blacks and other people of color.) As a member of the Washington, D.C.-based organization TransAfrica, Waters was committed to the use of economic sanctions to bring an end to apartheid.

In 1979, when Waters first introduced a bill into the California state legislature to withdraw all state pension funds from businesses with ties to South Africa, the bill did not get a single vote of support. In 1986, after seven years of Waters's tirelessly promoting the bill, plus the pressure generated by three years of sustained demonstrations by University of California students, it passed the state assembly.

---

practice of discriminating against lesbians. She also criticized Los Angeles police chief Daryl Gates for his "insensitivity" toward the black community.

Waters played a leadership role in the 1980 presidential campaign of Senator Edward Kennedy, as well as in Jesse Jackson's two presidential campaigns (in 1984 and 1988). Throughout the 1980s, in addition to being the majority whip (Democratic party manager) in the state assembly, she sat on the boards of directors of several organizations, such as *Essence* (a magazine for black women) and the Ms. Foundation for Women.

Wins election to the U.S. House of Representatives

Waters was elected to the U.S. Congress in 1990, to take the place of retiring Representative Augustus F. Hawkins. She was elected to represent the twenty-ninth district, which includes the south-central Los Angeles communities of (predominantly black and Hispanic) Watts and (predominantly white) Downey.

When Waters was elected to Congress, she became just the second black woman in the institution, joining Representative Cardiss Collins of Chicago. "We've had to overcome the problems of racism and sexism," stated Waters in a 1991 *Ebony* article, by way of explanation of the small numbers of elected black women. "So our time has really come."

Among the issues Waters has worked on in the House of Representatives are: reducing the dropout rate of African American and Latino youth; stemming the flow of drugs in minority communities; securing the rights of veterans; supporting minority-owned and woman-owned businesses; and providing programs in job training, child care, and employment. Waters has consistently fought for federal funds for inner-city economic development. She supports a woman's right to abortion (termination of pregnancy), restrictions on handguns and assault weapons, and the civil rights of lesbians and gay men.

Waters voted for the Family and Medical Leave Act, and against the North American Free Trade Agreement (NAFTA), the Defense of Marriage Act (DOMA), and welfare reform. (The Family and Medical Leave Act allows workers to take unpaid leave following the arrival of a child, or to deal with personal illness or the illness of a family member; NAFTA created a common economic market between the U.S., Canada, and Mexico, thereby allowing U.S. corporations to freely relocate factories to Mexico; DOMA defines marriage as the union of one man and one woman, thereby excluding same-sex marriage; and welfare reform narrowly redefined the criteria for receiving welfare, thereby removing the primary source of government support for many poor people.)

Waters was elected to the House Democratic leadership in 1996. That same year she was elected chair of the Congressional Black Caucus (CBC; an organization of African American representatives that gathers to create legislative strategy). Her term as CBC chair ended in 1998.

The 1992 Los Angeles riots

Waters's congressional district made international headlines in April and May 1992, when four days of rioting in south-central Los Angeles left 52 people dead and 2,383 injured. There were 8,801 arrests and about 3,700 buildings were burned to the ground. Property damage was estimated to be between $735 million and $1 billion.

The event that sparked the riots was a "not-guilty" verdict handed down by an all-white jury in the trial of four white police officers—Sgt. Stacey Koon and officers Laurence Powell, Theodore Briseno, and Timothy Wind—accused of brutally beating black motorist Rodney King. The officers' beating of King in March 1991 had been captured on videotape and broadcast around the world. In a span of eighty-one seconds, the four officers had struck or kicked King fifty-six times and had twice zapped him with 50,000 volts of electricity from a cattle prod.

The nation reacted to news of the rioting, and footage of burning and looting, with shock and dismay. The press turned to Waters for comment. Waters took a position that was widely interpreted (or misinterpreted) as supporting the rioters. She asserted that the hopelessness, frustration, and despair that accompany poverty, a lack of jobs, and police brutality were really at fault for the disturbance. "Our children are hurting, our mothers are tired and our young men are angry," Waters stated at a rally shortly after the riots.

The CIA crack cocaine scandal

Waters again made headlines in 1996 and 1997 by calling for a congressional investigation into accusations that the Central Intelligence Agency (CIA) had been involved in the sale of illegal drugs in the 1980s, the profits of which went to finance the Nicaraguan counterrevolutionary army (known as the contras). The allegations of crack-cocaine sales in inner-city Los Angeles surfaced in August 1996, in a series of articles published by the [San Jose, California] *Mercury News*. Editors for the *Mercury News,* facing a barrage of criticism by governmental and nongovernmental sources, later conceded that some of the conclusions in the articles were unfounded and that their reporters' research had been flawed.

Waters quickly embraced the theory that the government played a role in starting the crack epidemic in inner cities. "I think it is unconscionable," Waters stated at a rally in south-central Los Angeles in late 1996 (before the *Mercury News* retraction was printed), "that the intelligence community or the CIA could think so little of people of color that they would be willing to destroy generations to try to win the war in Nicaragua."

Even after the *Mercury News* retraction, Waters argued that the underlying story could still be sound. "I've never cared how much was sold," stated Waters in May 1997. "I've only cared that some profits did support the contras from the sale of drugs, and that shouldn't have happened in America." Waters has been roundly criticized for promoting the theory that there is a government conspiracy to harm minority communities.

Sometimes supports, sometimes opposes Bill Clinton

Waters wholeheartedly endorsed presidential candidate Bill Clinton in 1992. She seconded his nomination on the Democratic convention floor and served as national cochair of his campaign. Following Clinton's election, he appointed Waters's husband ambassador to the Bahamas.

One of Waters's earliest clashes with President Clinton, however, was over Clinton's policy reversal regarding Haitian refugees. During his campaign, Clinton had condemned President George Bush's policy of denying Haitian political refugees asylum. (Tens of thousands of Haitians had been fleeing the violence and terror that followed the military coup in their country.) Once he became president, however, Clinton made it even more difficult for Haitians to enter the United States. In 1994 Waters was arrested outside the White House with other prominent activists, in a protest over Clinton's denial of Haitian refugees.

Waters again butted heads with Clinton in 1997 over welfare reform. Waters argued that it is cruel to withdraw government support from the nation's poorest and most vulnerable citizens. "It is a real understanding I have about the unfairness [of the] inability of poor and powerless people to get a decent shake from the government and from life in general," Waters explained in a 1998 *Los Angeles* magazine article.

While Waters asserts that the government needs to provide a safety net for poor people, she also stresses the importance of all people to provide for themselves. "I have twelve brothers and sisters. We were on welfare most of my life. Off and on welfare. So we were very, very poor," Waters told an assembly of students at south-central Los Angeles's George Washington Preparatory High School in the fall of 1998. "But guess what? Many of us learned at some point in our lives to just take responsibility for ourselves no matter what's going on. If you put a little more effort into it, no matter what's going on at home, you can do it."

During the impeachment proceedings against Bill Clinton in late 1998 and early 1999, Waters renewed her support for the president. She pledged, on behalf of the Congressional Black Caucus (CBC), to act as the "fairness police" in the proceedings. "I think the right wing [conservative politicians] feels absolutely threatened by Hillary and Bill Clinton," Waters stated in *Los Angeles* magazine in November 1998. "Through their good work, they have caused the right wing to turn on progressive politics in ways that people never thought could happen again in this country."

"We're not fair weather friends," Waters said to Clinton at a CBC fundraiser in August 1998. "We will be with you to the end."

Sources for further reading

Beyette, Beverly. "A Day in the Life of Maxine Waters: A Legislator Who Takes Risks." *Ms.* January 1984: pp. 42–46.

"Black Caucus Chair Rep. Maxine Waters Lauds Clinton at D.C. Fundraiser." *Jet.* August 24, 1998: pp. 32+.

Brown, Roxanne, Richette Haywood, and Aldore Collier. "A Black Woman's Place is in the ... House of Representatives." *Ebony.* January 1991: pp. 104–5.

Carey, Pete. "Handling of CIA-Crack Probes Decried; Rep. Waters Demands Release of Reports." Knight-Ridder/Tribune News Service. December 19, 1997.

Geary, Robyn. "Troubled Waters: Outspokenness of Congressional Black Caucus Chairperson Maxine Waters." *New Republic.* June 30, 1997: pp. 11+.

Holmes, Steven A. "Call for C.I.A.-Cocaine Inquiry is Renewed." *New York Times.* May 15, 1997: p. A17.

Lindsey, Robert. "California's Tough Line on Apartheid." *New York Times.* August 31, 1986: p. E2.

"Maxine Water, D-California, 29th District." *Congressional Quarterly Weekly Report.* November 10, 1990: p. 3809.

National School Network. "Congresswoman Maxine Waters." [Online] Available http://nsn.bbn.com/community/bl_hist/waters_bio.html, (accessed May 29, 1999).

Newman, Maria. "Lawmaker from Riot Zone Insists on a New Role for Black Politicians." *New York Times.* May 19, 1992: p. A10.

Reynolds, Barbara. "A Conversation With ... Congresswoman Maxine Waters." *Essence.* January 1999: pp. 80+.

Voter Information Services. "VIS Ratings for Representatives of California." [Online] Available. http://world.std.com/~voteinfo/ascii_reports/CA/35.html(accessed June 25, 1999).

Warren Chris. "Running Water: Congresswoman Maxine Waters' Politics." *Los Angeles Magazine.* November 1998: pp. 64+.

William Julius Wilson

*Born December 20, 1935
Derry Township, Pennsylvania
Urban sociologist, educator, author*

William Julius Wilson is a leading scholar on the issues of poverty and unemployment among African Americans in urban ghettos. He argues that class (social and economic standing) is a greater factor than race in one's potential for economic advancement, and that an ambitious federal jobs program is needed to revitalize America's inner cities. Such assertions have made him friends and foes across the political spectrum.

Left-leaning (favoring extensive social reform) politicians and scholars have criticized Wilson for harping on the shortcomings of black Americans while letting white Americans and the government off the hook; conservative (favoring existing political conditions or gradual change) figures have denounced Wilson for his insistence upon greater social spending as a solution to the seemingly intractable problem of ghetto poverty.

After twenty-five years of teaching at the University of Chicago, Wilson joined the faculty of Harvard University in

"You can walk into any maternity ward in [ghetto areas] and look at the rows of babies and predict with almost unerring certainty what their lives are going to be."

Portrait: Reproduced by permission of William Julius Wilson.

1996. His major books include: *The Declining Significance of Race* (1978); *The Truly Disadvantaged* (1987); and *When Work Disappears* (1996).

Experiences poverty as a child

Wilson was born on December 20, 1935, the eldest of six children of Esco and Pauline Wilson. He grew up in the working-class community of Blairsville, just east of Pittsburgh. The Wilson family's house had two bedrooms: one for the parents and the other for the six children.

Wilson's father, a coal miner, died of lung disease when Wilson was twelve years old. After Esco's death, the family had to scramble to make ends meet. Wilson recalls that the family shared just one quart of milk per week.

While Wilson admits that his family was "struggling all the time," he is quick to point out that his experience growing up was very different than the experiences of the urban poor he studies. For instance the adults in his community, although poor, had jobs—unlike the majority of ghetto dwellers. In addition, Wilson's youth was filled with hope and expectations. "Even though my parents didn't go past the ninth or tenth grades," Wilson commented in 1996 in the *New Yorker,* "it never occurred to me that I wasn't going to college." Wilson and all five of his siblings eventually earned advanced degrees.

A major influence on Wilson during his childhood was his aunt, Janice Wardlaw, a psychiatric social worker living in New York City. Wardlaw encouraged Wilson's intellectual and cultural development. After Wilson completed high school, Wardlaw helped pay for his college education.

Training as a sociologist

Wilson began his college career at the predominantly black Wilberforce College in Wilberforce, Ohio. At college Wilson was introduced to the writings of African American scholar and civil rights activist W.E.B. Du Bois (1868–1963; see entry in volume 1) and urban sociologist Robert Park of the University of Chicago. From their works and others, Wilson developed a great interest in social sciences—in particular, the politics of race.

Wilson earned his bachelor of arts degree from Wilberforce in 1958. After a short stint in the army, Wilson enrolled in the master's program in sociology at Bowling Green State University in Ohio. He earned his master's degree in 1961, then went to Washington State University, where he completed his doctorate in sociology in 1966.

Teaching career at University of Chicago

Wilson's first teaching post, which he began the year before completing his doctoral dissertation, was at the University of Massachusetts. He spent six years at the East Coast school, earning the title "Teacher of the Year" in 1970. That same year Wilson married Beverly Ann Heubner, a manuscript editor. The couple have a son, Carter, and a daughter, Paula.

In 1971 Wilson was hired by the University of Chicago's department of sociology to be an associate professor. Wilson was promoted to full professor in 1975. He became chairman of the sociology department in 1978 and two years later was named to the distinguished Lucy Flower Chair in Urban Sociology. In 1990 Wilson rose to the level of university professor—the highest academic designation for a faculty member.

Promotes scientifically sound research methods

Even before arriving at the University of Chicago Wilson had become skeptical of the research methods used by social scientists of the 1960s and early 1970s. He felt that many social scientists were biased in their approach and did not conduct adequate research to support their conclusions. Wilson believed that social science, like natural science (such as biology and physics), should be supported by facts and that conclusions should be arrived at through rigorous research. It became Wilson's hallmark to include extensive graphs, tables, and statistics in his reports.

Wilson's credibility as a scientist—albeit a social scientist—was recognized in 1991 with his election to the National Academy of Sciences. That high honor is typically reserved for scholars in the natural sciences.

Shifts emphasis from race to class

As a new professor at the University of Chicago, Wilson concentrated on the same topic as many other urban sociologists at the time: race relations. It was during this phase of Wilson's career, in 1973, that he published his first book: *Power, Racism, and Privilege: Race Relations in Theoretical and Sociohistorical Perspectives*. The book compared race relations in the United States and South Africa (at that time South Africa was governed by apartheid—the policy of racial segregation [legal separation] and discrimination against blacks and other people of color).

Shortly after the publication of that book Wilson forged an independent path in the field of urban sociology. He began to look at issues of class above race in analyzing poverty and other social ills in black inner cities.

Stirs up controversy with *The Declining Significance of Race*

In 1978 Wilson published the work that thrust him into the spotlight and sparked a national debate over the root causes of ghetto poverty: *The Declining Significance of Race: Blacks and Changing American Institutions*. In this book Wilson argued that in the years following the civil rights movement (since 1965, when racial discrimination was made illegal), class had taken the place of race as the greatest roadblock to economic and social progress for black city dwellers. Wilson further stated that the economic opportunities opened up to African Americans by the gains made by the civil rights movement had resulted in a more clearly delineated class system among blacks. The more successful, middle-class blacks had joined whites and employers in the migration to the suburbs, leaving poor blacks behind in inner cities with few job prospects. The jobs left behind in inner cities were mostly service jobs (such as working at fast-food restaurants), offering low wages with no benefits—gone were the manufacturing jobs that had paid higher wages and offered health and other benefits.

While not denying the existence of racial discrimination, Wilson argued that poor blacks in the ghettos suffered more from lack of economic opportunity than from racism.

Response by the right and the left

The Declining Significance of Race was alternately hailed as masterful and denounced as an affront to the struggle for racial equality. While the American Sociological Association honored the book with its prestigious Sydney Spivack Award, the Association of Black Sociologists condemned the book, claiming to be "outraged over the misrepresentation of the black experience."

Wilson's book came under a hailstorm of criticism from politically progressive scholars, politicians, and prominent black newspapers such as the New York *Amsterdam News* and the *Chicago Defender*. Among the criticisms of *The Declining Significance of Race* was that Wilson had blamed the poverty, crime, and substance abuse problems plaguing black inner cities on the dysfunctional patterns of living of the members of those communities. In other words, the critics asserted, Wilson had parroted the conservatives' argument that the victims were to blame. Wilson was also attacked for suggesting that since the government and society were not responsible for the creation of the black underclass, neither were they responsible for curing its ills. "By identifying the poor as cut off—as an underclass with no relation to anyone else," commented sociologist Charles Willie in a 1996 *New Yorker* article, "[the book] absolved the rest of society of responsibility."

While Wilson was dismayed by his critics' comments, he was even more troubled by the right-wing's (politically conservative camp's) rush to embrace him as one of their own. As Wilson received letters of congratulations from conservative organizations, he rejected the label of "neoconservative" (a member of the far-right wing, especially one who regards societal ills as consequences of individuals' failings) that was being thrust upon him.

Wilson was even invited to meet with President Ronald Reagan—a conservative president intent on enlisting the aid and advice of black conservatives. Wilson refused the invitation, telling the president's aide who contacted him: "Where did you get the idea that I'm a conservative? To the contrary, I'm a member of the Democratic left."

Explores causes of poverty in *The Truly Disadvantaged*

In his next book, *The Truly Disadvantaged: The Inner City, The Underclass, and Public Policy,* Wilson challenged the "culture of dependency" model put forward by conservative scholars. (In the 1980s, Charles Murray [author of *The Bell Curve*] and other social scientists asserted that welfare and other forms of government aid were not only not helping poor people, but were harming them by making them dependent on handouts and making them forget the meaning of hard work and responsibility.) Wilson rebutted the "culture-of-dependency" theorists, claiming that while behavioral problems of ghetto-dwellers could not be ignored, the major causes of ghetto poverty—such as the loss of manufacturing jobs, inadequate schools, and isolation from people of other classes and races—were beyond residents' control. Furthermore, Wilson's research showed that unemployed ghetto residents continued to value hard work and honesty.

Wilson also discussed how a legacy of joblessness, hopelessness, and a sense of isolation is passed down from one generation to the next. "You can walk into any maternity ward in these areas and look at the rows of babies and predict with almost unerring certainty what their lives are going to be," Wilson told journalist David Remnick of *The New Yorker.* "Chances are they've been born to a family in which there is no steady breadwinner.... The child will be exposed almost entirely to families like his or her own—an almost total social isolation.... Most of these kids have practically no contact at all with white people, and when they do encounter white people they are intimidated.... they are exposed to an environment that provides a vast opportunity for crime, drugs, hustling, illicit sex."

Proposes solutions

As a remedy for inner-city despair, Wilson recommended the implementation of social programs, including affirmative action, based not on race but on class. (Affirmative action is a set of federal government policies that provide increased educational and employment opportunities to racial minorities and women, in order to overcome past patterns of discrimination.) In other words, Wilson advocated that jobs, child care, health care, and other forms of social support be made available to poor people in inner cities, regardless of race.

Responses to *The Truly Disadvantaged*

The Truly Disadvantaged was widely hailed as an important and well-researched work; however, it was not uncontroversial. Because Wilson called for the expenditure of government dollars in inner cities, the conservative camp (which claims that the best way to aid poor people is to let them fend for themselves) no longer embraced him as one of their own. At the same time, the left wing criticized him for the way he described the social ills plaguing the ghetto poor.

Adolph Reed Jr., in a book review in the politically progressive magazine *The Nation,* took Wilson to task for including female-headed households among the list of social "pathologies" (ills) prevalent in ghettos and for asserting that job programs should target young males since males have greater earning potential than females. "One might think that point would lead him to call for pay equity, universal day care and other initiatives to buttress women's capacities for living independently in the world," wrote Reed, "but Wilson goes in exactly the opposite direction."

Advises President Clinton

Since the late 1980s Wilson has become a much sought after advisor to Democratic politicians. Among those who have turned to Wilson include Chicago mayor Richard M. Daley, Senators Bill Bradley of New Jersey and Paul Simon of Illinois (both recently retired), and former governor of New York Mario Cuomo.

Wilson was tapped by Bill Clinton in the early 1990s to be an advisor for his 1992 presidential campaign. Clinton, who continued to rely heavily on Wilson's input throughout the first few years of his presidency, was quoted in *The New Yorker* as saying: "*The Truly Disadvantaged* made me see race and poverty and the problems of the inner city in a different light."

Wilson and Clinton parted ways over the president's "welfare reform" policy. Implemented in 1996, this legislation dismantled the federal government's welfare program, Aid to Families with Dependent Children, and transferred responsibility for welfare programs to the states. Although Wilson had voiced a need to alter the existing welfare system to include time limits for able-bodied recipients, he felt it was a tragic error to take away poor people's sole source of support without an accompanying public-sector jobs program.

Founds Center for the Study of Urban Inequality

In the late 1980s Wilson initiated the Urban Poverty and Family Life Study—a vast survey of the attitudes and experiences of urban poor people. Wilson employed a team of graduate students from the University of Chicago to help him conduct interviews with some 2,500 Chicago ghetto residents and about 190 employers in the area.

The study, the results of which were presented at a 1991 conference, was most remarkable for its finding that employers, overall, were reluctant to hire African Americans living in the ghettos. The majority of employers (even those who were African American) stated they would rather hire Hispanic men than African American men.

The study spawned the establishment of the Center for the Study of Urban Inequality at the University of Chicago. The center conducts ongoing research on the city's ghetto poor and makes policy recommendations to the city government. Some of the center's suggestions include increased job-training programs and job-referral services, coordination of car pools, and the scattering of low-income housing throughout the city (to break up the economically isolated ghettos).

Calls for government jobs programs in *When Work Disappears*

The year 1996 saw the publication of Wilson's fourth book, *When Work Disappears: The World of the New Urban Poor*. The focus of this book was the importance of work in people's lives and the consequences of unemployment on families and a community. The book was based on Wilson's years of research in Chicago ghettos, where virtually all manufacturing jobs have disappeared, the majority of adults are unemployed, and the poverty rate is between 40 and 50 percent.

In *When Work Disappears* Wilson explained that employment provides structure in the lives of adults and that working adults serve as role models for young people. "Regular employment provides the anchor for the spatial and temporal aspects of daily life," Wilson wrote in *When Work Disappears*. "It determines where you are going to be and when you are going to be there. In the absence of regular employment, life, including family life, becomes less coherent."

Wilson fingered joblessness as the primary cause of a host of social ills, including crime, substance abuse, gangs, and teenage parenthood. He also underscored that social ills are passed from one generation to the next. "High neighborhood joblessness," stressed Wilson, "has a far more devastating effect than high neighborhood poverty."

Wilson suggested as a remedy for inner cities the implementation of a massive government jobs program—similar to the New Deal programs of President Franklin D. Roosevelt (1882–1945; the New Deal was a group of public works programs that employed large numbers of people in a variety of construction and neighborhood improvement projects during the 1930s.)

Joins Harvard's African American "Dream Team"

In 1996 Wilson left the University of Chicago for a faculty position at Harvard University's John F. Kennedy School of Government. Wilson was recruited by professors Cornel West and Henry Louis Gates Jr. (1950– ; see entry in volume 2)—members of Harvard's African American "dream team." (The "dream team" includes several of the nation's most highly respected black intellectuals.) Wilson also joined the faculty of Harvard's program in Afro-American studies.

The same year that Wilson went to Harvard he was named by *Time* magazine as one of the twenty-five most influential people in America. "No thinker has done more than the sixty-year-old sociologist," stated a *Time* article of June 1996, "to explain why the black underclass sank into such misery and isolation at the same time millions of other African Americans were escaping from the ghetto to create a vibrant middle class."

Sources for further reading

Early, Gerald. "William Julius Wilson: A Leading Scholar of Urban Poverty Has a Prescription for the Ghetto—Jobs." *Mother Jones*. September-October 1996: pp. 20+

Erikson, Kai. "When Work Disappears: The World of the New Urban Poor." *Yale Review*. April 1998: pp. 121+.

Kalb, Claudia, and Mark Starr. "Education: Up From Mediocrity—Now Black Studies at Harvard is Famous For Its Stars." *Newsweek*. February 19, 1996: p. 64.

Morley, Jefferson. "The New Anti-Poverty Debate." *The Nation*. February 13, 1988: pp. 196+.

Reed, Adolph Jr. "Dissing the Underclass." *The Progressive*. December 1996: pp. 20+.

Reed, Adolph Jr. "The Truly Disadvantaged: The Inner City, the Underclass, and Public Policy" (book review). *The Nation*. February 6, 1988: pp. 167+.

Remnick, David. "Dr. Wilson's Neighborhood." *The New Yorker*. April 29, 1996: pp. 96+.

Reynolds, Gretchen. "The Rising Significance of Race." *Chicago*. December 1992: pp. 80+.

"The *Time* 25: *Time*'s Most Influential Americans—William Julius Wilson." *Time*. June 17, 1996: pp. 56+.

White, Jack E. "The Black Brain Trust: Harvard University's Revitalized Afro-American Studies Department." *Time*. February 26, 1996: pp. 58+.

White, Jack E. "Let Them Eat Birthday Cake: Clinton's Welfare Reform Dismays the President's Favorite Poverty Scholar." *Time*. September 2, 1996: pp. 45+.

Wilson, William Julius. *The Declining Significance of Race: Blacks and Changing American Institutions*. Chicago: University of Chicago Press, 1978.

Wilson, William Julius. *The Truly Disadvantaged: The Inner City, The Underclass, and Public Policy*. Chicago: University of Chicago Press, 1987.

Wilson, William Julius. *When Work Disappears: The World of the New Urban Poor*. New York: Alfred A. Knopf, 1996.

Coleman Young

Born May 24, 1918
Tuscaloosa, Alabama
Died November 29, 1997
Detroit, Michigan
Mayor, state senator, civil rights activist

UPDATE

Coleman Young, the mayor of Detroit for twenty years, died of respiratory failure in November 1997. At the time of his death, he was seventy-nine years old. Young was a controversial figure, regarded as a hero by some and a corrupt and ineffective politician by others. Prior to his election as mayor of Detroit in 1973, Young was a resolute fighter for the rights of African Americans and working people. He challenged segregation in the U.S. military, antiunionism at the Ford Motor Company, and repression of political freedoms by the House Un-American Activities Committee (HUAC). As mayor of one of the nation's largest cities, Young revitalized the downtown riverfront district—at the expense of crumbling neighborhoods, say his critics. **(See original entry on Young in volume 4.)**

Early experiences with discrimination

In 1923, when Young was five years old, his family moved from his birthplace, Tuscaloosa, Alabama, to Detroit,

Coleman Young was a controversial figure, regarded as a hero by some and a corrupt and ineffective politician by others.

Portrait: Reproduced by permission of Corbis-Bettmann.

Michigan. Like so many other southern blacks during that era, the Young family migrated to a northern city to escape racial intimidation by the Ku Klux Klan and to seek better employment. (The Ku Klux Klan [KKK] is an anti-black terrorist group that originally formed in the South after the Civil War [1861–65]. For decades, the KKK has intimidated and committed acts of violence against black Americans and members of other racial and ethnic minorities.)

Young experienced racial discrimination at an early age when he was denied a scholarship to a Catholic high school because of the color of his skin (placing among the top ten students in Detroit's parochial schools should have automatically entitled him to a scholarship). To make matters worse, Young was not allowed to attend the graduation party with other members of his parochial school at Detroit's Boblo Island, a "whites-only" amusement park

After attending public high school, Young took a job as an assembly-line worker at the Ford Motor Plant. When Young was suspected of supporting the formation of a union at a plant, he was confronted by members of Ford's private security force. (Henry Ford [1863–1947], founder of the Ford Motor Company, hired a security force to keep his plant free of unions.) A skirmish broke out and Young was fired for fighting. Young continued to aid union organizers from outside the plant; in 1941, after a long and bitter battle, the auto workers voted in favor of the union.

Challenges segregation in military

In 1942, following the U.S. entry into World War II (1939–45), Young was drafted into the army. At that time the military was segregated (separated by race); African American infantrymen and officers alike were mistreated and made to suffer numerous indignities. Young achieved the rank of second lieutenant, then entered the air force training school for bombardiers and pilots at the Tuskegee Institute in Alabama. On at least two occasions Young, with other African American officers, challenged the air force's segregationist policies by occupying whites-only officers' clubs. In 1946, the year after Young received his honorable discharge, President Harry S. Truman (1884–1972) issued an executive order desegregating the military.

Activism in post-war years

After his military stint Young returned to Detroit and resumed his union organizing activities. He served for a short time on the board of directors of the Congress of Industrial Organizations (CIO), until he and other leftists (people favoring extensive social reform) were purged in a consolidation of power by CIO president Walter Reuther. Young then organized postal workers with the United Public Workers union and helped members of the Garbage Workers Union secure a new contract.

In 1951 Young was elected executive secretary of the National Negro Labor Council (NNLC), an organization of progressive (reform-minded) African American unionists. The following year Young, as an officer of a group deemed "subversive" by the attorney general, was called to answer questions before the House Un-American Activities Committee (HUAC). (HUAC conducted public investigations into alleged subversive or communist activity in the 1940s and 1950s.) Young refused to answer many of the committee's questions and accused the committee chairman of racism—in Young's view, an un-American activity.

Becomes mayor of Detroit

Young made his first bid for public office, unsuccessfully, for Detroit city council in 1959. In 1964 he won his first of two elections to the Michigan state senate. Young left the state senate in 1973 and launched a victorious campaign for the mayor of Detroit. Young became the first African American mayor of a large city, sharing that distinction with Tom Bradley of Los Angeles. Young served a record five terms as mayor, for a total of twenty years.

When Young took over the reins of Detroit, the city was still feeling the effects of the 1967 race riots that left forty-three people dead and more than two thousand injured. Among the factors that led to the rioting, issues that continued to simmer when Young took office, were unemployment (many industrial employers had left the city since 1960) and police brutality (Detroit's 95-percent-white police force was notorious for harassing and assaulting black males on street corners). One of Young's first initiatives was to integrate the police force and to establish a citizens' committee to oversee police actions.

Another important element of Young's legacy was the revitalization of the downtown riverfront district—including the construction of high-rise office buildings, entertainment centers, marinas, hotels, and a monorail called the "people mover"—at a cost of hundreds of millions of dollars in federal aid. Young's critics charged that the downtown renovation did little more than line the pockets of Young's cronies in the development and construction industries, and claimed that the money would have been better spent restoring the city's decaying neighborhoods.

Retires after two decades in office

After retiring from the mayor's office in 1993 Young joined the faculty of Wayne State University (in Detroit) as a professor of urban affairs. Young published his memoirs, *Hard Stuff: The Autobiography of Mayor Coleman Young,* in 1994. In the years that followed, Young's health began to fail. He suffered from emphysema and heart problems and was hospitalized several times. Young died of respiratory failure on November 29, 1997.

Young's body laid in state at the African American History Museum for two days, during which time some eighty thousand people came to pay their final respects. On December 4 thousands of Detroiters lined the streets to witness the motorcade that brought Young's body to its final resting place.

Sources for further reading

Davis, Karen A. "Two American Heroes Children Should Know." *The Providence Journal-Bulletin.* December 10, 1997.

Ensign, Tod. "Hard Stuff: The Autobiography of Mayor Coleman Young" (book review). *The Progressive.* June 1994: pp. 37+.

Gallagher, John, Jennifer Dixon, and Joe Swickard. "His Efforts Set the Stage for Rebirth of His City." *Detroit Free Press.* November 30, 1997.

Kulman, Linda. "Detroit's Resilient Mayor." *U.S. News & World Report.* December 15, 1997: p. 14.

McGraw, Bill. "Today, the Last Motorcade Through the City He Loved." *Detroit Free Press.* December 4, 1997.

"Requiem for an Urban Giant." *Ebony.* February 1998: pp. 140+.

Thieme, Darius L. "Coleman A. Young" in *Notable Black American Men,* edited by Jessie Carney Smith. Farmington Hills, MI: The Gale Group, 1999, pp. 1285–89.

Index

Italic type indicates volume number; **boldface** indicates main entries and their page numbers; (ill.) indicates photos and illustrations. For a fields of endeavor index, see p. ix.

Nina Simone

Portrait: Reproduced by permission of Archive Photos, Inc.

A

A. Philip Randolph Institute, *3:* 640, 642
Aaron, Hank, *1:* **1–3,** 1 (ill.); *2:* 313
Abbott, Robert S., *6:* **1–8**
ABC News, *4:* 670, 671
ABC Sports, *5:* 210
Abdalla, Kenneth, *5:* 215
Abdul-Jabbar, Kareem, *1:* **3–5,** 4 (ill.); *2:* 401; *5:* 143
Abernathy, Ralph David, *1:* **5–8,** 6 (ill.); *3:* 457, 483, 545
Abolitionists, *5:* 31, 34
Absence (dance), *2:* 411, 412
Acquired Immune Deficiency Syndrome (AIDS), *1:* 27; *2:* 400, 402, 412; *5:* 128, 129; *6:* 84
Adams, John Quincy, *5:* 31, 36, 38, 39

Adventures in Black and White, 6: 189
Advocates Scene, 4: 659
African Journey, 3: 619, 620
Affirmative action, *6:* 34, 35
African Liberation Support Committee, *2:* 276
Afro-American Association (AAA), *4:* 657
Afro-American, 5: 227–28
Afrocentric movement, *1:* 23, 25
Afrocentricity: The Theory of Social Change, 1: 25
AIDS. *See* Acquired Immune Deficiency Syndrome (AIDS)
Ailey, Alvin, *1:* **8–11,** 9 (ill.)
"Ain't Misbehavin'," *1:* 22
Al-Amin, Jamil Abdullah. *See* Brown, H. Rap
Albany Movement, *6:* 179
Alcindor, Lew. *See* Abdul-Jabbar, Kareem

Ali, Muhammad, *1:* 5, **11–14,** 12 (ill.) 76; *5:* 81, 84
All Afrikan People's Revolutionary Party, *1:* 119
All American Women: Lines that Divide, Ties that Bind, 1: 152
All God's Chillun Got Wings, 3: 622
All Hail the Queen, 3: 606
Allen, Debbie, *5:* 39
Alliance Against Racism and Political Repression, *1:* 183
Alpha Suffrage Club, *1:* 43
"Ambassador of Love," *1:* 29
Ambush, Kathy, *4:* 711
American Bandstand, 1: 168, 169
American Committee on Africa, *3:* 641
An American Dilemma, 1: 105
American Equal Rights Association, *4:* 730
American Federation of Labor and Congress of Industrial Organizations (AFL-CIO), *3:* 611
American Jewish Congress, *3:* 642
American Legion Boys Nation, *5:* 148
American Library Association, *3:* 629
American Medical Association, *2:* 230, 231
American Muslim Mission, *2:* 239
American Negro Theater, *3:* 581, 582; *6:* 65, 66
American Political Science Association, *1:* 106
American Red Cross, *1:* 208
American Society for the Prevention of Cruelty to Animals, *5:* 168
American Spectator, 5: 21

American Tennis Association, *2:* 267
American Theater for Poets, *1:* 39
American Woman Suffrage Association (AWSA), 6: *123, 124*
Amistad (ship) *5:* 31, 32, 33, 33 (ill.), 34
And the Walls Came Tumbling Down, 1: 6
Anderson, Marian, *1:* **14–17,** 102; *3:* 590
Anderson, Myers, *4:* 710–11
Angela Davis, 1: 183
Angelou, Maya, *1:* **17–20,** 18 (ill.)
Ann-Margret, *5:* 220, 221
Annan, Kofi, *5:* 131
Annie Allen, 1: 86
Ansen, David, *2:* 278
The Answer, 6: 158
Anthropology for the Nineties, 1: 152
Anti-Semitism, *5:* 72, 73
Apartheid, *5:* 149, 251; *6:* 139, 214
Arafat, Yasir, *2:* 381
Argaiz, Pedro Alcantara de, *5:* 35
Arkansas State Press, 1: 51
Armstrong, Louis, *1:* **20–23,** 22 (ill.), 189; *2:* 383; *4:* 757
Asante, Molefi Kete, *1:* **23–25,** 24 (ill.)
Ashe, Arthur, *1:* **25–28,** 26 (ill.)
Ashford, Evelyn, *5:* 104
Association for the Study of Afro-American Life and History, *4:* 799
Association for the Study of Negro Life and History, *4:* 798, 799–800
Association for Theatre in Higher Education, *5:* 28
Association of Black Anthropologists, *1:* 198

Atlanta Committee on Appeal for Human Rights (COHAR), *1:* 69
Atlanta, Georgia, *5:* 249, 252, 253, 254
Atlantic Monthly, 1: 134
Atlantic Records, *2:* 246
Atomic bomb, *3:* 603
Atomic reactor, *3:* 603
Ausbie, Geese, *2:* 320
Austin, Clyde, *2:* 320
The Autobiography of Malcolm X, 2: 302
The Autobiography of Miss Jane Pittman, 2: 253, 255
Avalon Community Center, *2:* 264
Aykroyd, Dan, *5:* 24
Aziz, Muhammad Abdul, *5:* 76

B

Bach, Erwin, *5:* 224
Bailey, F. Lee, *5:* 211, 213
Bailey, Joy, *2:* 313
Bailey, Pearl, *5:* 24, **28–30,** 29 (ill.)
Bailey's Cafe, 3: 559
Baker, Augusta, *1:* **30–32,** 30 (ill.); *6:* **9–12,** 9 (ill.)
Baker, Ella Jo, *6:* **13–20,** 13 (ill.)
Baker, Josephine, *1:* **32–34,** 33 (ill.)
Baldwin, James, *1:* **34–37,** 36 (ill.), 143; *4:* 687, 688, 800
Baldwin, Roger S., *5:* 34
Ballard, Florence, *3:* 630
Baltimore Elite Giants, *1:* 114
Banneker, Benjamin, *5:* **1–7,** 1 (ill.), 2 (ill.), 5 (ill.)
Baraka, Amiri, *1:* **37–40,** 39 (ill.); *2:* 276; *3:* 609; *4:* 650

Barker, Danny, *4:* 678
Barnard, James, *4:* 706
Barnett, Camille C., *5:* 12
Barnett, Charlie, *2:* 358
Barnett, Ida B. Wells, *1:* **40–43,** 41 (ill.); *6:* 106–7
Barnett, Marguerite Ross, *1:* **43–45,** 44 (ill.)
Barrow, Joseph Louis. *See* Louis, Joe
Barry, Marion, *1:* **45–47,** 47 (ill.); *2:* 330; *3:* 448; *5:* **9–12,** 9 (ill.), 182
Baryshnikov, Mikhail, *2:* 351
Baseball Hall of Fame, *1:* 116, *3:* 575, 626; *6:* 116
Basketball Hall of Fame, *1:* 67
Basie, Count, *1:* 28, **48–50,** 49 (ill.); *4:* 680
Bassett, Angela, *5:* 155, 167, 193, 217, 223–24
Bates, Daisy, *1:* **50–53,** 51 (ill.)
Battle, Kathleen, *1:* **53–55,** 54 (ill.)
Baumfree, Isabella, *4:* 728
Bearden, Romare, *6:* **21–29,** 21 (ill.)
Beastie Boys, *2:* 314
Beat cultural revolution, *1:* 38
Beatles, *1:* 22; *2:* 337; *5:* 220, 223
Beatty, Warren, *5:* 15
Beauvoir, Simone de, *4:* 803
Beckham, William, *4:* 805
Beckwith, Byron de la, *2:* 236
Bedford, David, *4:* 790
Before Columbus Foundation, *3:* 616
Behind the Scenes, Or, Thirty Years a Slave and Four Years in the White House, *3:* 443

Belafonte, Harry, *1:* **55–58,** 56 (ill.); *5:* 48, 49
Beloved, *3:* 543
Belushi, Jim, *5:* 204
Belushi, John, *5:* 24
Ben Folds Five, *5:* 28
Benjamin Banneker Historical Park and Museum, *5:* 6
Bennett College, *4:* 654
Bennett, Ned, *4:* 743
Bennett, Rolla, *4:* 743
Bennett, Tony, *5:* 78
Benny Goodman Quartet, *2:* 316
Benson, George W., *4:* 729
Bensonhurst shooting, *4:* 666
Benton, Robert, *2:* 277
Berlin, Germany, *3:* 571
Berlin, Irving, *2:* 244; *5:* 78
Bernstein, Leonard, *4:* 766, 768
Berry, Chu, *5:* 24
Berry, Chuck, *1:* **58–61,** 59 (ill.); *5:* 24, 222
Berry, Halle, *1:* **61–63,** 62 (ill.); *5:* **13–16,** 13 (ill.), 47, 52
Berry Park, *1:* 60
Bethune-Cookman College, *1:* 64
Bethune, Mary McLeod, *1:* 43, **63–65,** 63 (ill.); *2:* 334
The Beulah Show, *3:* 517
Beverly Hills Cop, *3:* 554
"Bhahiana," *1:* 216
Biafra, Jello, *2:* 372
Bicentennial Nigger, *3:* 598
Bing, Dave, *1:* **65–67,** 66 (ill.)
Bird, Daniel W., Jr., *4:* 775
Bird, Larry, *2:* 400–401; *5:* 128
Birmingham Barons, *5:* 141
Birmingham Black Barons, *3:* 510

Birth of a Nation, *5:* 166
Bizet, Georges, *5:* 49
Black America's Political Action Committee (BAMPAC), *5:* 154
Black Arts Movement, *1:* 37
Black Arts Repertory Theater School, *1:* 39
Black Boy, *4:* 802–3
Black History Month, *4:* 800
Black Horizons Theater Company, *4:* 791
Black Judgement, *2:* 272
"Black" language, *4:* 651
Black Magic, *1:* 156
Black Muslims, *4:* 650; *5:* 72
The Black Muslims in America, *3:* 550
Black nationalism, *1:* 39, 119; *2:* 256, 374
Black Panthers, *1:* 100, 119, 120, 143–46, 182; *3:* 560, 561, 562; *4:* 657–59; *5:* 199; *6:* 45, 47, 57, 58, 59, 69, 193, 195, 196, 196 (ill.)
Black Patti. *See* Jones, Sissieretta
Black Patti's Troubadors, *2:* 421
Black Periodical Literature Project, *2:* 262
Black Power: The Politics of Liberation in America, *1:* 120
Black Press Hall of Fame, *2:* 406
Black Street Hawkeyes, *2:* 279–80
Black Student Alliance (BSA), *4:* 701
Black supremacy, *5:* 73
Black Thunder, *1:* 75
Black Wings, *1:* 160
Black Writers Conference, *1:* 88
The Blackboard Jungle, *3:* 582

Blackburn, Jack, *3:* 479
Blacklock, Jimmy, *2:* 320
Blacks in America: With All Deliberate Speed, 1: 79
Blackthink, 3: 572
Blood, *1:* 207, 208
Bloodchild, 1: 109
Bloom, Allan, *5:* 148
Blouis, James, *4:* 705
Blow, Kurtis, *2:* 371
The Blues Brothers, 1: 113; *5:* 24
The Bluest Eye, 3: 542
Bluford, Guy, *5:* 159
Boghetti, Giuseppe, *1:* 15
Bogle, Donald, *2:* 278
Bolling v. Sharpe, 6: 134–35
Bond, Julian, *1:* **67–71,** 68 (ill.); *6:* **31–35,** 31 (ill.)
The Bonds: An American Family, 1: 69
Bonilla, Bobby, *1:* **71–73,** 72 (ill.)
Bontemps, Arna, *1:* **73–75,** 74 (ill.), 151, 180; *4:* 715
The Book of American Negro Poetry, 2: 405
Booker T. Washington (BTW) Burial Insurance Company, *2:* 259; *5:* 89;
Booker T. Washington (BTW) Business College, *2:* 260
Booker T. Washington (BTW) Insurance Company, *2:* 258
Books about Negro Life for Children, 1: 31; *6:* 10
Borg, Bjorn, *1:* 27
Bork, Robert, *4:* 669
Bosnia, *5:* 18
Boston Celtics, *2:* 401; *3:* 638, 639; *5:* 128
Boukmann, *4:* 719
Bowe, Riddick, *1:* **75–78,** 76 (ill.)
Boycotts, *3:* 455, 457, 482, 579, 612, 641

"The Boys of Summer," *1:* 115
Boyz N the Hood, 4: 675–76
Bradley, Ed, *1:* **78–80,** 80 (ill.)
Bradshaw, Terry, *5:* 111
Braugher, Andre, *5:* 229, 230
Braun, Carol Moseley, *1:* **80–83,** 82 (ill.)
Brawley, Tawana, *4:* 666
Breaking Barriers: A Memoir, 3: 634
Bridges, Richard, *4:* 686
Briggs, Bunny, *2:* 351
Bring the Pain, 5: 180
Broadside Press, *3:* 607, 608
Broadus, Doc, *5:* 82, 83
Brontë, Emily, *5:* 67
Brooke, Edward W., III, *1:* **83–85,** 84 (ill.)
Brooklyn Dodgers, *1:* 114; *3:* 625
Brooks, Gwendolyn, *1:* **86–88,** 87 (ill.); *3:* 609, 629
Brother Ray, 1: 130
Brotherhood of Sleeping Car Porters, *3:* 611
Brown, Bobby, *2:* 362
Brown, Claude, *1:* **88–91,** 90 (ill.)
Brown Girl, Brownstones, 3: 502
Brown, H. Rap, *1:* **91–93,** 92 (ill.); *3:* 449
Brown, James, *1:* **93–95,** 94 (ill.), 169; *2:* 312; *4:* 665
Brown, Jim, *5:* 82
Brown, Ron, *1:* **95–99,** 98 (ill.); *5:* **17–22,** 17 (ill.), 19 (ill.), 116
Brown, Tracey, *5:* 19
Brown v. Board of Education, 3: 504, 505, 545, 633; *4:* 777
Bryant, William Cullen, *5:* 35
Buchanan, James, *4:* 653

Buckley, Tom, *4:* 807
Buffalo Bills, *5:* 208–9
Bugs Bunny, *5:* 141, 142 (ill.)
Bullins, Ed, *1:* **99–101,** 100 (ill.)
Bullock, Anna Mae, *5:* 218
Bumbry, Grace, *1:* **101–4,** 103 (ill.)
Bunche, Ralph, *1:* **104–6,** 105 (ill.)
Burke, Yvonne Brathwaite, *1:* **106–9,** 108 (ill.)
Burns, Kephera, *4:* 704
"Burrell House," *1:* 216
Burrell, Stanley, *2:* 312
Burrill, Mamie, *2:* 293
Burroughs, James, *4:* 758
Bus boycotts, *1:* 7; *5:* 250
Busby, Jheryl, *5:* 130
Bush, George, *2:* 356, 402; *4:* 671, 710, 712, 713, 805; *5:* 18, 128, 172, 173, 174
Bush, George W., *5:* 175
Butler, Octavia E., *1:* **109–11,** 110 (ill.)
Butterfly Ballet, 3: 526

C

"Cablinasian," *5:* 244
Caldwell, Erskine, *5:* 97
California General Assembly, *1:* 107, 108
California State University, *1:* 148
Call & Post, 3: 540
Callahan, John F., *5:* 68–69
Callahan, Tom, *5:* 246
Callender, Clive O., *6:* **37–43,** 37 (ill.)
Calloway, Cab, *1:* **111–14,** 113 (ill.); *5:* **23–25,** 23 (ill.)
Calloway, Nuffie, *5:* 25
Campaign for Nuclear Disarmament, *3:* 641

Campanella, Roy, *1:* **114–16,** 115 (ill.)
Campbell, Naomi, *1:* **116–18,** 117 (ill.)
Cancer research, *1:* 148
Cane, 4: 713, 715–16
Cantor, Mickey, *5:* 19
Capitol Records, *1:* 157
Carbon filaments, *6:* 151
The Caribbean Poetry of Derek Walcott and the Art of Romare Bearden, 6: 28
Carlucci, Frank, *5:* 172
Carmen Jones, 5: 49, 52
Carmichael, Stokely, *1:* **118–21,** 120 (ill.); *6:* **45–49,** 45 (ill.)
Carnegie, Andrew, *4:* 760
Carnegie Hall, *1:* 102, 155; *2:* 270; *3:* 453
Carson, Benjamin, *1:* **121–24,** 122 (ill.)
Carson, Johnny, *2:* 304–5, 306
Carter, Art, *5:* 227–28
Carter, Greg, *5:* 99
Carter, Jimmy, *1:* 70; *2:* 329, 392, 432; *4:* 656, 805; *5:* 116, 135, 174, 249, 251
Cartwright, Marguerite, *4:* 649
Carver Club, *1:* 198
Carver, George Washington, *1:* 75, **124–27,** 124 (ill.); *4:* 760
Casey, Robert P., *4:* 693
Castro, Fidel, *1:* 145, 2: 381
Catherine Carmier, 4: 254
Catholic Church, *4:* 683–86
CBS Radio, *1:* 79
CBS Sports, *5:* 111, 112, 113
CBS This Morning, 5: 111
CBS-TV, *1:* 79
Center for the Study of Urban Inequality, *6:* 228–29
Challenge of Change, 1: 85

Challenger Center for Space Science Exploration, *5:* 163
Challenger (space shuttle), *2:* 396; *5:* 159, 162, 163
Chamberlain, Wilt, *1:* 5, **127–29,** 127 (ill.); *3:* 639; *5:* 143
Chambre Syndicale du Prêt-à-Porter, *3:* 445
Chapin, Katherine Garrison, *4:* 691
Chapman, Tracy, *5:* 223
Charles, Ray, *1:* **130–32,** 131 (ill.); *2:* 417; *5:* 24
Charleston, South Carolina, *4:* 742–44
Chase, Richard, *4:* 717
Chattanooga Lookouts, *3:* 573
Chavis, Benjamin, *5:* 73
Chesnutt, Charles Waddell, *1:* **132–35,** 133 (ill.)
Chicago Bulls, *2:* 427, 428–29; *5:* 140–41
Chicago Business Hall of Fame, *2:* 406
Chicago Conservator, 1: 42
Chicago Defender, 6: 1, 3, 4, 6, 7, 22
"Chicago Eight," *4:* 658
Chicago, Illinois, *5:* 124–25, 140
Chicago White Sox, *5:* 141
Chiffons, *5:* 219
The Children of Ham, 1: 89, 90
Children's Defense Fund (CDF), *2:* 223, 224
Childress, Alice, *1:* **135–38,** 136 (ill.); *5:* **27–29,** 27 (ill.)
Chisholm, Shirley, *1:* **138–40,** 139 (ill.); *6:* **51–55,** 51 (ill.)
Chopin, Frédéric, *4:* 766
The Chosen Place, the Timeless People, 3: 502

Christophe, Henri, *4:* 720–21
Chuckie D, *3:* 599–602; *5:* 201
Church of the Advocate, *2:* 324
Cinque, *5:* **31–40,** 31 (ill.), 33 (ill.)
Citadel (magazine), *1:* 100
Citizens Against Government Waste, *5:* 153
Citizens Federal Savings Bank, *2:* 258
Civil Rights Act (1964), *3:* 578
Civil Rights movement, *5:* 37, 63, 151
Civil War, *5:* 60, 151, 166; *6:* 122
Claessen, David, *2:* 281
Clapton, Eric, *5:* 223
Clara's Ole Man, 1: *100*
Clark, Dick, *1:* 168, 169
Clark, Joe, *1:* **140–43,** 141 (ill.)
Clark, John L., *4:* 695
Clark, Marcia, *5:* 211
Clark, Ramsey, *4:* 808
Clay, Cassius. *See* Ali, Muhammad
Clay's Ark, 1: 111
Clayton, E., *4:* 648
Cleaver, Eldridge, *1:* 37, 120, **143–46,** 144 (ill.); *3:* 561; *6:* **57–61,** 57 (ill.)
Clements, George, *1:* **146–48;** 147 (ill.)
Cleveland Call, 3: 538, 540
Cleveland Job Corps Center for Women, *5:* 94–95
Clinton, Bill, *1:* 5, 20, 96, 200; *3:* 567, 589; *5:* 17, 18, 19, 20, 21, 71, 79, 101, 106, 107, 115, 117–18, 134, 136, 148, 172–73, 174, 181; *6:* 51, 55, 85, 88, 143, 146, 217, 218, 227, 228
Clinton, George, *5:* 223

Clinton, Hillary Rodham, *5:* 64, 118
Cobb, Jewel Plummer, *1:* **148–50,** 149 (ill.)
Cochran, Johnnie, *5:* 211, 211 (ill.), 213
Cole, Johnnetta Betsch, *1:* 150, **151–53,** 151 (ill.)
Cole, Nat "King," *1:* **153–55,** 154 (ill.)
Cole, Natalie, *1:* **155–58,** 157 (ill.)
Coleman, Bessie, *1:* **158–60,** 159 (ill.)
Coleman, J. Marshall, *4:* 776
Coleridge-Taylor, Samuel, *4:* 689
Collier, Aldore, *2:* 377
Collins, Marva, *1:* **160–63,** 162 (ill.)
The Colonel's Dream, 1: 135
Color, 1: 179
Color Me Flo: My Hard Life and Good Times, 3: 448
The Color Purple, 2: 277–78, 280, 281; *4:* 749
Coltrane, John, *1:* **163–65,** 164 (ill.), 187; *3:* 495, 535
Columbia Records, *2:* 246, 383
Columbus, Christopher, *5:* 36
Combs, Sean "Puff Daddy," *5:* 180, 203, 222, 223
Comedy Central, *5:* 180
Comic Relief, *2:* 281
Commission on Immigration Reform (CIR), *5:* 135–36
Committee on Fair Employment Practice, *3:* 640; *6:* 134
Committee on Un-American Activities, *3:* 620; *4:* 804
Committee to Support South African Resistance, *3:* 641
Communism, *3:* 623

Communist Party, *1:* 182; *4:* 801; *6:* 173
Community Relations Commission (CRC), *5:* 251
Compton, Malaak, *5:* 177
Con Funk Shun, *2:* 313
Congress of African Peoples, *1:* 40; *3:* 538
Congress of Racial Equality (CORE), *1:* 119; *2:* 237, 238, 291, 374, 375, 376, 380; *3:* 520, 521, 522, 556, 640; *4:* 686
Congressional Gold Medal, *3:* 573
Conjure, 3: 617
The Conjure Woman, 1: 134
Connie's Hot Chocolates, 1: 112
Connors, Jimmy, *1:* 27
"Conservative," *5:* 150–51
Constitution, *4:* 653, 654; *5:* 38
Content, Marjorie, *4:* 715
Contraception, *6:* 85, 86
Cookman Institute, *1:* 64
Cooney, Gerry, *5:* 85
Cooper, Anna J., *1:* **165–67,** 167 (ill.)
Cooper, Samuel, *4:* 773
Coppola, Francis Ford, *2:* 350
Cornelius, Don, *1:* **168–70,** 169 (ill.)
Cornell University, *5:* 148
Cornish, James, *4:* 781
Cosby, Bill, *1:* **170–73,** 172 (ill.), 188; *3:* 597; *5:* 25, **41–45,** 41 (ill.), 64
Cosby, Camille, *5:* 41, 42–43, 64
Cosby, Ennis, *5:* 41, 43, 44
The Cosby Show, 1: 171, 173; *5:* 42
Cosmetics, *4:* 674
Cosmopolitan, 1: 116
Cotten, Elizabeth, *1:* **173–75,** 174 (ill.)

"Cotten style," *1:* 173, 174
Cotton Club, *1:* 112; *2:* 228, 357; *5:* 48
"Cotton picking," *1:* 174
Council of Planned Parenthood Federation of America (PPFA), *4:* 763, 764–66
Council on African Affairs, *3:* 620
Counter, S. Allen, *2:* 341
Cowlings, Al, *5:* 210
Craft, Ellen, *1:* **175–78,** 177 (ill.)
Crawford, Cindy, *5:* 15
Creedence Clearwater Revival, *5:* 217
Creole Jazz Band, *1:* 21
Crisis, 1: 210, 212
Croatia, *5:* 17, 18
Crown Heights riots, *1:* 200
Crystal, Billy, *2:* 351
Cuba, *5:* 32
Cullen, Countee, *1:* 74, **178–80,** 179 (ill.)
Curtis, Lemuel R., *5:* 227

D

Da Gama, Vasco, *5:* 36
Dafoe, Willem, *2:* 351
Daily American, 2: 403
Daley, Richard, *4:* 649
Daley, William, *5:* 19, 20
Dandridge, Dorothy, *5:* 15, **47–52,** 47 (ill.), 50 (ill.), 167
Danforth, John, *4:* 711
Dante, Madam, *4:* 756
Darden, Christopher, *5:* 212
Daughters of the American Revolution (DAR), *1:* 16; *3:* 585
Dau Tranh, 6: 190
Davies, Roger, *5:* 221–22
Davis, Angela, *1:* **180–83,** 181 (ill.), 193

Davis, Benjamin, *5:* 225, 228, 229, 230–31
Davis, Benjamin O., Sr., *1:* **183–86,** 185 (ill.)
Davis, Clive, *2:* 361
Davis Cup, *1:* 26
Davis, Mike, *2:* 313
Davis, Miles, *1:* 164, **186–88,** 187 (ill.); *3:* 495; *4:* 662
Davis, Nelson, *4:* 733
Davis, Ossie, *1:* **188–91,** 190 (ill.); *6:* 63, 66, 67, 68
Davis, Sammy, Jr., *1:* **191–93,** 192 (ill.); *2:* 351; *5:* 50 (ill.)
Dawes, Dominique, *5:* **53–57,** 53 (ill.), 55 (ill.)
Dawson, William, *4:* 649
A Day Late and a Dollar Short, *5:* 157
"Day of Atonement," *5:* 76
Dayton Tattler, *1:* 213
Daytona Normal and Industrial School for Negro Girls, *1:* 64
D. C. Organ Donor Program, *6:* 41
Dead Kennedys, *2:* 372
Death Row Records, *5:* 203
DeBarge, James, *2:* 377
Debow, Charles, *5:* 227
Declaration of Independence, *5:* 2, 4, 37
The Declining Significance of Race: Blacks and Changing American Institutions, *6:* 224–25
Dee, Ruby, *6:* **63–71,** 63 (ill.), 65 (ill.)
Def Jam, *3:* 600
Delany Sisters (Sadie and Bessie), *5:* **59–65,** 59 (ill.)
Delgado Museum, *2:* 367
Delta Sigma Theta, *2:* 334
Demery, Larry, *5:* 141

Democratic National Committee (DNC), *1:* 96, 97; *5:* 17, 18, 117
Democratic National Convention (1984 and 1988), *6:* 140
Democratic Party, *1:* 70, 108; *2:* 381; *3:* 445; *4:* 658; *5:* 108, 134, 150–51
DeNiro, Robert, *2:* 362
Denison, Jack, *5:* 51
Department of Peace, *5:* 6
Derricotte, Juliette, *1:* **193–96,** 194 (ill.)
Desert Shield/Storm, *3:* 586, 588, 589; *5:* 172
Dessa Rose, *4:* 789
Dessalines, Jean Jacques, *4:* 721
Detroit, Michigan, *2:* 286; *3:* 607; *4:* 803–6
Detroit Pistons, *2:* 314
Devine, Loretta, *5:* 155
Dexter Avenue Baptist Church, *3:* 457
Dickens, Charles, *5:* 235
Die Nigger Die!, *1:* 91, 92
Diggs, Irene, *1:* **196–98**
Digital Underground (DU), *5:* 200
Dillard, Annie, *4:* 687
Dinkins, David, *1:* 97, **198–200,** 199 (ill.); *2:* 376; *5:* 18
Dire Straits, *5:* 222
Disabled children, *2:* 298
Disappearing Acts, *3:* 522, 524; *5:* 156, 158, 524
Distinguished Services Award, *6:* 12
District of Columbia. *See* Washington, D.C.
Dixie Fliers, *1:* 33
Dixson, Joyce, *6:* **73–79,** 73 (ill.)
Do the Right Thing, *3:* 470; *6:* 159
Dole, Bob, *5:* 154, 173
Domino, Fats, *5:* 222

Donahue, Phil, *4:* 794
Dorsey, Thomas A., *1:* **201–04,** 202 (ill.); *2:* 383
Dostoevski, Fedor, *4:* 687
Douglas, Michael, *2:* 402
Douglass, Frederick, *1:* 42, 75, 135, 181, **204–7,** 205 (ill.), 214; *4:* 653–54, 688, 729, 779, 781
Drayton, William, *3:* 600
"Dream Team," *6:* 230
Dred Scott v. John Sanford, *4:* 653
Drew, Charles Richard, *1:* **207–9,** 208 (ill.)
Drug treatment programs, *2:* 251
Du Bois, William Edward Burgardt (W. E. B.), *1:* 190, 196, **209–12,** 211 (ill.); *2:* 257; *3:* 561, 610; *4:* 662, 724, 726, 777, 800
Dugan, Alan, *4:* 783
Dukakis, Michael, *2:* 382; *5:* 18, 123
Duke, David, *3:* 530
Dumont, John J., *4:* 728
Dunbar, Paul Laurence, *1:* 86, 180, **212–15,** 215 (ill.)
Dunham, Katherine, *1:* **215–17,** 216 (ill.)
Durocher, Leo, *3:* 511
Dutchman, 1: 39
Duvalier, Jean-Claude "Baby Doc," *5:* 18
Dylan, Bob, *2:* 411
"Dynamite Hill," *1:* 181

E

Eakins, Thomas, *4:* 697
Earl, Nancy, *5:* 134
Eastwood, Clint, *4:* 738, 739
Ebony magazine, *2:* 405, *2:* 407; *4:* 649

Ebony Man magazine, *2:* 408
Eckford, Elizabeth, *1:* 52
Eckstine, Billy, *4:* 740–41
Economic Regulatory Administration, *3:* 566
Edelman, Marian Wright, *2:* **223–25,** 225 (ill.)
Edison General Electric Company, *6:* 152
Edison Pioneers, *6:* 154
Edison, Thomas Alva, *6:* 149, 151, 152, 153 (ill.)
Edwards, Eli. *See* McKay, Claude
Eisenhower, Dwight D., *1:* 17, 52, 183; *2:* 265; *5:* 94
Elder, Lee, *5:* 245
Elders, Joycelyn, *6:* **81–90,** 81 (ill.), 87 (ill.)
Eldridge, Elleanor, 225–27
The Electronic Nigger, 1: 100
Eley, LeRoy, *5:* 229
Eliot, T. S., *5:* 67–68
Elizabeth, Queen, *1:* 16
Elle, 1: 116
Ellicott, Andrew, *5:* 4
Ellington, Duke, *1:* 112; *2:* **227–30,** 229 (ill.)
Ellington, Mercer, *2:* 228
Ellis, Effie O'Neal, *2:* **230–32,** 231 (ill.)
Ellison, Ralph, *2:* **232–34,** 233 (ill.); *4:* 716, 790, 800; *5:* 66, **67–70,** 67 (ill.), 99
Elma Lewis School of Fine Arts, *3:* 473, 474, 475
Emerson, John, *4:* 652
The Emperor Jones, 3: 622
ENABLE (Education and Neighborhood Action for a Better Living Environment), *2:* 390
Endeavour (space shuttle), *2:* 394, 397
Episcopal Church, *2:* 323, 324; *3:* 557

Equal Employment Opportunity Commission (EEOC), *2:* 341, 342; *4:* 711–12
Erwiah, Alex, *4:* 674
Eskimos, *2:* 339–40
ESPN (Entertainment and Sports Programming Network), *5:* 111
Essence magazine, *4:* 702–4
Ethiopian Orthodox Church of North and South America, *3:* 538
Evans, Robert, *2:* 350
Evening Shade, 1: 188
Evers, Medgar, *2:* **234–36,** 236 (ill.); *4:* 668; *5:* 195; *6:* 203, 207
Evers-Williams, Myrlie, *2:* 236; *4:* 668; *5:* 195
"Executive Order 8802," *3:* 612
Experimental Black Actors Guild, *4:* 722

F

Fagan, Eleanora. *See* Holiday, Billie
Faggs-Starr, Mae, *5:* 187
Fair Deal (production company), *1:* 94
Fair Employment Practice Committee, *3:* 612
The Family, 6: 26 (ill.)
Fard, Wallace D., *3:* 549
Farley, Chris, *5:* 183
Farmer, James, *2:* **237–39,** 238 (ill.); *3:* 522; *4:* 807; *6:* 53
Farrakhan, Louis, *2:* **239–42,** 241 (ill.); *3:* 549; *5:* 21, 37, **71–76,** 71 (ill.), 74 (ill.), 151, 193–94, 254
Farrell, Perry, *2:* 374
Fat Albert and the Cosby Kids, 5: 42

Father Divine, *6:* **91–99,** 91 (ill.), 94 (ill.)
Federal Bureau of Investigation (FBI), *1:* 92, 144, 182; *2:* 236; *6:* 193, 196, 197
Federal Committee on Fair Employment Practices, *1:* 65
Federal Communications Commission (FCC), *2:* 355
Federal Energy Administration, *3:* 566
Fellowship of Reconciliation, *3:* 640
Feminist Party, *3:* 449
Fenger, Christian, *4:* 781
Ferraro, Geraldine, *5:* 135
Field, Sally, *2:* 277
Fields, Freddie, *4:* 786
Findlay, Michael, *4:* 674
Finley, Charley, *2:* 312–13
The Fire Next Time, 1: 37
First African Methodist Episcopal Church, *3:* 507, 509
First World Festival of Negro Art, *1:* 217
Fishburne, Laurence, *5:* 217, 223, 225, 230
Fisher, Orpheus, *1:* 17
Fisk University, *1:* 193, 196
Fitzgerald, Ella, *1:* 156; *2:* **242–45,** 244 (ill.), 245; *4:* 740; *5:* **77–80,** 77 (ill.)
The Five Heartbeats, 4: 723–24
Flash Photography, 3: 577
Flavor Flav, *3:* 600
Fleisher, Leon, *4:* 768
Fletcher Henderson Band, *1:* 21
Floating Bear, 1: 39
Florence Griffith Joyner Youth Foundation, *5:* 107
Floyd, John, *4:* 736
Fokker airplane, *1:* 159
Folger, Ben, *4:* 729

Folies Bergère, *1:* 33
Folklore, *2:* 310, 368; *3:* 541
For Colored Girls Who Have Considered Suicide/When the Rainbow Is Enuf, *4:* 662, 663–64
For Malcolm: Poems on the Life and Death of Malcolm X, *3:* 609
Forbes, George Washington, *4:* 725
Ford, Gerald, *4:* 656, *5:* 174
Ford, Henry, II, *4:* 807
Ford-Taylor, Margaret, *5:* 95
Foreman, George, *1:* 13; *5:* **81–88**, 81 (ill.), 83 (ill.)
Forrester, William T., *4:* 754
Fortune, T. Thomas, *6:* **101–9**, 101 (ill.)
48 Hours, *3:* 554
Foster, Greg, *5:* 103
Foster, Vincent, *5:* 21
Four Little Girls, *6:* 161
Fox Sports, *5:* 113
Fox Television Network, *4:* 769
Fox, Vivica, *5:* 182
Franklin, Aretha, *1:* 169, 201; *2:* **245–47**, 246 (ill.), 360; *4:* 793; *5:* 222
Franklin, John Hope, *2:* **247–50**, 248 (ill.)
Frazier, Joe, *1:* 13; *5:* 81, 84
Free D.C. Movement, *1:* 46
The Free-Lance Pallbearers, *3:* 617
Free Speech, *1:* 40, 41
Free Speech and Headlight, *1:* 41
Freedman's Hospital, *4:* 781
Freedom, *2:* 317
Freedom Farm, *2:* 308
Freedom from Religion Foundation, *5:* 168
Freedom rides, *2:* 237, 238; *3:* 641
Freedom Singers, *6:* 179–80
Freeman Field, *5:* 229, 231

Freeman, Morgan, *1:* 142; *5:* 39
"Freight Train," *1:* 173
Frelinghuysen University, *1:* 167
French Resistance, *1:* 34
French Revolution, *4:* 719
Friedan, Betty, *2:* 342; *3:* 557
Frost, Robert, *4:* 791
Fruit of Islam, *2:* 240
Fugard, Athol, *2:* 277
Fugitive Slave Law *1:* 177; *4:* 733
Fuhrman, Mark, *5:* 212, 213
Futrell, Mary Hatwood, *2:* **250–53**, 252 (ill.)

G

G.A. Morgan Hair Refining Cream, *3:* 539
Gagarin, Yuri, *5:* 160
Gaines, Ernest J., *2:* **253–55**, 254 (ill.)
Gandhi, Mohandas K., *1:* 126; *5:* 250
"Gangsta rap," *5:* 197–204
Garland, William, *5:* 199, 204
Garrison, William Lloyd, *1:* 205, 206; *4:* 729
Garry, Charles, *4:* 658
Garvey, Marcus, *2:* **255–58**, 257 (ill.); *3:* 474, 536, 611; *6:* 96, 97, 97 (ill.), 102, 171, 172
Gas mask, *3:* 538, 539
Gass, William, *4:* 687
Gaston, Arthur, *2:* **258–61**, 259 (ill.); *5:* **89–92**, 89 (ill.)
Gates, Henry Louis, Jr., *2:* **261–63**, 262 (ill.)
Gaye, Marvin, *2:* 378
Gee, Jack, *4:* 679–80
George, Clayborne, *5:* 94
George VI, King, *1:* 16

George, Zelma Watson, *2:* **263–66**, 265 (ill.); *5:* **93–95**, 93 (ill.)
Georgia Democratic Party Forum, *6:* 33
Georgia Georgia, *1:* 19
Georgia Music Hall of Fame, *1:* 204
"Georgia on My Mind," *1:* 132
Get on the Bus, *6:* 160
Giant Steps, *1:* 5
Gibbs, Marla, *4:* 661
Gibson, Althea, *2:* **266–68**, 267 (ill.); *5:* 236
Gibson, Josh, *6:* **111–17**, 111 (ill.)
Gibson, Mel, *2:* 278; *5:* 177, 221 (ill.), 222
Gilbert, Olive, *4:* 729
Gillespie, Dizzy, *1:* 186; *2:* **268–71**, 270 (ill.), 417; *3:* 495; *4:* 662, 741; *5:* 24
Gimelstob, Justin, *5:* 237
Giovanni, Nikki, *2:* **271–73**, 273 (ill.)
Girl Scouts, *4:* 654–57
Giuliani, Rudolph W., *1:* 199, 200
Givens, Robin, *2:* **273–76**, 275 (ill.)
Glamour magazine, *2:* 397, 398
Glenn, John, *5:* 160
Glover, Danny, *1:* 188; *2:* **276–78**, 277 (ill.); *5:* 177
Glover v. Johnson, *6:* 76
Go Tell It on the Mountain, *1:* 36
Goldberg, Whoopi, *2:* 277, **278–81**, 280 (ill.); *5:* 182
Golden Lynx, *1:* 30
Goldman, Ronald, *5:* 207, 210, 212
Gone with the Wind, *3:* 515, 525, 526, 527; *5:* 165, 166–67, 168
Goode, W. Wilson, *2:* **281–84**, 282 (ill.)

Gooding, Cuba, *5:* 230
Goodman, Benny, *2:* 316; *4:* 680
Goodwill Games, *2:* 434
Gordon, Franklin, *4:* 764, 765
Gordone, Charles, *2:* **284–86,** 285 (ill.); *5:* **97–99,** 97 (ill.)
Gordy, Berry, Jr., *2:* **286–89,** 287 (ill.); *3:* 630
Gospel Music Association, *1:* 204
Gould, Glenn, *4:* 767–68
Grabeau, *5:* 33
Grand Negro Jubilee, *2:* 420
Grand Ole Opry, *3:* 594
Grant, Ulysses S., *4:* 730
Graphite lubricator, *6:* 167–68
Gray, Thomas, *4:* 736
Grazybowska, Magdalena, *5:* 235
Great Depression, *5:* 61; *6:* 14, 91
The Greatest: My Own Story, 1: 13
Greece, *5:* 36
Green, Charlie, *4:* 679
Green, Daniel, *5:* 141
Green, Mrs. Charles, *4:* 706
Gregory, Dick, *1:* 77; *2:* **289–91,** 290 (ill.); *3:* 597; *5:* 21
Grenada, *5:* 172
Grier, Rosie, *5:* 214
Griffin, Merv, *2:* 305
Griffith, D. W., *5:* 166
Griffith Joyner, Florence, *2:* 434; *5:* **101–8,** 101 (ill.), 105 (ill.)
Grimké, Angelina Weld, *2:* **291–94,** 293 (ill.)
Grimké, Archibald, *2:* 292
Grimké, Sarah, *2:* 292
"A Guide to Negro Music," *2:* 265

Gulf War, *5:* 18, 172. *See also* Operation Desert Shield/Storm
Gullah Jack, *4:* 743
Gumbel, Bryant, *2:* **294–96,** 295 (ill.); *5:* 109, 110
Gumbel, Greg, *5:* **109–13,** 109 (ill.), 112 (ill.)
Gunning, Lucille C., *2:* **297–99,** 297 (ill.)
Gurdjieff, George I., *4:* 715
Guyton, Eugene, *5:* 231

H

Hair straightener, *3:* 538
Hajj, *5:* 192, 193
Hale, Clara, *2:* 299–301, **300 (ill.)**
Hale House, *2:* 299, 301
Hale, Teddy, *2:* 349
Haley, Alex, *1:* 62; *2:* **301–4,** 303 (ill.)
Hall, Arsenio, *2:* **304–6,** 305 (ill.); *4:* 770; *5:* 179
Hall, Charles B., *5:* 227
Halley's comet, *5:* 62, 162
Hamer, Fannie Lou, *2:* **307–9,** 308 (ill.); *6:* 18
Hamilton, Virginia, *2:* **309–12,** 311 (ill.)
Hammer, *2:* **312–14,** 313 (ill.)
Hammond, John, *4:* 677, 680
Hampton, Lionel, *2:* **314–17,** 316 (ill.); *4:* 680
Hancock, Herbie, *5:* 14
Handy, W. C., *4:* 690
Hansberry, Lorraine, *2:* **317–19,** 318 (ill.)
A Hard Road to Glory, 1: 27
Hard Stuff: The Autobiography of Mayor Coleman Young, 6: 236
Hardy, Thomas, *5:* 67

Harlem Art Workshop, *3:* 465
Harlem Globetrotters, *1:* 127, 128; *2:* **320–22,** 322 (ill.)
Harlem Renaissance, *1:* 73, 74, 178; *2:* 294, 362, 370; *4:* 713, 715
Harlem riots (1964), *3:* 641
Harlem Writers Guild, *3:* 523
Harper, Frances Ellen Watkins, *6:* **119–25,** 119 (ill.)
Harpo Productions, *4:* 795
Harriet Tubman Association, *3:* 537
Harriet Tubman Society, *1:* 139; *6:* 52
Harris, Barbara, *2:* **323–25,** 324 (ill.)
Harris, Frank, *3:* 519
Harris, Joel Chandler, *4:* 718
Harris, Marcelite J., *2:* **325–28,** 327 (ill.)
Harris, Patricia, 328–30, 328 (ill.)
Harrison, William Henry, *5:* 38
Hart, Moss, *5:* 97
Hartman, Phil, *5:* 183
Hartzell, Joseph, *4:* 697
Harvard Law Review, 6: 128
Hatch, Orrin G., *4:* 669
Havens, Richie, *5:* 223
Hawkins, Yusef, *1:* 200
Hayden, Robert, Jr., *2:* **330–33,** 331 (ill.); *3:* 609
Hayes, Lester, *5:* 82
Haynes, Marques, *2:* 320
Hearth, Amy Hill, *5:* 59, 62, 63–64
Heavy D and the Boyz, *2:* 314
He Got Game, 6: 160–61
Height, Dorothy, *2:* **333–35,** 334 (ill.)
Heisman Trophy, *5:* 208

Hello Dolly!, *1:* 22, 29
Helms, Jesse, *3:* 530
Hemingway, Ernest, *4:* 687, 700; *5:* 98
Hendrix, Jimi, *2:* **336–38,** 336 (ill.); *5:* 223
Henson, Matthew, *2:* **338–41,** 340 (ill.)
Here I Stand, 3: 622
Herman, Alexis, *5:* **115–19,** 115 (ill.), 117 (ill.)
Hernandez, Aileen, *2:* **341–43,** 343 (ill.)
A Hero Ain't Nothin' but a Sandwich, 1: 137
"Hero of the 80s," *3:* 596
Hertz Rental Car Agency, *5:* 209
Hewitt, Don, *1:* 79
"Hi-De-Ho Man," *5:* 24
Hickey, James A., *4:* 684
Hill, Anita, *1:* 81; *2:* **344–46,** 344 (ill.); *3:* 618; *4:* 710, 712–13
Hill, Kelli, *5:* 54
Hill, Raymond, *5:* 218
Himes, Chester, *2:* **346–49,** 347 (ill.)
Hines, Earl, *4:* 740
Hines, Gregory, *2:* **349–51,** 350 (ill.)
Hines, Maurice, *2:* 349, 350
Hingis, Martina, *5:* 237
Hitler, Adolf, *2:* 240; *3:* 480, 571; *5:* 227
HIV, *2:* 400, 402; *5:* 129
Hobley, Billy Ray, *2:* 320
Hoffman, Julius, *4:* 658–59
Holiday, Billie, *2:* **351–54,** 352 (ill.); *3:* 449; *4:* 677
Hollywood Shuffle, 4: 723
Holy Angels Church (Chicago), *1:* 146, 148
Holy Ghost Boys, *2:* 313
Holyfield, Evander, *5:* 81, 86
Hooks, Benjamin L., *2:* **354–57,** 356 (ill.); *4:* 668, 688

Hoover, J. Edgar, *1:* 144
Hope, Bob, *1:* 62; *5:* 14, 240
Hopkins, Anthony, *5:* 39
Hopwood Award, *2:* 331
Horne, Lena, *1:* 189; *2:* **357–59,** 359 (ill.); *5:* 24
The Hotel Messenger, 3: 611
Hounsou, Djimon, *5:* 39
The House Behind the Cedars, 1: 135
House Un-American Activities Commitee (HUAC), *6:* 235
Housing segregation, *6:* 98
Houston, Charles Hamilton, *4:* 692; *6:* **127–36,** 127 (ill.), 135 (ill.)
Houston, Whitney, *2:* **359–62,** 360 (ill.); *5:* 52, 155, 167, 222
How Stella Got Her Groove Back, 5: 155, 157
Howard Beach shooting, *4:* 666
Howard University, *5:* 183
Howard University Law School, *6:* 129, 130, 131, 132
Howlin' Wolf, *5:* 223
Huang, John, *5:* 20
Hue magazine, *2:* 408
Hughes, Langston, *1:* 74, 86; *2:* 233, 331, **362–65,** 363 (ill.), 370; *3:* 629; *4:* 690–91, 748, 790; *5:* 68
Humphrey, Hubert, *5:* 186
Hunter, Clementine, *2:* **366–68,** 367 (ill.)
Hurok, Sol, *1:* 16
Hurston, Zora Neale, *2:* **368–71,** 369 (ill.); *3:* 558; *4:* 748
Hussein, Saddam, *5:* 172
Hybl, Bill, *5:* 107
Hyde, Henry, *5:* 125

I

"I Have a Dream" speech, *3:* 458; *5:* 73
I Have Changed, 3: 572
I Know Why the Caged Bird Sings, 1: 19
I Shall Not Be Moved, 1: 19
I Spy, 1: 171; *5:* 41, 42
Ibsen, Henrik, *4:* 714
Ice Cube, *2:* 371
Ice-T, *2:* **371–74,** 373 (ill.); *5:* 201
"If We Must Die," *3:* 517, 519
I'm Gonna Git You Sucka!, 4: 769
Imani Temple African American Catholic Congregation, *4:* 683, 684
Incandescent Electric Lighting: A Practical Description of the Edison System, 6: 152
Independent Old Catholic Church, *4:* 686
Independent Order of Saint Luke (IOSL), *4:* 753–54
Indiana State University *2:* 400; *5:* 128
Indianapolis Clowns Negro League, *1:* 1
In Living Color, 4: 769, 770, 771; *5:* 179
The Inner Circle, *2:* 316
Innis, Roy, *2:* **374–76,** 375 (ill.)
Interracial Ministerial Alliance, *1:* 52
Interracial romance, *5:* 49–50
Invisible Man, 2: 232, 233, 234; *5:* 67, 68
Iola Leroy; or, Shadows Uplifted, 6: 119, 121, 123
Iran, *5:* 75
Iraq, *5:* 75, 172
Isaac, Lorrain, *4:* 783
Islam, *1:* 4, 93; *3:* 489

Italy, *5:* 227
Ito, Lance, *5:* 212
It's My Party, 2: 417

J

Jackson, Autumn, *5:* 43–44
Jackson Five, *2:* 288, 377, 384–86
Jackson, Jacqueline, *5:* 122
Jackson, Janet, *2:* 362, **376–78;** 377 (ill.); *5:* 25, 52, 130, 197, 201
Jackson, Jermaine, *2:* 361
Jackson, Jesse, *1:* 96, 200, 240, 378, 380 (ill.), 432; *2:* **378–82;** *4:* 666–67, 712, 770, 778–79; *5:* 18, 71, 72–73, 116, 121, 124 (ill.), 149, 151, 153, 160, 182; *6:* **137–42,** 137 (ill.)
Jackson, Jesse, Jr., *5:* **121–26,** 121 (ill.), 124 (ill.)
Jackson, Mahalia, *1:* 203; *2:* **382–84,** 383 (ill.); *4:* 677
Jackson, Maynard, *5:* 253
Jackson, Michael, *1:* 93; *2:* 377, 378, **384–87,** 386 (ill.), 402, 418, 682
Jackson, Sandra, *5:* 123, 126
Jackson, Shirley Ann, *2:* **387–89,** 388 (ill.)
Jacob, John, *2:* **389–92,** 390 (ill.)
Jagger, Mick, *5:* 220, 223
James, Daniel, Jr., *2:* **392–94,** 393 (ill.)
James, Mark, *3:* 606
James, Rick, *2:* 314
James Weldon Johnson Memorial Collection, *6:* 10
Jane's Addiction, *2:* 374
Jarvis, Gregory B., *5:* 163
Jazz, 3: 543
Jazz Messengers, *3:* 496

Jefferson, Thomas, *1:* 83; *4:* 774; *5:* 1–2, 4–5, 150
Jemison, Mae C., *2:* **394–97,** 395 (ill.)
Jesse Owens National Youth Games, *5:* 102
Jesus of Nazareth, *1:* 145
Jet magazine, *2:* 405, 408
Jim Crow laws, *5:* 61; *6:* 104–5, 207
Jimmy Jam, *2:* 378
Job Corps, *5:* 82, 83, 87
Joe's Bed-Stuy Barbership: We Cut Heads, 3: 468
John XXIII, Pope, *3:* 636
Johns Hopkins Hospital, *1:* 122
Johnson, Alice, *4:* 781
Johnson, Beverly, *2:* **397–99,** 399 (ill.)
Johnson, Caryn, *2:* 279
Johnson, Earletha "Cookie," *2:* 402; *5:* 127, 128
Johnson, Earvin "Magic," *1:* 5; *2:* **400–402,** 401 (ill.); *5:* **127–32,** 127 (ill.), 131 (ill.)
Johnson Gospel Singers, *2:* 383
Johnson, James P., *4:* 679
Johnson, James Weldon, *2:* **402–5,** 403 (ill.)
Johnson, John H., *2:* **405–8,** 406 (ill.)
Johnson, Lyndon B., *1:* 91, 95, 108, 203; *2:* 329, 342; *3:* 546, 634; *4:* 693, 807, 808
Johnson, Marguerite. *See* Angelou, Maya
Johnson Publishing Company, *2:* 408
Johnson, Robert, *2:* **409–11,** 410 (ill.)
Johnston, Buddy, *5:* 231
Joint Chiefs of Staff, *3:* 586, 587; *5:* 172
Jones, Bill T., *2:* **411–13,** 412 (ill.)

Jones, Cheri, *4:* 723
Jones, Emil, *5:* 125
Jones, James Earl, *2:* **413–16,** 415 (ill.); *4:* 792
Jones, LeRoi. *See* Baraka, Amiri
Jones, Quincy, *2:* 385, 386, **416–19,** 418 (ill.); *4:* 794; *5:* 122
Jones, Sissieretta, *2:* **419–21,** 420 (ill.)
Jones, Williams Augustus, *4:* 667
Joplin, Scott, *2:* **421–24,** 422 (ill.)
Jordan, Barbara, *2:* **424–27,** 425 (ill.); *5:* **133–37,** 133 (ill.)
Jordan, James, *2:* 427, 430; *5:* 139, 141
Jordan, Louis, *5:* 24
Jordan, Michael, *2:* 274, **427–30,** 429 (ill.); *5:* **139–45,** 139 (ill.), 140 (ill.), 142 (ill.)
Jordan, Vernon E., Jr., *2:* 390, **430–32,** 431 (ill.); *6:* **143–48, 143 (ill.)**
Journal of Black Studies, 1: 23
"Journey of reconciliation," *3:* 521, 641
Joyner, Al, *5:* 103
Joyner-Kersee, Jackie, *2:* **432–35,** 434 (ill.); *5:* 106–7, 186
Judaism, *1:* 193
Judicial Watch, *5:* 21
Judson, Andrew T., *5:* 35
Juilliard School of Music, *3:* 590
Jungle Fever, 1: 62
Jungle Saints, 6: 189
Junior World Golf Championship, *5:* 240
Justice, David, *1:* 62, *5:* 13, 14–15

K

Kaddafi, Muammar, *2:* 240, 241; *5:* 75, 172
Kale (slave), *5:* 31, 37
Kane, William, *4:* 685
Katleman, Harris, *4:* 770
Keats, John, *1:* 179
Keckley, Elizabeth, *3:* **441–43,** 442 (ill.)
Kellogg, Clark, *5:* 112 (ill.)
Kelly, Patrick, *3:* **443–45,** 444 (ill.)
Kelly, Sharon Pratt, *3:* **445–48,** 447 (ill.); *5:* 11
Kennedy, Edward, *2:* 224; *5:* 18
Kennedy, Flo, *3:* **448–50,** 450 (ill.)
Kennedy, John F., *1:* 20, 49, 155; *3:* 458, 528, 529, 636; *4:* 660, 693, 807; *5:* 148, 150
Kennedy, Robert, *2:* 319
Kersee, Bobby, *2:* 433–34; *5:* 103, 104, 107
Keyes, Alan, *5:* 21, **147–54,** 147 (ill.), 149 (ill.)
Khan, Chaka, *2:* 360
Kindred, 1: 111
King, B. B., *3:* **451–53,** 453 (ill.); *5:* 218, 223
King, Coretta Scott, *3:* **453–56,** 455 (ill.), 457; *4:* 661; *5:* 190, 195
King David, 2: 316
"The Kingdom" *6:* 96
Kingdom of Dreams, 6: 189
King, Edward, *4:* 706
King, Lonnie, *6:* 32
King, Martin Luther, Jr., *1:* 5, 6, 17, 58, 61, 69, 91, 106, 118, 146, 193, 203; *2:* 260, 324, 355, 380; *3:* 454, **456–59,** 459 (ill.), 460, 482, 545, 580, 613, 641; *4:* 659, 661, 688, 711, 779, 798, 807; *5:* 61, 73, 90, 115–16, 121–22, 190, 195, 214, 249, 250–51; *6:* 15, 16, 137, 138, 139
King of Delta Blues Singers, 2: 411
King, Yolanda, *3:* **459–62,** 460 (ill.), 459; *4:* 659, 661
Kinte clan, *2:* 302, 303
Kirchwey, George, *4:* 647
Klein, David, *2:* 306
Knight, Marion "Suge," *5:* 203
Knock on Any Door, 3: 546, 547, 548, 549
Knopfler, Mark, *5:* 222
Koch, Edward I, *1:* 199
Kochiyama, Yuri, *5:* 195
Koenigswarter, Baroness de, *3:* 535
Korean War, *2:* 393
Koslow, Pamela, *2:* 350
Kournikova, Anna, *5:* 237
Kouyomjian, Susan, *5:* 99
Kravitz, Lennie, *5:* 223
Kruger, Joanette, *5:* 233, 237
Ku Klux Klan (KKK), *1:* 178, 181, 184; *2:* 258; *5:* 166, 250
Kunstler, William, *4:* 658
Kunta Kinte, *2:* 303
Kuwait, *5:* 172

L

L'Enfant, Pierre Charles, *5:* 4
Ladies Fresh, *3:* 606
Lady Sings the Blues, 3: 598, 631
Lafontant, Jewel Stradford, *3:* **462–64,** 463 (ill.)
LaMotta, Jake, *4:* 771
Lamp, Virginia, *4:* 713
Lancaster, Abna Aggrey, *4:* 716–17
Lane, Randall, *5:* 86
Lange, Jessica, *1:* 62
The Last Days of Louisiana Red, 3: 618
Latimer, Lewis Howard, *6:* **149–55,** 149 (ill.)
Latimer, Margery, *4:* 715
Lawford, Peter, *5:* 51
Lawrence, David L., *4:* 693
Lawrence, Jacob, *3:* **464–67,** 466 (ill.)
Lay Bare the Heart, 2: 239
League for Non-Violent Civil Disobedience Against Military Segregation, *3:* 612
Lean on Me, 1: 142
Lear, Norman, *2:* 377
The Learning Tree, 3: 577
Leavitt, Joshua, *5:* 34
LeClerc, Captain-General, *4:* 720–21
Led Zeppelin, *5:* 223
Lee, Bill Lann, *5:* 175
Lee, Edward T., *4:* 647
Lee, Spike, *1:* 62; *3:* **467–70,** 468 (ill.), 490; *4:* 682, 770; *5:* 14, 142, 193; *6:* **157–62,** 157 (ill.)
"Left," *5:* 150–51
Legion of Honor, *1:* 34
Lehmann, Lotte, *1:* 102
Lemon, Meadowlark, *2:* 320
Lenin, Vladimir, *1:* 143
Lennon, John, *2:* 301
Leno, Jay, *3:* 498; *5:* 130
A Lesson Before Dying, 2: 255
LeTang, Henry, *2:* 349
"Letter from Birmingham City Jail," *3:* 458
Letterman, David, *2:* 306; *5:* 130
Levant, Brian, *5:* 13, 15
Leventhal, Melvyn, *4:* 748, 749
Levi, Josef, *5:* 3
Levi, Primo, *4:* 687
Levin, Sander, *5:* 17
Lewinsky, Monica, *6:* 147

Lewis, Carl, *3:* **471–73,** 471 (ill.)
Lewis, Elma, *3:* **473–76,** 475 (ill.)
Lewis, Lennox, *1:* 77
Lewis, Terry, *2:* 378
"Liberal," *5:* 150–51
Library of Congress, *2:* 330, 332
Libya, *5:* 75, 172
Life magazine, *3:* 576, 577
Lifetime Achievement Award, *1:* 150; *3:* 453
Lilies of the Field, 3: 582
Lincoln, Abraham, *3:* 441; *4:* 730, 774; *5:* 150
Lincoln, Mary Todd, *3:* 441, 442
Lincoln University, *4:* 693–94, 695–96
Linden Hills, 3: 559
Linkletter, Art, *5:* 44
Lister, Joseph, *4:* 779
Liszt, Franz, *4:* 766
Little, Malcolm. *See* Malcolm X
Little Richard, *3:* **476–78,** 477 (ill.); *5:* 222
"Live Aid," *3:* 497
Living Color, 5: 223
Living Colours, 2: 374
Locke, John, *5:* 36–37
Lollapalooza, 2: 374
Long, Lutz, *3:* 571
Long, Vicki, *3:* 494
A Long Way from Home, 3: 520
Lopate, Phillip, *4:* 687
Lori, William, *4:* 684
Los Angeles Lakers, *1:* 3; *2:* 400, 401–2; *5:* 127, 128, 129
Los Angeles riots (1992), *6:* 215–16
Losing Isaiah, 1: 62
Lotus Press, *3:* 486
Lou, Sweet, *2:* 320

Louis, Joe, *3:* **479–82,** 480 (ill.)
Louisiana State University, *3:* 569
Lowery, Joseph E., *3:* **482–84,** 483 (ill.); *4:* 779
Lubricator cup, *6:* 163, 165
"Lucille" (guitar), *3:* 451
Lyle, Ron, *5:* 84
Lynching, *6:* 4
Lyrics of Lowly Life, 1: 214

M

Ma Rainey's Black Bottom, 4: 791
Mabley, Jackie "Moms," *5:* 28
Macci, Ric, *5:* 234
Madgett, Naomi Long, *3:* **484–87,** 485 (ill.)
Magellan, Ferdinand, *5:* 36
Mahogany, 3: 631
Majors and Minors, 1: 214
Make, Vusumzi, *1:* 19
Malcolm X, *1:* 5, 12, 39, 143, 190, 193; *2:* 239, 240, 302; *3:* **487–90,** 489 (ill.), 551, 561, 609, 617; *4:* 650, 659–61, 681, 763; *5:* 72, 73, 76, 189, 190, 191–92, 195, 214
Malcolm X, 3: 470; *6:* 160
Malone, Annie Turnbo, *3:* **490–93,** 492 (ill.)
Mama, 3: 523
Mama Day, 3: 559
Manchild in the Promised Land, 1: 88, 90
Mandela, Nelson, *1:* 58; *4:* 671
Manhattan Project, *3:* 603
Mao Zedong, *1:* 145
"Maple Leaf Rag," *2:* 423
March on Washington (1963), *3:* 458, 613, 640, 641; *6:* 68

Marino, Eugene A., *3:* **493–95,** 494 (ill.)
Markhasev, Mikail, *5:* 44
The Marrow of Tradition, 1: 135
Marrow, Tracey, *2:* 371
Marsalis, Branford, *3:* **495–98,** 497 (ill.)
Marsalis, Wynton, *3:* 495, **498–501,** 499 (ill.)
Marsh, Henry, *4:* 775
Marshall, James, *4:* 672
Marshall, Paule, *3:* **501–4,** 501 (ill.)
Marshall, Ray, *5:* 116
Marshall, Thurgood, *3:* **504–7,** 506 (ill.), 521, 544; *4:* 694, 710; *6:* 127, 130, 131, 133
Martel, Joyce, *5:* 154
Martin, Susan, *5:* 136
Marx, Karl, *1:* 143; *3:* 610
Maslin, Janet, *2:* 278
Mason, Biddy, *3:* **507–9,** 508 (ill.)
Mason, Bridget, *See* Mason, Biddy
Massachusetts Institute of Technology (MIT), *5:* 161–62, 163
Masters tournament, *5:* 239, 242, 244, 245
Mathabane, Mark, *4:* 795
Matthews, James Newton, *1:* 213
Matthews, Robert (Matthias), *4:* 728
Matthias, *4:* 728–29
"Maybellene," *1:* 59
Mayo, Charles, *4:* 780
Mays, Willie, *3:* **509–12,** 510 (ill.); *5:* 208
McAuliffe, Christa, *5:* 159, 162
McBride, Clara. *See* Hale, Clara
McCarthy, Eugene, *2:* 365
McCarthy, Joseph, *3:* 620

McCartney, Paul, *2:* 337
McClain, John, *2:* 378
McClellan, George Marion, *3:* **512–15,** 513 (ill.)
McCone Commission, *1:* 108
McCoy, Elijah, *6:* **163–69,** 163 (ill.)
McDaniel, Hattie, *3:* **515–17,** 515 (ill.); *5:* 166, 167
McDonald, Chris, *5:* 230
McEnroe, John, *5:* 234
McKay, Claude, *1:* 74; *3:* **517–20,** 519 (ill.)
McKinley, William, *1:* 42
McKissick, Floyd B., *2:* 375; *3:* **520–22,** 521 (ill.)
McMillan, Terry, *3:* **522–25,** 524 (ill.); *5:* **155–58,** 155 (ill.), 167
McMillen, Tom, *5:* 106
McNair, Cheryl, *5:* 161 (ill.), 163–64
McNair, Ronald, *5:* **159–64,** 159 (ill.), 161 (ill.)
McQueen, Thelma "Butterfly," *3:* **525–27,** 526 (ill.); *5:* **165–70,** 165 (ill.)
McWilliams, Moses, *4:* 750
Meadman, Dhimah, *4:* 802
Media Workshop, *3:* 449
Mehta, Zubin, *4:* 768
Melanoma research, *1:* 150
Mellman, Michael, *2:* 402
Mencken, H. L., *4:* 801
Mercury Records, *2:* 417
Meredith, James, *1:* 119; *3:* **527–30,** 528 (ill.)
The Messenger, *3:* 611
Metro-Goldwyn-Mayer (MGM), *2:* 358
Metropolitan Opera, *1:* 55
Michigan State University, *2:* 400; *5:* 128
Middle East, *1:* 105; *2:* 381
Mignon, François, *2:* 366

"Migration of the Negro," *3:* 466
Mikulski, Barbara, *5:* 153
Miller, Arthur, *4:* 792
Miller, Shannon, *5:* 56
Miller, Zell, *5:* 253
Millet, Jean-François, *4:* 697
Million Man March, *5:* 71, 73, 74, 75, 194, 254
Milner, Ron, *3:* **530–33,** 531 (ill.)
Milne School, *6:* 10
Milwaukee Braves, *1:* 1
Mind of My Mind, *1:* 111
Minneapolis Millers, *3:* 511
"Minnie the Moocher," *1:* 113; *5:* 23, 24
Minority Organ and Tissue Transplant Education Program, *6:* 41
Miss USA pageant, *5:* 14
Miss World pageant, *5:* 14
Mississippi Freedom Democratic Party (MFDP), *2:* 307; *6:* 18
"Mississippi Goddam," *6:* 203, 207
Missouri Compromise, *4:* 652, 653
Mitchell, Clarence, *4:* 669
Mitchell, Timothy, *4:* 667
Mobutu, Sese Seko, *4:* 768
Moceanu, Dominique, *5:* 56
Momyer, William, *5:* 228
Mondale, Walter, *5:* 135
Monk, Thelonious, *1:* 50, 164; *3:* **533–35,** 534 (ill.)
Monroe, Marilyn, *5:* 47
Montes, Pedro, *5:* 32, 33–34, 35
Montgomery, Alabama, *3:* 578; *5:* 250
Montgomery Improvement Association, *1:* 7; *3:* 580; *6:* 15
Moore, Audley, *3:* **536–38,** 537 (ill.); *6:* **171–76,** 171 (ill.)

Moore, Emerson, *4:* 684, 686
Moore, Thomas, *4:* 735
Moorer, Michael, *5:* 82, 86
Morehouse College, *1:* 69
Morgan, Garrett, *3:* **538–41,** 539 (ill.)
Morgan, Richard, *4:* 680
Morgan State College, *1:* 197
Morgan University, *1:* 198
Morris, Stevland, *4:* 796
Morrison, Tommy, *5:* 86
Morrison, Toni, *3:* **541–43,** 543 (ill.), 558; *4:* 687, 795
Morton Thiokol, *5:* 163
Moses: A Story of the Nile, *6:* 122
Moss, Tom, *4:* 709
Mother Hale. *See* Hale, Clara
Motley, Constance Baker, *3:* **544–46,** 545 (ill.)
Motley, Willard, *3:* **546–49,** 548 (ill.)
Motown Records, *2:* 286, 287, 288; *3:* 630; *4:* 796–97
MOVE, *2:* 283
Muhammad, Elijah, *2:* 239; *3:* 488, 489, **549–52,** 550 (ill.); *5:* 72, 191, 192
Muhammad, Warith Deen, *5:* 72
Mulattoes, *4:* 719–21; *5:* 47
Multiple sclerosis, *3:* 599
Mumbo Jumbo, *3:* 617
Murphy, Dwayne, *2:* 313
Murphy, Eddie, *2:* 274, 306, 362; *3:* **552–55,** 553 (ill.); *4:* 723, 769, 770; *5:* 14, 179
Murray, Albert, *5:* 68
Murray, Bill, *5:* 142 (ill.)
Murray, David, *4:* 664
Murray, Pauli, *3:* **555–57,** 556 (ill.)

Murray v. University of Maryland, 6: 131
Muslim Mosque, Inc., 3: 489
Mutiny, 5: 31–39
Mythology, 2: 310; 3: 541

N

Napoleon Bonaparte, 4: 720, 721
Nation of Islam, 1: 12; 2: 239, 240; 3: 488, 549, 551; 4: 650, 660; 5: 72, 151, 190, 191, 192
National Aeronautics and Space Administration (NASA), 2: 396; 5: 159, 162, 163
National Afro-American Council, 6: 105
National AIDS Commission, 2: 402; 5: 128
National Alliance Against Racist and Political Repression, 1: 180
National Amateur Athletic Union (AAU), 3: 636
National Association for the Advancement of Colored People (NAACP), 1: 40, 43, 50, 52, 64, 70, 106, 107, 135, 196, 211; 2: 223, 234, 235, 249, 292, 354, 356, 402, 404, 430, 431; 3: 504, 505, 521, 544; 4: 668–69, 707, 712, 726, 776, 777–79; 5: 21, 73; 6: 14, 15, 34, 129, 131, 132, 133, 144
National Association of Black Journalists, 5: 75
National Association of Colored Women (NACW), 1: 43; 4: 707, 709; 6: 124
National Basketball Association (NBA), 1: 3, 127; 2: 400–2, 427, 428–29; 5: 127, 140–41, 143

National Black Political Assembly, 1: 40
National Center of Afro-American Artists, 3: 473, 475
National Collegiate Athletic Association (NCAA), 2: 428; 5: 128
National Convention of Gospel Choirs and Choruses, 1: 203
National Council of Churches, 5: 250
National Council of Negro Women (NCNW), 1: 64; 2: 333, 334, 335; 3: 537; 4: 648
National Education Association (NEA), 2: 250, 251, 252
National Enquirer, 5: 44
National Equal Rights League, 4: 726
National Football League (NFL), 5: 111, 113, 208–9
National Low Income Housing Coalition, 1: 85
National Newspaper Publishers Association/Black Press of America, 5: 75
National Organization for Women (NOW), 2: 341, 342; 3: 555, 557
National Safety Device Company, 3: 539
National Science Foundation, 1: 150
National Security Council (NSC), 3: 587; 5: 172
National Sports Council, 5: 186
National Track and Field Hall of Fame, 5: 107
National Urban League, 1: 96; 2: 389, 390, 430, 431; 4: 806, 807; 5: 17; 6: 15, 145

National Woman Suffrage Association (NWSA), 6: 124
National Women's Hall of Fame, 5: 186
National Youth Administration, 1: 63, 65
Naylor, Gloria, 3: 557–60, 559 (ill.)
Nazism, 3: 572
NBC Sports, 3: 639; 5: 112, 113, 210
NBC-TV, 1: 153; 4: 671
Neal, Frederic Douglas "Curly," 2: 320
Negro American Labor Council, 3: 611
Negro Dance Group, 1: 216
Negro Digest, 2: 407
Negro Eastern League, 3: 573
Negro League, 6: 111, 113, 114
Negro National League, 1: 114; 3: 573
The Negro Soldier, 1: 185
Negro World, 2: 257; 6: 108
Negro World Series, 3: 574
Neurosurgery, 1: 122
Never Blue Productions, 2: 276
New Jack City, 4: 682, 739
New Lafayette Theater, 1: 100
New Orleans Philharmonic Orchestra, 3: 498
New York Age, 1: 40
New York Giants, 3: 511
New York Metropolitan Opera, 1: 103
New York National Guard, 1: 185
New York, New York, 1: 198, 200
New York Philharmonic Orchestra, 4: 766, 767, 768
New York Public Library, 1: 31

New York State Assembly, *1:* 139, 199
New York State Senate, *3:* 546
Newport Jazz Festival, *1:* 187
Newton, Huey P., *1:* 120, 144; *3:* **560–62,** 561 (ill.); *4:* 657
New York Age, *6:* 101, 104, 108
NFL Live, *5:* 210
The NFL on NBC, *5:* 112
The NFL Today, *5:* 112
Niagara Movement, *1:* 210, 211; *4:* 726; *6:* 105
Nicholas, Harold, *2:* 351; *5:* 48
Nichols, John F., *4:* 804
Nicholson, Jack, *2:* 402
Nicklaus, Jack, *5:* 241–42, 244
Nike, *5:* 141, 143, 144, 244, 254
Nine Inch Nails, *2:* 374
Nixon, Richard M., *1:* 29, 193; *2:* 230, 239, 424; *3:* 463; *4:* 746, 778, 808; *5:* 94–95, 133, 135, 172
Nkrumah, Kwame, *4:* 694
No Place to Be Somebody, *2:* 284, 285; *5:* 97, 98–99
No Way Out, *3:* 582
Nobel Peace Prize, *1:* 104, 106; *3:* 456, 458
Nobody Knows My Name, *1:* 37
Nonviolent Action Group, *1:* 91
Noriega, Manuel, *5:* 172
Norman, Jessye, *3:* **562–65,** 564 (ill.)
North Africa, *5:* 227
North American Air Defense Command (NORAD), *2:* 392, 394
North Pole, *2:* 338–41
North Star, *1:* 206

Northern States Power Company, *3:* 566
Norvell, James, *3:* 529
Notorious B.I.G., *5:* 201, 203
Nucleus (theater company), *3:* 462
Nucleus Inc., *4:* 659, 661
N.W.A., *2:* 314; 371

O

O'Connor, Katie, *4:* 705
O'Jays, *2:* 312
O'Leary, Hazel, *3:* **565–67,** 566 (ill.)
O'Neal, Shaquille, *3:* **567–70,** 569 (ill.)
Oak and Ivy, *1:* 214
Oakland A's, *2:* 312–13
Of Love and Dust, *2:* 255
Old Greenbottom Inn and Other Stories, *3:* 514
Oliver, King, *1:* 21
Olivier, Laurence, *1:* 79
Olssen, Jessie, *4:* 698
Olympic Games, Summer (1936), *3:* 570, 571
Olympic Games, Summer (1956), *3:* 638; *5:* 185–86
Olympic Games, Summer (1960), *1:* 12; *3:* 636; *5:* 185, 186
Olympic Games, Summer (1968), *5:* 83
Olympic Games, Summer (1980), *2:* 433
Olympic Games, Summer (1984), *2:* 434; *3:* 472; *5:* 103, 140
Olympic Games, Summer (1988), *1:* 77; *3:* 473; *5:* 101, 104
Olympic Games, Summer (1992), *2:* 402; *5:* 53, 55, 111, 128

Olympic Games, Summer (1996), *5:* 53, 56, 109, 112–13, 253
Olympic Games, Winter (1994), *5:* 109, 111
Once Upon a Time, *1:* 30
One Church, One Child, *1:* 147
One Way Productions, *3:* 559
Onizuka, Ellison, *5:* 163
Ono, Yoko, *2:* 301
Onyx Club, *2:* 269
Operation Breadbasket, *2:* 380; *3:* 484
Operation Champion, *3:* 636
Operation Desert Shield/Storm, *3:* 588, 589; *5:* 172
Operation Equality, *2:* 390
Operation PUSH (People United to Serve Humanity), *2:* 381; *5:* 123; *6:* 137, 139
Operation Woman Power, *2:* 335
Opportunity, *6:* 24
Organization of Afro-American Unity, *3:* 489
Organ transplants, *6:* 38, 39, 40
Orlando Magic, *3:* 570
Othello, *3:* 622
Our Nig, or Sketches from the Life of a Free Black, *2:* 262
Owens, Dana. *See* Queen Latifah
Owens, Jesse, *3:* 471, **570–73,** 571 (ill.)
Owens, Major, *4:* 667
OyamO, *5:* 98

P

Page, Jimmy, *5:* 223
Paige, Satchel, *3:* **573–75,** 574 (ill.); *6:* 114, 116

Paine, Thomas, *1:* 143
Painting, *3:* 465
Palestine Liberation Organization (PLO), *2:* 381; *5:* 252
Palmer, Henry, *4:* 780
Panella, Patricia, *2:* 350
Parents' Music Resource Center, *2:* 372
Parker, Charlie, *3:* 449; *4:* 662, 741, 783
Parks, Gordon, *3:* **575–78,** 577 (ill.)
Parks, Rosa, *1:* 6; *3:* 457, 462, 482, **578–80,** 578 (ill.); *4:* 778; *5:* 71
Parrish, Noel, *5:* 229
Partnerships for Progress Program, *1:* 45
Pasteur, Louis, *4:* 779, 780
The Path of Dreams, 3: 514
"Patternist" saga, *1:* 110
Patternmaster, 1: 111
Pay equalization, *3:* 545
Payne, Allen, *5:* 230
Payne, Billy, *5:* 253
Peace and Freedom Party, *4:* 658
Peace Corps, *1:* 56
Peace Mission, *6:* 98
Pearson, Pauletta, *4:* 763
Pearson's Magazine, 3: 519
Peary, Robert E., *2:* 338–40
Pendergrass, Teddy, *2:* 361
People Organized and Working for Economic Rebirth (POWER), *2:* 241
People's Political Party, *2:* 258
People's Voice, 3: 585
Perkins, Edward J., *4:* 667
Perpetual Help Mission, *4:* 744, 746
Persian Gulf War, *3:* 586
Pesci, Joe, *5:* 177
Peters, John, *4:* 773
Pharr, Pauline, *4:* 716

Philadelphia Council for Community Advancement, *2:* 282
"Philadelphia 11," *2:* 324
Philadelphia, Pennsylvania, *2:* 281, 283
Philadelphia 76ers, *1:* 128
Philadelphia Warriors, *1:* 128
Phong, Nguyen "Tiger," *5:* 240, 246
Pickett, Owen, *4:* 775
Pieh, Samuel H., *5:* 39
Pierson, Elijah, *4:* 728–29
Pierson, Sarah, *4:* 728
Pilate, Felton, *2:* 313
Pinckney, Brian, *5:* 6
Pindell, Geraldine, *4:* 725, 726
Pippen, Scottie, *5:* 142
The Pitiful and the Proud, 3: 633
The Places in the Heart, 2: 277
Plantation Club, *1:* 33
Plasma, *1:* 208
Playboy Club, *2:* 290
Plessy v. Ferguson, 4: 777; *6:* 130, 132
Plummer, Jonathan, *5:* 157
Poems, 3: 513
Poems of Life and Love, 6: 154
Poitier, Sidney, *3:* **580–83;** *4:* 722; *5:* 49, 167
Polio, *3:* 635
Polk, George, *1:* 80
Poole, Elijah. *See* Muhammad, Elijah
Poor People's Campaign, *3:* 459
Poor People's March, *3:* 455
Poplar, Ellen, *4:* 802
Porgy and Bess, 1: 19
Poro College, *3:* 491
Poro Company, *3:* 491, 492
Porter, Cole, *2:* 244; *5:* 78
Posse, 4: 739

"Potomac Watch," *3:* 614
Powell, Adam Clayton, Jr., *3:* **583–86,** 584 (ill.); *4:* 665
Powell, Alma, *5:* 174
Powell, Colin, *3:* **586–89,** 588 (ill.); *5:* 143, 153, **171–76,** 171 (ill.)
Powell, Shezwae, *5:* 98–99
Power, Racism, and Privilege: Race Relations in Theoretical and Sociohistorical Perspectives, 6: 224
Poyas, Peter, *4:* 743
Pozo, Chano, *2:* 270
Preminger, Otto, *5:* 49, 51
Presidential Transition Office, *5:* 118
President's Council on Physical Fitness and Sports, *5:* 101, 106
Presley, Elvis, *5:* 24, 222
Preston, Billy, *5:* 223
Price, Frank, *4:* 675
Price, Leontyne, *3:* **589–92,** 590 (ill.)
Pride, Charley, *3:* **592–94,** 593 (ill.)
Pride, Inc., *1:* 46; *5:* 9
Primettes, *3:* 630
Prince, *2:* 378; *5:* 223
Proctor & Gardner, *3:* 594, 595
Proctor, Barbara Gardner, *3:* **594–97,** 596 (ill.)
Professional Golfers' Association (PGA), *5:* 241
Project Alert, *2:* 390
Proud Shoes: The Story of an American Family, 3: 556
Prout, Mary, *4:* 753
Provincetown Players, *3:* 622
Pryor, Richard, *3:* 553, **597–99,** 598 (ill.)
Public Enemy, *3:* **599–602,** 601 (ill.); *5:* 201

Publishing Hall of Fame, *2:* 406
Purple Onion (nightclub), *1:* 18
Purvis, Robert, *4:* 654

Q

Qaddafi, Muammar Al-. *See* Kaddafi, Muammar
Quakers, *4:* 732–33; *5:* 3, 4
Quarterman, Lloyd Albert, *3:* **602–5,** 603 (ill.)
Quayle, Dan, *5:* 197
Queen, 1: 62
Queen Latifah, *3:* **605–7,** 606 (ill.)
"Queen of Soul." *See* Franklin, Aretha
"Queen of the Harlem Renaissance," *2:* 368
Qwest Records, *2:* 418

R

Rachel, 2: 293–94
Rackley, Alex, *4:* 659
Rainbow Coalition, *5:* 123
"Rainbow Tribe," *1:* 34
Rainey, Ma, *4:* 678, 680, 791
A Raisin in the Sun, 2: 317, 318
Raitt, Bonnie, *4:* 758
Ramsey, Buck, *5:* 97, 98
Randall, Dudley, *3:* **607–10,** 608 (ill.)
Randolph, A. Philip, *3:* **610–13,** 612 (ill.)
Rap music, *3:* 600, 605; *5:* 197–204
Rashad, Phylicia, *5:* 42
Raspberry, William, *3:* **613–16,** 615 (ill.)
Raw Pearl, 1: 29
Rawls, Lou, *2:* 360
Reach the American Dream foundation, *4:* 785–86

Reading Guidance Clinic, *3:* 628
Reagan, Ronald, *2:* 301, 390; *4:* 711, 779, 805; *5:* 149–50, 163, 172, 173
Reagon, Bernice Johnson, *6:* **177–84**
"Real McCoy," *6:* 166
Redding, Otis, *5:* 220
"Red Summer," *6:* 6
Reed, Ishmael, *3:* **616–18,** 617 (ill.)
Refigee, Derrick, *2:* 320
Reich, Robert B., *5:* 118
Reiser, Paul, *5:* 64
"Religious Right," *5:* 153
Remond, Charles, *4:* 654
Rendell, Edward, *5:* 75
Reno, Janet, *5:* 21, 119
Reparations, for slavery, *6:* 173, 174
Republic of New Africa, *3:* 538
Republican Party, *1:* 85; *5:* 150–51, 173–74
Resnick, Judith, *5:* 163
Revlon cosmetics, *5:* 15
Reynolds, Mel, *5:* 124
The Rhetoric of Black Revolution, 1: 24
Riccardi, Michael, *4:* 666
Rich, Frank, *2:* 350
Rickey, Branch, *3:* 625
Ride, Sally, *5:* 160
"Right," *5:* 150–51
Riley, Pat, *2:* 401
Ritchie, Lionel, *2:* 387
Rivers, Joan, *2:* 305
Robb, Charles, *4:* 775, 776
Roberts, George S., *5:* 227
Robeson, Eslanda Goode, *3:* **618–21,** 619 (ill.)
Robeson, Paul, *1:* 189; *3:* 619, **621–24,** 622 (ill.)
Robinor, Genia, *4:* 767
Robinson, Bradley, *2:* 341

Robinson, Jackie, *1:* 1; *3:* 511, 574, **624–27,** 625 (ill.); *6: 114*
Robinson, Ray Charles. *See* Charles, Ray
Robinson, Sugar Ray, *2:* 266; *4:* 771
Rochon, Lela, *5:* 155
"A Rock, A River, A Tree," *1:* 20
Rock, Chris, *5:* **177–84,** 177 (ill.), 182 (ill.)
Rogers, Norman, *3:* 600
Rolling Stones, *1:* 60; *5:* 220
Rollins, Charlemae Hill, *3:* **627–29,** 627 (ill.)
Roman Catholic Church, *3:* 450, 493
Rome, Italy, *5:* 36
Ronettes, *5:* 219
Roosevelt, Eleanor, *1:* 16; *2:* 407; *5:* 227
Roosevelt, Franklin D., *1:* 16, 63, 65, 185; *3:* 612, 640
Roosevelt, Theodore, *4:* 760
Roots: The Saga of an American Family, 1: 19; *2:* 301, 303
Rosenberg, Julius and Ethel, *6:* 68
Ross, Diana, *2:* 288, 378; *3:* **629–32,** 631 (ill.); *5:* 222
Ross, Lucy, *2:* 340
Ross, Mac, *5:* 227
Rowan, Carl T., *3:* **632–34,** 633 (ill.)
Royal Garden Blues, 3: 497
Royal Roost Nightclub, *1:* 57
RPM International, *1:* 132
Rubin, Rick, *3:* 600
Rudolph, Wilma, *1:* 5; *3:* **634–37,** 635 (ill.); *4:* 762; *5:* **185–88,** 185 (ill.)
Ruffner, Viola, *4:* 759
Ruiz (*Amistad* slave owner), *5:* 32, 33–34, 35

Index | xlvii

Running a Thousand Miles for Freedom, 1: 176
Russell, Bill, *3:* **637–39,** 637 (ill.)
Russert, Tim, *5:* 75
Rustin, Bayard, *3:* **639–42,** 642 (ill.)
Ruth, Babe, *1:* 2

S

Sacramento Kings, *3:* 639
Saint Domingue, *4:* 718–21, 742–43
Sajak, Pat, *2:* 306
Sampras, Pete, *5:* 234
Sampson, Edith, *4:* **647–49,** 647 (ill.); *5:* 134
Sampson, Rufus, *4:* 648
San Francisco 49ers, *5:* 209
Sanchez, Sonia, *3:* 609; *4:* **649–52,** 651 (ill.)
Sandburg, Carl, *4:* 791
Sandler, Stanley, *5:* 230
Sanford, John, *4:* 652, 653
Saperstein, Abe, *2:* 320, 321
Sarbanes, Paul, *5:* 152
Sargent, John Singer, *4:* 698
Sartre, Jean-Paul, *4:* 803
Satchmo. *See* Armstrong, Louis
Saturday Night Live, 3: 552, 553; *5:* 179
Sawamatsu, Naoko, *5:* 235
Scat singing, *1:* 21, 112; *2:* 244; *5:* 77
Schiffer, Claudia, *5:* 15
Schmeling, Max, *3:* 480
Schomberg Center for Research, *5:* 168
School Daze, 3: 470; *6:* 159
School dropout program, *2:* 251
Schroeder, Joyce Tanac, *5:* 55
Schuyler, Philippa Duke, *6:* **185–91,** 185 (ill.)

Schwarzenegger, Arnold, *5:* 131 (ill.)
Schwarzkopf, Norman, *3:* 586
Scobee, Dick, *5:* 163
Scobee, June, *5:* 163
Scott, Dred, *4:* **652–54,** 653 (ill.)
Scott, Gloria, *4:* **654–57,** 655 (ill.)
Scott, Oz, *4:* 663–64
Scott, Will Braxton, *4:* 656
Seale, Bobby, *1:* 120, 144; *4:* **657–59,** 658 (ill.)
Seals, Frank, *4:* 756
Seattle Supersonics, *3:* 639
Seeger, Charles, *1:* 175
Seeger, Pete, *1:* 175
Seeger, Ruth, *1:* 175
Segal, George, *4:* 762
Seinfeld, Jerry, *5:* 14, 64
Sengbe Pieh, *5:* 32
Sengstacke, John H., *6:* 7
Serbia, *5:* 18; *6:* 141
Sesame Street, 5: 25
Sewing machines, *3:* 538
Sexual harassment, *2:* 344, 346
Shabazz, Attalah, *3:* 462; *4:* **659–61,** 660 (ill.)
Shabazz, Betty, *4:* 660; *5:* 73, **189–96,** 189 (ill.), 194 (ill.)
Shabazz, Qubilah, *5:* 73, 194
Shaker, Ted, *5:* 111
Shakur, Afeni, *5:* 199, 200, 202, 204
Shakur, Assata, *6:* **193–201**
Shakur, Lumumba Abdul, *5:* 199
Shakur, Tupac, *5:* **197–205,** 197 (ill.), 198 (ill.), 222
Shange, Ntozake, *4:* **662–64,** 663 (ill.)
Shapiro, Robert, *5:* 211, 211 (ill.), 213
Sharpton, Al, *4:* **664–67,** 666 (ill.)

Shaw, George Bernard, *4:* 714
Shaw, Robert Gould, *4:* 762–63
Shepard, Alan B., *5:* 160
She's Gotta Have It, 3: 469; *6:* 159
Shocklee, Hank, *3:* 600
Shore, Dinah, *2:* 305
Shriver, Pam, *5:* 237
Sierra Leone, *5:* 32, 37, 38, 39
Sifford, Charles, *5:* 245
"Silent March," *3:* 484
Simmons, Althea T. L., *4:* **667–70,** 668 (ill.)
Simone, Nina, *6:* **203–10,** 203 (ill.), 209 (ill.)
Simpson, Carole, *4:* **670–72,** 671 (ill.)
Simpson, Nicole Brown, *5:* 207, 210, 212, 214
Simpson, O. J., *5:* 182, **207–16,** 207 (ill.), 209 (ill.), 211 (ill.), 244
Sims, Naomi, *4:* **672–74,** 673 (ill.)
Sims, Sandman, *2:* 349, 351
Singleton, John, *4:* **674–77,** 676 (ill.); *5:* 197
Siouxie and the Banshees, *2:* 374
Sir John's Trio, *1:* 59
Sit-ins, *1:* 46, 69; *2:* 223, 237
60 Minutes, 1: 78, 79, 163
Skelton, Red, *4:* 722
Sketches of Southern Life, 6: 122
Slave insurrections, *4:* 733–36, 742–44
Slavery, *1:* 40, 63, 124, 166, 176, 204–6, 213; *2:* 225, 302–3, 317, 379, 419; *3:* 441, 504, 507–9, 518, 610, 621; *4:* 652–54, 718–21, 730–33, 733–36, 742–44; *5:* 36–37, 62, 75, 166–67

Sleeping Car Porters Union, *3:* 640
Sly & the Family Stone, *2:* 378; *5:* 220, 223
Slyde, Jimmy, *2:* 351
Smalls, Biggie, *5:* 201
Smith, Arthur Lee, Jr. *See* Asante, Molefi Kete
Smith, Bessie, *1:* 21; *4:* **677–80,** 679 (ill.), 789
Smith, Clara, *4:* 678
Smith, Dean, *5:* 112 (ill.)
Smith, Eula Mae, *4:* 692
Smith, Joe, *4:* 679
Smith, Lewis C., *5:* 228
Smith, Mamie, *4:* 678
Smith, Mike, *5:* 163
Smith, Trixie, *4:* 678
Snipes, Wesley, *4:* **680–83,** 681 (ill.); *5:* 14
Snoop Doggy Dogg, *5:* 201, 203
Song of Solomon, 3: 542, 543
Songs of Jamaica, 3: 518
Songs to a Phantom Nightingale, 3: 485
Sons and Daughters of the Incarcerated (SADOI), *6:* 78
Soul City, *3:* 522
Soul of the Game, 6: 113, 115 (ill.)
Soul on Ice, 1: 143; *6:* 57, 58
Soul Train, 1: 168, 169, 170
Soul Train Records, *1:* 170
"Soulja's Story," *5:* 197, 200
The Souls of Black Folk, 1: 211
South of Freedom, 3: 633
Southern Christian Leadership Conference (SCLC), *1:* 5, 19, 58, 69; *2:* 307, 380; *3:* 457, 458, 482; *4:* 665; *5:* 249, 250; *6:* 15, 16
Soviet Union, *3:* 623
Space Jam, 5: 142

Spector, Phil, *5:* 219
Spelling, Aaron, *1:* 62; *5:* 14
Spelman College, *1:* 150, 153, 173; *5:* 42
Spielberg, Steven, *4:* 675; *5:* 39
Spingarn Medal, *1:* 135; *2:* 236, 303, 405; *3:* 575
Spirlea, Irena, *5:* 237
Spivey, Victoria, *4:* 757
Spurlock, Charles T., *4:* 649
Spurlock, Oliver, *4:* 649
Sputnik, 5: 160
Stafford, Shaun, *5:* 235
Stallings, George A., Jr., *4:* **683–86,** 683 (ill.)
Stanford University, *5:* 242
Stapleton, Jean, *2:* 280
"State of Black America," *2:* 391
States' Laws on Race and Color, 3: 556
Steele, Shelby, *4:* **686–89,** 687 (ill.)
Steinbeck, John, *5:* 97
Steinem, Gloria, *1:* 85; *3:* 444, 449
Stepping into Tomorrow, 3: 462
Stewart, Rod, *5:* 222
Still, William Grant, *4:* **689–91,** 689 (ill.)
Sting, *3:* 497
Stir Crazy, 3: 583
Stone, Sharon, *5:* 14
Storytelling, *1:* 31; *3:* 627, 628
Storytelling: Art and Technique, 6: 12
Stout, Charles Otis, *4:* 691–92, 693
Stout, Juanita Kidd, *4:* **691–93,** 692 (ill.)
Stowe, Harriet Beecher, *4:* 729, 802
"Strange Fruit," *2:* 353
Street Stories, 1: 80
Strone, Dan, *5:* 64

Student Nonviolent Coordinating Committee (SNCC), *1:* 45, 46, 69, 91, 92, 118, 119, 182; *2:* 272, 291, 307; *3:* 458; *5:* 254; *6:* 16, 17, 32, 33, 45, 46, 178, 179
Styron, William, *4:* 736
Sudan, *5:* 37, 75
Sudarkasa, Niara, *4:* **693–96,** 695 (ill.)
Suffrage, *1:* 206
Sula, 3: 542
Summer of Sam, 6: 161
Supremes, *3:* 630, 631
Survivor, 1: 111
Susan Smith McKinney-Steward Medical Society, *2:* 298
Sweet Honey In The Rock, *6:* 180, 181, 181 (ill.), 182

T

Taft, William Howard, *2:* 341
"Take My Hand, Precious Lord," *1:* 203
Talking to Myself, 1: 29
Talking Tree, 1: 30
Tan magazine, *2:* 408
Taney, Roger B., *4:* 653; *5:* 35
Tanner, Henry Ossawa, *4:* **696–99,** 698 (ill.)
Tappan, Lewis, *5:* 34
Tar Baby, 3: 543
Tatum, Goose, *2:* 320
Tauziat, Natalie, *5:* 235
Taylor, Clarice, *5:* 28
Taylor, Mildred, *4:* **699–702,** 701 (ill.)
Taylor, Russell L., *4:* 707
Taylor, Susan, *4:* **702–4,** 703 (ill.)
Taylor, Susie Baker King, *4:* **704–7,** 706 (ill.)

Técora, 5: *32, 33*
Teddy Hill Orchestra, 2: 269
Temple, Edward, 5: 186–87
Temple of Islam, 3: 550
Tennis Hall of Fame, *1:* 26
Tereshkova, Valentina, 5: 160
Terminator X, 3: 600
Terrell, Jean, 3: 631
Terrell, Mary Church, 4: **707–9,** 708 (ill.)
Terrell, Robert, 4: 709
Terry, Roger, 5: 229
Texas Medley Quartette, 2: 423
That Nigger's Crazy, 3: 598
Thicke, Alan, 2: 305
Thomas, Beulah Belle, 4: 755
Thomas, Bigger, 4: 802
Thomas, Clarence, *1:* 81; 2: 344, 345, 356; 4: **710–13,** 712 (ill.); 5: 153
Thomas, George, 4: 756, 757
Thomas, Hersal, 4: 756, 757
Thomas, Isiah, *1:* 67
"Three O'Clock Blues," 3: 452
Thriller, 2: 416, 418
The Today Show, 2: 294, 295; 3: 444
Tommy Boy Records, 3: 606
Tone-Loc, 2: 314
The Tonight Show, 1: 171; 3: 498
Toomer, Jean, 4: **713–16,** 714 (ill.)
Torme, Mel, 5: 77, 78
Torrence, Jackie, 4: **716–18,** 717 (ill.)
Tosca, 3: 591
Totem Press, *1:* 38
Toussaint, François-Dominique, 4: 718
Toussaint-Louverture, 4: **718–21,** 719 (ill.)
Towns, Edolphus, 4: 667
Townsend, Robert, 4: **721–24,** 724 (ill.), 770; 5: 15

Trading Places, 3: 554
Travis, Joseph, 4: 735
Treadwell, George, 4: 741
Trotter, William Monroe, 4: **724–27,** 726 (ill.)
Trouble in the Mind, 1: 136
The Truly Disadvantaged: the Inner City, the Underclass, and Public Policy, 6: 226, 227
Truman, Harry S., *1:* 106; 3: 613; 4: 648; 5: 226, 230; 6: 134
Truth, Sojourner, *1:* 181; 4: **727–30,** 728 (ill.)
Tubman, Harriet, *1:* 181; 4: **730–33,** 732 (ill.)
Tubman, John, 4: 731–32
Tucker, C. DeLores, 5: 204
Tupac Amaru, 5: 200
Turner, Ike, 5: 217, 218, 220, 223
Turner, Mabel G., 4: 692
Turner, Nat, 4: **733–36,** 734 (ill.)
Turner, Tina, 5: **217–24,** 217 (ill.), 221 (ill.)
Tuskegee Airmen, 4: 804; 5: **225–32,** 225 (ill.), 228 (ill.); 6: 234
Tuskegee Institute, *1:* 126, 184, 185; 2: 232; 4: 758, 759–61; 6: 234
Tuskegee Machine, *1:* 211
"Tutti Frutti," 3: 478
Tutu, 1: 186
Tutu, Desmond, 5: 253
2 Live Crew, 2: 263
Tyler, John, 5: 38
Tyson, Cicely, 2: 255
Tyson, Mike, 2: 273, 274, 275

U

U.S. Air Force, 2: 325, 326, 327; 5: 21
U.S. Amateurs, 5: 242

U.S. House Committee on Education and Labor, 3: 585
U.S. House Judiciary Committee, 2: 424, 426; 5: 135
U.S. House Un-American Activities Committee, 3: 620; 4: 804
U.S. Information Agency (USIA), 3: 634
U.S. Junior Amateurs, 5: 239, 241
U.S. Open Championship, *1:* 27; 5: 237
U.S. Postal Service, *1:* 160; 5: 6
U.S. Senate Judiciary Committee, 2: 344, 345
U.S. State Department, 5: 148–50
U.S. Supreme Court, 2: 344; 3: 504, 506, 507
"Uncle Remus" stories, 4: 718
Uncle Tom's Children, 4: 802
Underground Railroad, 4: 730, 732–33; 6: 120
"Unforgettable," *1:* 155, 158
Union Missionary Society, 5: 38
United Christian Youth Movement, 2: 333
United Church of Christ, 5: 250
United Nations (UN), *1:* 17, 29, 105, 106; 4: 648; 5: 93, 94, 131, 249, 251–52; 6: 81, 88
United Nations Children's Fund, *1:* 56
United Nations Educational, Scientific, and Cultural Organization, 5: 151
United Negro College Fund (UNCF), 2: 431

United Negro Improvement Association (UNIA), *2:* 256; *6:* 171, 172
United Parcel Service (UPS), *5:* 115, 118
United Service Organization (USO), *1:* 28, 62; *3:* 536; *5:* 14
United States Lawn Tennis Association, *2:* 267
Universal Remnant Church of God, *3:* 478
University of California at Los Angeles (UCLA), *1:* 3, 182
University of Mississippi, *3:* 528, 529
University of North Carolina, *2:* 427–28; *5:* 139–40
University of Southern California (USC), *5:* 208

V

Van Buren, Martin, *5:* 34, 35, 38
Van, Lythi Bich, *5:* 246
Van Peebles, Mario, *4:* 682, **737–39,** 737 (ill.)
Van Wagener, Isaac, *4:* 728
Van Wagener, Maria, *4:* 728
Vance, Courtney B., *5:* 230
Vandross, Luther, *2:* 351
Vantage (theater), *2:* 284
Varèse, Edgard, *4:* 690
Vaudeville, *1:* 192; *2:* 421
Vaughan, Sarah, *1:* 156; *4:* **739–42,** 740 (ill.)
Vegetarianism, *2:* 291
Very Young Poets, *1:* 86
Vesey, Denmark, *4:* 735, **742–44**
Vesey, Joseph, *4:* 742
Vicario, Arantxa Sanchez, *5:* 235
Victor, Don, *2:* 279

Vietnam War, *1:* 13; *2:* 393; *3:* 586; *5:* 171; *6:* 189, 190
Village Voice, *5:* 254
Vogue magazine, *1:* 116; *2:* 397, 398; *3:* 576
A Voice from the South: By a Black Woman from the South, *1:* 167
Volunteerism, *2:* 264, 265; *5:* 174
Voter Education Project, *2:* 431; *6:* 145
Voters for Choice, *1:* 85
Voting, *2:* 307; *3:* 459

W

Waddles, Charleszetta, *4:* **744–46,** 745 (ill.)
Waddles, Payton, *4:* 746
Wagner Festival, *1:* 101
Waiting to Exhale, *3:* 522, 524; *5:* 155, 156, 157, 167
Wake Forest University, *1:* 20
"Walk Against Fear," *3:* 529
Walker, Alice, *2:* 371; *4:* **747–50,** 747 (ill.)
Walker, Armstead, *4:* 753
Walker, C. J., *4:* 751
Walker, Clifford, *4:* 745
Walker, Lelia, *4:* 752
Walker, Leroy, *5:* 186
Walker, Madame C. J., *3:* 490; *4:* **750–52,** 751 (ill.)
Walker, Maggie L., *4:* **752–55,** 754 (ill.)
Wallace, Christopher, *5:* 203
Wallace, George, *6:* 53
Wallace, Matt, *4:* 756
Wallace, Mike, *1:* 79
Wallace, Sippie, *4:* **755–58,** 756 (ill.)
War Resisters League, *3:* 641

Warner, Malcolm-Jamal, *5:* 43, 230
Warwick, Dee Dee, *2:* 360
Warwick, Dionne, *2:* 360, 361
Washington, Booker T., *1:* 126, 211; *2:* 256; *4:* 724, 725–26, **758–61,** 759 (ill.), 781; *5:* 91; *6:* 106
Washington Bullets, *1:* 66
Washington, D.C., *3:* 447, 448; *5:* 3, 9–12
Washington, Denzel, *4:* **761–63,** 762 (ill.)
Washington, George, *4:* 773; *5:* 4, 150
Washington Post, *3:* 614
Washington Urban League, *2:* 390
Watergate scandal, *2:* 426; *5:* 135
Waters, Maxine, *5:* 21; *6:* **211–14,** 211 (ill.)
Waters, Muddy, *1:* 59; *5:* 223
Watson, Carolyn, *5:* 253
Wattleton, Faye, *4:* **763–66,** 765 (ill.)
Watts, André, *4:* **766–68,** 767 (ill.)
Watts, J. C., Jr., *5:* 182
Wayans, Keenan Ivory, *4:* **769–71,** 770 (ill.); *5:* 144
"We Are the World," *1:* 56; *2:* 418
Webb, Chick, *2:* 243; *5:* 77
Webster, Ben, *5:* 24
Welch, Leonard, *5:* 156
Western Association of Writers, *1:* 213
Westhead, Paul, *2:* 401
Westside Preparatory School, *1:* 162
What the Wine Sellers Buy, *3:* 532
Wheatley, John, *4:* 772, 773
Wheatley, Phillis, *4:* **771–73,** 772 (ill.)

When Work Disappears: The World of the New Urban Poor, 6: 229
Whistler, James McNeill, 4: 698
White Citizens Council, 2: 236
Whitefield, George, 4: 772
Whitehead, John C., 5: 151
Who Killed the Congo?, 6: 189
"The Wife of His Youth, and Other Stories of the Color Line," 1: 134
Wigs, 4: 673–74
Wilberforce University, 1: 184
Wild Seed, 1: 111
Wilder, L. Douglas, 1: 97; 4: **773–76,** 774 (ill.); 5: 18
Wilkins, Roger, 4: 688
Wilkins, Roy, 4: 668, **776–79,** 777 (ill.), 807
Williams, Alice Faye, 5: 199
Williams, Clarence, 4: 678
Williams, Daniel Hale, 4: **779–82,** 780 (ill.)
Williams, Jayson, 5: 129
Williams, John A., 4: **782–84,** 783 (ill.)
Williams, Maggie, 5: 118
Williams, Montel, 4: **784–87,** 785 (ill.)
Williams, Paulette, 4: 662
Williams, Richard, 5: 234
Williams, Robert, 5: 230
Williams, Serena, 5: 234, 235, 237, 238
Williams, Sherley Anne, 4: **787–89,** 788 (ill.)
Williams, Venus, 5: **233–38,** 233 (ill.), 236 (ill.)
Williams, Walter, 4: 688
Willke, John, 4: 765
Wilson, August, 4: **790–92,** 790 (ill.)
Wilson, Harriet E., 2: 262

Wilson, Martin, 4: 688
Wilson, Mary, 3: 630
Wilson, Nancy, 2: 305
Wilson, William Julius, 6: **221–31,** 221 (ill.)
Wilson, Woodrow, 4: 726–27
Wimbledon, 2: 268
Winfrey, Oprah, 4: 770, **792–95,** 794 (ill.); 5: 15
Witter Bynner Poetry Contest, 1: 179
The Wiz, 3: 631
Wofford, Chloe Anthony. *See* Morrison, Toni
The Women of Brewster Place, 3: 557, 558
Women's Bureau, 5: 116
Women's Committee of the Baltimore Art Museum, 1: 197
Women's Medical College of Pennsylvania, 2: 298
Women's Political Council, 3: 579
Women's Tennis Association (WTA), 5: 233, 234, 235, 237
Wonder, Stevie, 2: 286; 4: **795–98,** 797 (ill.); 5: 222
Wonderful Hair Grower, 3: 491
Woodard, Lynette, 2: 322
Woods, Earl, 5: 240, 241, 246
Woods, Eldrick "Tiger," 5: **239–47,** 239 (ill.), 241 (ill.), 243 (ill.)
Woodson, Carter G., 4: **798–800,** 799 (ill.)
Woodward, Nathan, 5: 28
World Boxing Association, 1: 13
World Federation of African People, 3: 538
World Town Hall Seminar, 4: 648
World War I, 2: 259

World War II, 1: 183; 2: 358; 5: 225, 226
World's Student Christian Federation, 1: 195
Worthy, William, 4: 649
Wright, Orville, 1: 213
Wright, Richard, 1: 36; 2: 233; 4: 716, 788, 790, **800–3,** 802 (ill.); 5: 68
Wright, Syreeta, 4: 797

Y

Yancy, Marvin, 1: 156, 157
Yeakey, Lamont H., 4: 736
Yellow Back Radio Broke-Down, 3: 617
Young, Andrew, 5: **249–55,** 249 (ill.), 252 (ill.)
Young, Coleman A., 4: **803–6,** 805 (ill.); 5: 227; 6: **233–37,** 233 (ill.)
Young Communist League, 3: 640
Young Ideas, 5: 252
Young, Jean, 5: 252 (ill.), 253
Young, Jimmy, 5: 84
Young Negroes Cooperative League, 6: 14
Young Poet's Primer, 1: 86
Young, Whitney M., Jr., 4: **806–8,** 807 (ill.)
Young Women's Christian Association (YWCA), 1: 193, 194
Yugen, 1: 38
Yugoslavia, 5: 18

Z

Zane, Arnie, 2: 412
Zea-Daly, Errol, 4: 701
Zeely, 2: 310

transferred to JR 8/2009

For Reference

Not to be taken from this room

RECEIVED MAR 1 3 2002 52.00

South Huntington Public Library
Huntington Station, New York
11746-7699

GAYLORD M